The Neurotic Organization

Manfred F. R. Kets de Vries
Danny Miller

HarperBusiness

A Division of HarperCollins*Publishers*

Library of Congress Cataloging in Publication Data
Kets de Vries, Manfred F. R.
    The neurotic organization.

    Bibliography: p. 211
    Includes index.
    1. Organizational behavior. 2. Psychology, Industrial.
3. Management. I. Miller, Danny. II. Title.
HD58.7.K465   1984   658.4′001′9   84-5754
ISBN 0-87589-606-5 (cloth)   ISBN 0-88730-488-5 (paper)

Contents

Preface to the Paperback Edition

In the six years since the publication of *The Neurotic Organization*, much has occurred in the world of business to heighten public awareness of the themes we presented in the book. More attention is being paid to the "non-rational" aspects of management that surface as managers face the challenges and opportunities of the day. Three major developments over the past decade reflect the pathological themes and types of organizations that were introduced in our book.

First, our "dramatic organization"—with its aggressive leaders, its risk-embracing growth strategies, and its highly leveraged capital structure—became more common due to new developments in corporate finance. The takeover mania of the 1980s, which was financed by junk bonds and leveraged buyouts, brought the dramatic organization to the fore. It became possible for a few ambitious executives and financiers to control huge chunks of capital. Innovative financing techniques were often stretched to the limit as overconfident executives attempted ever larger and riskier takeovers. In many cases, sensible expansion gave way to uncontrolled greed. Before long, many highly leveraged firms began to find it difficult to support their mountains of debt. The problems of the Campeau Corporation seem to stem from the overconfidence of its entrepreneurial leader, and his excessive use of financial leverage. Similarly, Donald Trump earned his reputation with his propitious New York real estate investments, but his appetite for grandiose projects that garner media attention seems to have provoked his present cash crunch. Even the investment banks were not immune to such excesses. The celebrated Drexel, Burnham, Lambert is a classic example of a dramatic organization whose managers took financial entrepreneurship too far. Episodes of grandiosity were also in evidence at normally reserved and circumspect firms such as Salomon Brothers, as reported in Michael Lewis' recent book *Liar's Poker*.[1]

The takeover boom spawned by the new methods of financing engendered the second of our common types: "the paranoid organization," which spends so much time tracking and fighting its enemies that it neglects to evolve a concerted strategy to cater to its customers. A climate of paranoia prevailed within many takeover candidates during the 1980s. Executives devoted more attention to politicking, defensive legal maneuvers, golden parachutes, and proxy fights than to the substance of corporate strategies. As this atmosphere of suspicion took hold, fight and flight considerations began to supercede manufacturing and marketing strategy. The recent bestseller, *Barbarians at the Gate*[2], reflects the curious mixture of distrust and greed that is evoked in some managers by a hostile takeover.

The third type of neurotic organization, "the depressive firm"—an unresponsive, rigid organization that is frequently found in besieged or dying industries—has also received much attention in the last decade. In these organizations attitudes of passivity, pessimism, and helplessness prevail. This defeatism is often caused by—and frequently contributes to—stagnating industrial environments. Much has been written about the massive bureaucratic, finance-dominated corporations of America's mature industries, such as the steel industry and automobile manufacturing. David Halberstam's

---

[1]Lewis, Michael. *Liar's Poker*. New York: Norton, 1989.
[2]Burrough, Bryan, and John Helyar. *Barbarians at the Gate*. New York: Harper & Row, 1989.

brilliant book, *The Reckoning*[3], as well as Maryann Keller's *Rude Awakening*[4], show how firms such as Ford and General Motors became moribund bureaucracies whose conservative, complacent leaders let design and manufacturing capacities stagnate as their compulsive finance and cost control groups discouraged all corporate initiative. Lee Iacocca called attention to this problem in his popular account of his turnaround of Chrysler. In the auto firms, an oppressive bureaucracy stifled all innovation, enthusiasm, and creativity. It often took years to make the smallest changes in design— changes that were more likely to stem from a desire to cut costs than to adapt to customers' needs or improve products. The result: major inroads were made by Japanese auto firms which paid much more attention to quality and performance.

The above examples of greed, fear, and oppression illustrate how the personalities of top managers contribute to the strategic and cultural pathologies of their organizations. They also reveal the ways in which these personal predilections affect the emerging business practices, industrial policies, and challenges of the day. Each of these aspects of the *zeitgeist* highlights the non-rational aspects of many modern organizations and their executives.

Aside from the three trends discussed above, there are a number of deeper and less fleeting reasons for the book's enduring popularity. First, there is a growing realization that the rational models of management and organization are, in large part, incomplete and unrealistic. They fail to describe or account for the behavior of managers, they provide prescriptions that are impossible to implement, and they give little insight into why and how organizations go wrong—topics dealt with in some detail in Danny Miller's *The Icarus Paradox*[5]. Indeed, a recent cover story in *Business Week* criticizes much of the literature on strategic planning because its assumptions are too unrealistic to be properly implemented. Rational models and the quick fix, it seems, work only on paper, as do the facile schemes of most management consultants.

Second, there has been a growing interest in organizational cul-

---

[3]Halberstram, David. *The Reckoning*. New York: William Morrow, 1986.
[4]Keller, Maryann. *Rude Awakening*. New York: William Morrow, 1984.
[5]Miller, Danny. *The Icarus Paradox*. New York: HarperCollins, 1990.

ture. Bestselling books such as *Corporate Cultures*[6] by Terrence Deal and Allen Kennedy, *In Search of Excellence*[7] by Tom Peters and Robert Waterman, and *Theory Z*[8] by William Ouchi have had an unprecedented impact on the thinking of modern managers. These authors argue that the goals and values of managers, the way they instill ideals and meaning into their organizations, and their use of cultural rituals are all extremely important to corporate success. They not only claim that leaders and their attitudes are important to their firms, but that societal values play a role in the success of organizations as well. In short, these theorists go well beyond the dictates of rational management to look at the emotional and affective basis of corporate success.

But if non-rational factors such as emotions and values can contribute to success, they can also be a factor in failure. Increasing attention is now being paid to organizational pathologies. The United States appears to have lost its place as the leader of the industrial world. Japan, Korea, Taiwan, and much of Europe have outstripped our economic growth, and many U.S. and Canadian companies have fallen far behind their foreign rivals. The growing realization that the United States is lagging in international competition has made American managers more interested in the pathologies—social, industrial, and personal—that underlie this problem. As a result, managers have become more introspective about their shortcomings and wish to understand better not only their objective deficiencies, but also the problematic basic values, assumptions, and leadership attitudes that engender them. *The Neurotic Organization* represents one attempt to address these problems.

Manfred F.R. Kets de Vries, *Paris*
Danny Miller, *Montreal*
June 1990

[6]Deal, Terrence, and Allen A. Kennedy. *Corporate Cultures*. Reading, Mass.: Addison Wesley, 1982.
[7]Peters, Tom, and Robert Waterman. *In Search of Excellence*. New York: Harper & Row, 1982.
[8]Ouchi, William G. *Theory Z*. Reading, Mass.: Addison Wesley, 1981.

Preface

Freud's often-cited dictum about the dream being the "royal road to the unconscious" has, perhaps, a wider applicability than he intended. Our explorations of organizations have suggested that the royal road to understanding their central dynamics is also paved with the fantasies or "world view" of their top executives. The predominant fantasies, beliefs, and aspirations of key decision makers seem so pervasively to influence the nature of their organizations. Of course, we are referring here not to fantasies of the whimsical, fleeting sort but to those that come to characterize one's "internal theater." They compose one's picture of the world, which underlies and ultimately determines so much of behavior and which comes to broadly influence, even epitomize, what is often called "character" or "personality."

   One of the authors (Kets de Vries) underwent clinical training at the Canadian Institute of Psychoanalysis. There he developed his interest in the relations among fantasy, decision making, and action. This concern grew during his work as a practicing psychoanalyst with top executives. The knowledge gained from these clinical encounters proved extremely useful in analyzing organizational pathologies and carrying out consulting interventions. It helped sharpen diagnostic and prescriptive skills, creating a greater awareness of the complexities of the interactions between executives and their organizations. The problems and orientations of organizations seemed so often to mirror the personalities of their top executives.

The other author (Miller) has done extensive research to identify recurrent organizational problem syndromes. These seemed to form very common configurations, or "gestalts," among a wide variety of symptoms. They highlighted the integral interdependencies among elements of organizational strategy, organizational structure, and executive personality. Sporadic forays into the psychiatric literature seemed to point to the power of using common clinical insights and frameworks as organizing schemes for understanding the roots of organizational problems.

Our collaboration started with an unstructured dialogue concerning "fantasy and strategy." Soon we began to struggle to discover the links between organizational and human pathology, trying in the process to make the best of our extremely disparate backgrounds. A complementary interchange resulted that produced a series of highly speculative working papers, all elaborations on the theme of relating intrapsychic and organizational dynamics. The enthusiastic responses from colleagues and executives to these tentative, controversial, and exploratory papers gave us the courage to knit them into a book. As the reader will plainly see, our objective is to excite debate and to raise questions with our bold conjectures. Let the academic reader be forewarned that nowhere have we supplied any final answers or any airtight logical or empirical substantiation. The area of inquiry is still far too young and unexplored for this.

The clinical and theoretical perspectives of psychoanalysis provide our points of departure throughout. In sharp contrast to most of the literature on organizations, we will try, to paraphrase George Homans, to bring *the person* back into the organization. We do not attempt to understand organizations simply by resorting to the common sociological or strategic ("policy") frameworks. Instead, we examine the *human* psychological roots of organizational strategy, structure, group processes, and leadership. The mental, or intrapsychic, processes of executives are characterized in the richest way possible. Indeed, throughout the text we make use of psychoanalytically based models of the mind. We eschew the far more common piecemeal and narrow views that tend to dominate much of the research on cognition, affect, motivation, and personality.

The book is divided into two major parts. Part One treats the nature and genesis of some very prevalent organizational problems from a clinical perspective. The analysis commences at a high level of aggregation—the total organization—and proceeds over successive chapters to lower levels: the group, the dyad, and the individual. The literature on neurotic behavior patterns, group and family dynamics, transference, and the life cycle is used to help understand, respectively, strategic, structural, leadership, and motivational problems in organizations. Part Two deals with the issue of organizational change: Given the nature and causes of the problems discussed in Part One, how can we help to resolve them by changing the organization? First the sources of dysfunctional resistance to change and adaptation are investigated. The process of organizational change is then discussed by comparing it to the course of a successful psychoanalytic intervention. Finally, normative implications are drawn. The book concludes with an integrative case example of organizational diagnosis and prescription. (All our case material, in fact, has been disguised.) Our central objective is to present the reader with a body of knowledge and principles that will be of use in understanding, diagnosing, and perhaps ultimately dealing with organizational problems.

We believe that this book has a very broad potential audience. Its first ranks should include managers, organization development consultants, and management training specialists. The problems we discuss will all be very familiar to them, and the proposed explanations and recommendations are, we think, quite to the point. The nontechnical treatment of sometimes-complex subject matter should also appeal to this audience.

Academics teaching and studying policy, organizational behavior, and other social/behavioral sciences should find our theme stimulating, if somewhat aberrant. So will many of their students. To this audience, the book will serve as a departure from —one is tempted to say "antidote to"—the much more common structuralist perspective. Finally, psychotherapists, clinical psychologists, and other mental health professionals concerned with human problems in organizations may also benefit from this book.

A preface inevitably calls for a short statement of intellectual and emotional indebtedness. There is one unofficial group of helpers who must remain anonymous for reasons of discretion; but to them we owe perhaps the greatest debt. We are referring to our patients and clients, who managed to teach us a great deal while we were trying to help them. This book is dedicated to them.

Manfred Kets de Vries would like to express his gratitude to three of his teachers, Eva P. Lester, James Naiman, and W. Clifford Scott, of the Canadian Institute of Psychoanalysis and the McGill University Department of Psychiatry, for the invaluable clinical advice they have provided over the years. Clifford Scott, in particular, was instrumental in clarifying the meaning of fantasy, stressing both its ability to surprise and its elusive boundaries. The generosity of Maurice Dongier, chairman of psychiatry at McGill University, is hard to put into words. It created a touch of the Mediterranean sun in what can otherwise be a pessimistic profession. There is, in addition, an overall indebtedness to Abraham Zaleznik of the Harvard Business School, a pioneer in the application of psychoanalysis to the study of organizations and one who played an important mentor role.

Danny Miller would like to thank Peter H. Friesen and Pradip N. Khandwalla for the healthy doses of positivism that continue to sustain his skeptical point of view and his empirical bent. He would also like to thank Henry Mintzberg, Henry Tutsch, and Thomas Kubicek for the enthusiasm that occasionally emboldens him to take the risky inferential leaps that a book of this sort requires. Special thanks for moral support and intellectual stimulation go to family and to philosopher-friends Robert Feinstein, Edward G. Lesko, and Victor I. Levin.

In the process of rewriting and editing this book a number of people were extremely helpful in giving critical comments. We are particularly grateful to Gilles Amado, Warren Bennis, Claude Faucheux, William E. Henry, Harvey Kolodny, Richard O. Mason, Henry Mintzberg, Ian I. Mitroff, Lawrence A. Nadler, Roland Reitter, and Georges Trepo. We are also most indebted to Sidney Perzow of the Montreal General Hospital Department of Psychiatry, whose clinical insights have been particularly helpful. Sidney Perzow's work with Balint groups of managerial personnel has been a considerable source of inspiration. In addition, we are grateful for the editorial contributions of Anne Hodgsdon.

The typing of the various drafts has been done in good cheer and with great competence and alacrity by Cheryl Kelahear, Sandra Guadagnino, Martine Guyot, and Hélène Schieder.

Finally, we would like to thank the wife of one of the authors, Elisabet Kets de Vries, who helped as a guide in assessing the readability of the various chapters as they progressed. For this we are extremely grateful.

June 1984   Manfred F. R. Kets de Vries
                                                 Boston, Massachusetts

                                                 Danny Miller
                                                 Montreal, Quebec

Introduction

Tracing Problems
from Organizational
to Individual Levels

> Remember, it is the secret force hidden deep within us that
> manipulates our strings; there lies the voice of persuasion,
> there the very life, there, we might even say, is the man
> himself.   —Marcus Aurelius, *Meditations*

The great economist Adam Smith believed that people
were led, as if by an invisible hand, to promote unintended
ends. By acting in their self-interest, they would bring about un-
anticipated but salutary economic developments. We believe
there is an invisible hand at work in organizations as well as in
economies. Decision making, leadership, strategy formation,
structuring, and organizational change are influenced in subtle
and complex ways by "invisible," long-standing psychological
forces of which the individual is usually unaware. These covert
forces often act to produce organizational outcomes that appear
extremely irrational and dysfunctional. Whereas the self-centered
motives discussed by Smith are said to bring about positive results, the forces we shall describe are frequently quite pernicious
and often downright destructive.

We wish to examine covert psychological processes generally ignored by management theorists: those that are the prov-

1

ince of psychiatrists, clinical psychologists, and psychoanalysts. We have decided to examine common dysfunctional managerial styles and to study their organizational manifestations and repercussions. Much is known about neurotic behavior patterns, dysfunctional organizational climates, disturbing interpersonal interactions, and rigidified defense mechanisms. The pervasiveness of these phenomena has been pointed to time and time again in the psychiatric and psychoanalytic literature. Yet we virtually never see these issues discussed in the managerial literature. As management consultants and psychoanalysts, we are able to identify the symptomatology of organizations, particularly those that are performing poorly or are undergoing a disruptive period of change. The ways in which strategies, leadership styles, decision making, and even structure are influenced by the broadly defined psychological orientations of managers seem both remarkable and dramatic.

The study of irrational psychological forces in organizations is a time-honored practice. There is nothing new in acknowledging their importance. Our contribution will therefore be mainly in the orientation we shall employ. Traditionally, scholars of organizations have dealt with psychological matters in one of three ways. The first is epitomized by the *human relations school,* which points to the existence of crucial social needs and their impact on job performance. The human relations theorists showed that it is important to treat workers with consideration, to behave toward them in ways that imply that they are responsible, sensitive human beings. It was shown, for example, how by giving people more interesting work, more power or discretion, or more attention, their productivity and contentment might sometimes be enhanced. There are, however, important limitations to this type of research. For one, the focus is usually on first-line workers rather than managers. Furthermore, there is little attempt to explain the genesis of human needs or their specific manifestations. More important, perhaps, is the failure to examine or explain individual differences. Most theorists are simply content to point out the gross nature of "extrarational" (that is, nontask) factors in organizations and to discuss their importance for managing all people.[1]

The second school, the *trait or attribute school,* examines various psychological traits among managers in order to discern their repercussions and determine how functional they are. Typically, particular individual personality or cognitive attributes are examined to determine how they might influence risk taking, decision making, leadership, and so forth. Here there *is* a focus on individual differences. For example, it is shown how the need for power or achievement can influence leadership behavior,[2] how locus of control can affect strategy formulation,[3] and how cognitive styles can influence decision making.[4] This orientation too has some shortcomings. Perhaps the most important is that individuals are generally characterized along one simple psychological dimension or trait. So many aspects of personality and context are ignored that it is possible to unearth only the most general tendencies. We wish to be able to obtain more encompassing, more elaborate, and more realistic descriptions of managerial psychological states and behavior in order to relate them to key organizational problems.

Still a third school, the *cognitive constraint theorists,* looks at the general psychological limitations of individuals as they are manifested in an organizational context. The seminal work of Simon,[5] March and Simon,[6] and Cyert and March[7] has shown how universal cognitive limitations evoke, indeed necessitate, particular styles of decision making and limit rationality. For example, our mental limitations require that we consider only relatively few alternatives in choosing solutions to problems. Decisions are triggered by pressing problems rather than opportunities. Moreover, organizations focus on short-term goals in making any one decision, possibly supplanting these with contradictory goals in making the next decision. Finally, most decisions are incremental and remedial, rather than dramatically innovative or bold. Although cognitive theorists have discovered important organizational tendencies, they, like the human relations theorists, have ignored individual differences. These differences are critical to any understanding of the genesis of organizational dysfunction.

Our approach will be quite different from the three just described. This book tries to systematize our insights. It constructs a set of frameworks for classifying some of the most prevalent forms of dysfunction, particularly as they character- ize individual managers, superior/subordinate relationships, the experiences of groups, and the adaptive style of the entire or- ganization. These frameworks are erected with the help of an extensive study of the psychiatric, psychoanalytic, and family therapy literature. They are used to understand, predict, and classify the most common managerial problems. For example, the neurotic personality styles of top managers are used to help understand organizational failures; the literature on analytic group dynamics is used to understand problems of leadership and decision making.

We should emphasize that our approach is in many ways quite distinctive. First, it concentrates on dysfunctional psycho- logical states and "neurotic" behavior rather than on "normal" behavior or relationships. We believe, however, that the differ- ence between "normal" and "neurotic" is one of degree. Neither term is easy to define, in part because the two fall along the same continuum. We would not have concentrated so much on neurotic behavior had we been concerned mainly with general tendencies in healthy firms. Second, given our attention to or- ganizational dysfunction, we felt it would be impossible to make progress on this topic by drawing broad psychological generalizations. There are many types of dysfunctions, and so it is necessary to pay attention to individual differences or at least to use a contingency approach to distinguish among the com- mon "types" that emerge. Finally, we strive for a much richer characterization of behavior than the three schools just men- tioned. We believe that the human psyche is complex, that it is made up of a broad array of tightly interdependent components that develop in channeled ways over long periods. The psyche is not terribly malleable, nor is it easy to understand without much study. We believe that it simply is not good enough to examine one or two personality dimensions ("along a 7-point scale") if one hopes to obtain any insight into the primary causes of individual, group, or organizational dysfunction. Far more detailed, complex, and encompassing characterizations of mental behavior are needed. We believe these are more common in the psychiatric and psychoanalytic literature than in the traditional behavioristic writings.

Our book is speculative. It takes findings and frameworks from one field and applies them to another. This process is always somewhat risky, since the shift in contexts may render the frameworks inappropriate for or irrelevant to organizations. Three points must be made in this regard. First, we shall not be focusing on all organizations, departments, or leadership situations. We concern ourselves mainly with organizational dysfunctions and therefore look at "sick" organizations or groups or at destructive interpersonal interactions and relationships in organizations. Second, we focus on common neurotic rather than severely incapacitating "psychotic" behavior. Third, we try to relate psychiatric and psychoanalytic findings to organizational functioning using our personal experiences in organizations. As both consultants and clinicians, we have long been involved in the diagnosis and treatment of organizational, group, and interpersonal dysfunction. The many examples we shall use to translate the theoretical into the practical are based on our own work with organizations and patients.

All this is not to say that the frameworks we shall apply to understand organizational pathology are inviolate or uniquely appropriate. There are always a number of ways of conceptualizing, categorizing, and explaining organizational problems. All we can claim is that the frameworks we apply do in fact mirror our personal experiences in organizations, that they have helped us to diagnose organizational problems more quickly and accurately, and, most important, that they have allowed us to help organizations and individuals in organizations to grapple more effectively with these problems.

All the chapters of the book mix theory with examples. We evolve frameworks to understand the covert intrapsychic influences behind organizational, group, and interpersonal dysfunctioning and individual resistances. In every case there is an attempt to explicate the frameworks and, more important, to make their implications more concrete to the reader by giving many actual case examples. Such examples should make more apparent the relevance of the theoretical material.

We have taken both descriptive and normative positions throughout. The initial chapters are concerned mostly with pointing out the nature of hidden forces in organizations and showing how they inhibit effective strategy making, structuring, group dynamics, leadership, and decision making. These chapters deemphasize prescription. The last chapters, however, focus on organizational change. Here we are concerned with how we make organizations more effective by discovering dysfunctional patterns, bringing them out into the open, and helping managers to eradicate them.

A brief overview of each of our chapters will provide readers with the overall flavor and orientation of the book and allow them to more easily peruse its contents. As we progress, our focus shifts from the total organization to the group to dyadic relationships to the individual (see Table 1). In addition, whereas Part One (Chapters One through Five) deals with organizational problems that result from psychodynamic forces, Part Two (Chapters Six through Nine) deals with organizational resistance and change as they may be constrained or facilitated by these problems.

Chapter One is the longest and perhaps the most complex. It examines the influences that top executives' neurotic styles of behavior can have on overall organizational functioning. The psychiatric and psychoanalytic literature identifies a number of such styles. We have selected the five neurotic styles that relate to the five most common types of dysfunctional corporations. The five types of organizational problem syndromes seem to be strongly influenced by the five neurotic styles of their top managers. We call these paranoid, compulsive, dramatic, depressive, and schizoid. Each of these styles is shown to give rise to particular problems of strategy, structure, decision making, and managerial culture. The organizational configuration seems to broadly mirror the psychodynamic neurotic configuration of the top executives. Case examples of the five resulting organizational pathologies are given.

Chapter Two is based on the pioneering work by Bion[8] on group functioning. Bion discovered that many groups evolve particular fantasies, which their members all tend to share.

Table 1. Outline of This Book.

	Psychological Problem or Dimension	Level of Aggregation	Organizational Problem Area
	Part One: Organizational Problems		
1.	Neurotic personality styles of top executives of troubled firms	Overall organization	Strategy Strategy making Structure Organizational culture
2.	Dysfunctional group processes detracting from the primary organizational task; shared fantasies and organizational myths	Departments Work groups Small organizations	Decision making Structure Organizational culture
3.	Transferential patterns of subordinates or superiors that lead to frustration, anger, and confusion in interpersonal situations	Two-person relationships	Leadership Decision making
4.	Improper modes by which a superior "binds," "abandons," or "proxies" his or her subordinates	Superior/subordinate interactions	Leadership
5.	Life-cycle-related crises during a manager's career	The individual	Satisfaction with work and the organization
	Part Two: Overcoming Resistance to Change		
6.	Psychodynamic defense mechanisms and resistances	The individual	Resistance to change
7.	Disappointment, "mourning," and resistance caused by loss of status, security, or power	Primarily the individual	Developing insight and coping with disappointment in order to facilitate lasting organizational change; intervention techniques to aid the change process
8.	All of the above	All levels	Therapeutic prescriptions
9.	All of the above	All levels	Management consulting and organizational intervention

These are founded in the predominant needs of their members and can be very unrealistic and dysfunctional. For example, some group fantasies become vehicles for expressing members' hostilities toward a common enemy or for protecting members from the enemy. Bion claims that such "fight/flight" groups focus so much on the common enemy that they are often unproductive, shortsighted, and misdirected. Their energies are channeled into inappropriate and disruptive acts of aggression. Bion has also identified "dependency" groups, in which leaders are idealized and members refuse to take initiatives on their own. Bion's "pairing" groups, or what we call "utopian" groups, in contrast, have an abiding faith in a future utopian state that will arrive to rescue the group from any current problems. All these fantasies can seriously impair organizational decision making and strategy formation. We show just how this can occur and present case studies of each type of group.

Chapter Three explores transference, a concept that has been confined to the psychotherapy literature. Transference occurs when an individual, usually unconsciously, treats a current relationship as though it were an important relationship from the past. The past relationship is usually an intimate and intense one with parental figures or siblings that occurred early in life and had within it conflicts that remain unresolved. The person is said to reenact the past relationship in part to resolve some of these conflicts in a more satisfactory way. This reenactment almost inevitably involves intense and inappropriate behavior. Transference is a universal phenomenon, encroaching on all long-standing and close relationships, especially those in which power plays a key role. Superior/subordinate relationships are prominent among these. We shall discuss three common types of transference that occur in organizational settings. Each is argued to be responsible for very prevalent and persistent problems of decision making and leadership. These problems will be quite resistant to remedial measures until their transferential nature is recognized and explicitly addressed.

Our fourth chapter again focuses on dysfunctional superior/subordinate relationships, but it addresses their interactional and interpersonal dysfunctions using some of the findings of psychiatrists who have studied pathological dynamics within the family. These therapists have shown that family interactions often involve three destructive types of relationships, each characterized by the degree to which parents "bind," or control, their children. These apply to managerial situations in which superiors can *bind* their subordinates to the point of smothering their initiative and constraining their growth, essentially making them puppets. Alternatively, the superior can have the subordinate act as a *proxy*, serving as one who provides vicarious thrills and carries out dangerous and unacceptable missions for the boss. Finally, the *expelling* mode occurs when the superior takes no interest in his employees, offering them no guidance, support, or security. Each of these modes carries with it a multiplicity of injustices and dangers. The repercussions of each mode are discussed, and some remedial suggestions are given.

Chapter Five is the first to focus exclusively on the individual manager. It examines the challenges and opportunities present in the manager's work and family environment as she progresses through the stages of the life cycle. These stages have been identified from the psychiatric, psychological, sociological, and psychoanalytic literature. Satisfaction with work and with the organization is explained by making reference to the important psychological and emotional challenges that occur during different phases of the life cycle. Differences in these phases should discourage simplistic models that attempt to predict satisfaction based on rank, job performance, education, sex, and the like. They illustrate that managers must cope with specific problems at each phase of the life cycle. A case example is given for each of the five phases.

One of the reasons that effective organizational change is so difficult is that it involves taking authority, status, prestige, and security away from those in power, thereby threatening their self-images and giving rise to resistances, or defense mechanisms. There is a large variety of resistances. These are discussed in Chapter Six and include repression, regression, denial, reaction formation, and other mechanisms discussed by Freud and his followers. In all instances, these mechanisms block awareness of an important fact or inhibit an appropriate response to that fact. For example, a person may *deny* that he has lost something important to him, continuing to act as though nothing had happened. Examples are given of each type of resistance to show how it can prevent effective organizational change or disrupt interpersonal interactions in firms.

Chapter Seven examines organizational change to discover its key challenges and dynamics. Using psychoanalytic concepts, we attempt to show how, by using "confrontation, clarification, and interpretation" procedures, the trained organizational consultant can provide managers with insights into their problems, insights that are sufficiently poignant and concrete to motivate enduring change. Case examples are taken from our consulting and clinical psychoanalytic experiences to show these insight-generating processes at work. In addition, we describe how, after recognizing the need to change or after having change imposed on them, individuals must go through several trying stages as they abandon old methods and roles and adopt new ones. There is a process of "working through" in which the person must "mourn" his losses before being able to adopt new patterns of behavior. Our discussion of the therapist's role in fostering insight and the process of working through that everyone must experience in an important change situation can serve as a basis for changing the common approaches of management consultants and other change agents.

Chapter Eight begins to look for the action implications of what has gone before. It investigates what managers and organizational consultants should do to neutralize and take advantage of the psychodynamic forces we discussed.

The final chapter, on organizational therapy, is an integrative one. Using a complex case study based on our two-year consulting relationship with one firm, we try in Chapter Nine to illustrate the interrelationships among neurotic styles, group fantasies, transference patterns, resistances, and dysfunctional superior/subordinate interactions. Chapter Nine shows how these all interacted to create a serious organizational problem. It also describes what we did to try to correct the problem.

Throughout the book we have tended to simplify, categorize, and compartmentalize in order to clarify our presentation and enhance its memorability. Our frameworks are very neat, what with their five neurotic styles, three group cultures, three transferential relationships, and so on. Of course, things are not so simple in the real world. Our schemes point to important configurations and modes of behavior, but they do not exhaust reality. They do not describe all the types of dysfunctional groups, organizations, or superior/subordinate relationships, and most entities reflect a mixture of more than one "pure" type, as we shall see in the last chapter. As a final cautionary note, we urge the reader to distinguish between simplicity as an expository device, which we embrace, and simplicity as an implication about the structure of the intrapsychic world of individuals and groups, which we know to be illusory after years of sobering experience.

Part One

Organizational Problems

1

Neurotic Styles and Organizational Dysfunctioning

*Ils n'ont rien appris, ni rien oublié.**   —Talleyrand

Things began to change radically at Stevens Corporation after it was acquired by Pyrax International. Pyrax was a rapidly expanding conglomerate making new incursions into a number of vastly different industries. It had had a striking growth record, but its profits were already beginning to level off when it bought Stevens. Pyrax was run by Alex Herzog, a vain, ambitious, and domineering entrepreneur who was the founder, prime mover, and, many thought, the tyrant-in-chief. He drove his employees ruthlessly, arrogated the lion's share of decision-making power, and was noted for his boldness and audacity in acquiring firms larger than Pyrax itself. Herzog, a self-made man, had as his main objective to run a powerful and gigantic enterprise. By the zealous pursuit of growth through acquisition, he had gone a long way toward achieving his dream, incurring massive amounts of long-term debt in the process. Mounting interest rates were already starting to threaten Pyrax when it acquired Stevens.

*They have learnt nothing and have forgotten nothing.

15

Before the acquisition, Stevens was almost as large as Pyrax. It operated as a component and replacement parts manufacturer in the heavy equipment field. Stevens was a lively firm whose product innovations had produced a respectable growth rate and whose manufacturing economies had given it the highest rate of return on equity in the industry. The president, David Morse, was devoted to balancing innovation with efficiency and growth with financial strength. Stevens' products were known for their excellent quality.

Things soon began to change after the acquisition. Herzog disliked having strong managers in charge of *his* companies. He insisted on making all the major decisions at Stevens even though he knew nothing about the industry. He kept Stevens' top executives busy supplying him with trivial information and questioned—even scolded—them when they failed to consult him in deciding things. Morse rapidly became disenchanted with the situation. He quit after a final confrontation with Herzog during which the latter insisted on several misplaced cost-cutting measures that would ultimately damage product quality. It became more and more apparent that, in Stevens, Herzog simply saw a cash cow to finance his grandiose expansion plans.

The departure of Morse allowed Herzog to install Byron Gorsuch, one of his divisional controllers, as chief executive at Stevens. Gorsuch, a diminutive, shy, and insecure bureaucrat, knew little about Stevens' markets. His expertise lay in his ability to follow Herzog's directives to the letter. At Stevens he never took any initiatives. All managerial guidance had to come from Pyrax. Stevens' managers were forced to play a purely advisory role. As Herzog and Gorsuch generally failed to heed their advice, the most competent managers left. The more imaginative managers, those with initiative, were fired. The remaining personnel were passive and fearful; they simply did what they were told. Anxious about job security, they slavishly adhered to the rituals laid down by Herzog and the Pyrax Systems Department. Strategic issues and adaptation were ignored. Things just drifted along and the firm soon began to stagnate. Market share and profitability declined, as did real growth in sales.

The situation was not helped by recent events at Pyrax.

The stubborn, grandiose Herzog and his staff had become enmeshed in still more ambitious, and ultimately more disastrous, acquisitions. They were too busy to recognize the danger signs at Stevens and too ignorant of its markets to be able to do much about them. The depressive, passive group of managers at Stevens were too insecure to undertake any decisive measures to address the problem.

Both Pyrax and Stevens are examples of what we have called "neurotic organizations"—troubled firms whose symptoms and dysfunctions combine to form an integrated "syndrome" of pathology. Just as numerous symptoms combine to indicate a human disorder, similar patterns of strategic and structural defects often point to an integrated organizational pathology. Pyrax can be described as a *dramatic* company whose bold, grandiose leader caused the firm to overextend its financial and managerial resources. Stevens became a *depressive*, lethargic firm whose decline was due to strategic stagnation. In both firms the personalities of the top managers, Herzog and Gorsuch, were strongly reflected in the problematic strategies, structures, and managerial cultures. What surprised us in our experiences in organizations is that several types of organizational neuroses recur with such remarkable regularity. The same pathologies keep occurring again and again.

Human behavior is generally characterized by a mixture of neurotic styles. The same person may possess elements of many styles, each of which is triggered in different circumstances. In many individuals, however, we can discern the predominance of one particular style that consistently characterizes many aspects of behavior. Any extreme manifestations of a single style can eventually lead to psychopathology and serious impairment of functioning. Our experience with top executives and their organizations revealed that parallels could be drawn between individual pathology—excessive use of one neurotic style—and organizational pathology, the latter resulting in poorly functioning organizations. In dysfunctional, centralized firms, the rigid neurotic styles of the top executives were strongly mirrored in the nature of the inappropriate strategies, structures, and organizational cultures of their firms.

Admittedly, interdisciplinary research is fraught with hazards. It is all too easy to take a conceptual framework from one field and apply it blindly to another, very different field.[1] We therefore need a plausible rationale for making the link between intrapsychic phenomena, as manifested by neurotic style, and organizational adaptive characteristics. This we shall attempt to provide. Although the framework we are about to propose is quite speculative, we believe it is instructive and by no means facile.

Neurotic Styles and Organizations

The personality of the top manager can in very important ways influence strategy and even structure.[2] It can certainly influence organizational culture.[3] There is much formal, empirical, and anecdotal evidence to support these links. Unfortunately, the tendency has been to look at one simple aspect of personality, such as perceived control over one's life,[4] need for achievement,[5] or need for power,[6] and to relate it to one or two organizational variables, such as the participativeness of decision making[7] or formalization or bureaucratization.[8] Research built on single traits or attitudes, however, can be quite misleading. Complex situations are reduced to one dimension as though that dimension alone could explain much of the phenomenon under study or could exist independently of the broader aspects of personality.

We thought that the psychoanalytic and psychiatric literature[9] might be more useful than the standard psychological literature because it provides a relatively complete and far more integrated view of intrapsychic functioning and behavior. Instead of focusing on one narrow trait or attitude of the executive, it might be more useful to look at personality styles—those patterns of behavior by which individuals relate themselves to external reality and to their own internal dispositions. Personality styles can explain a multiplicity of behaviors. The focus is on clusters of behaviors that remain relatively stable over the years, as opposed to simple dimensions of behavior. These may better enable us to make a link between an executive's mentality and behavior in organizations.

Psychoanalytic object-relations[10] theoreticians stress that interpersonal interactions as well as instinctual needs are central in the development of personality.[11] Child observation studies reveal that behavior is determined by an individual's mental world, populated by enduring representations of oneself and others. These develop through the process of maturation and human interaction and become encoded as stable and directive forces. The mental representations become organizing units, enabling the individual to perceive, interpret, and react to her environment in a meaningful way. Instinctual needs are typically linked to these mental representations and are transformed into wishes of various kinds, which become articulated through "fantasies." Fantasies can be viewed as original rudimentary schemata that evolve in complexity, as "scripts (scenarios) of organized scenes which are capable of dramatization."[12] Here we are not talking about fantasies in the whimsical sense of daydreaming but about complex and stable psychological structures that underlie observable behavior. The dominant fantasies of an individual are the scenes that prevail in his "private theater,"[13] in his subjective world. They are the building blocks making for particular neurotic styles and are thereby determinants of enduring behavior.

We all have certain mildly dysfunctional neurotic traits. These might involve shyness, depression, irrational fears, suspicion, and so on. Everyone shows some of these characteristics sometimes. Indeed, "normality" entails many quite different neurotic traits. But occasionally people will exhibit a good number of characteristics that all appear to manifest a common neurotic style. They display these characteristics very frequently, so that their behavior becomes quite rigid and inappropriate. These individuals usually do not appear to be sick, they do not exhibit bizarre behavior, and they do not have to be treated by a psychiatrist in order to function well in day-to-day life. But their inflexible behavior does limit their effectiveness as top managers. It consistently distorts their perceptions of people and events and strongly influences their goals, their modes of decision making, and even their preferred social setting.

We believe that intrapsychic fantasies of key organization members are major factors influencing their prevailing neurotic

style and that these, in turn, give rise to shared fantasies that permeate all levels of functioning, color the organizational culture,
and make for a dominant organizational adaptive style. This
style will greatly influence decisions about strategy and structure. Many specific examples of the link between a leader's neurotic style and organizational behavior will follow; we can make
our argument more concrete by pointing to one now. Let us
take an organization in which power is highly centralized in a
leader with paranoid tendencies. The prevailing fantasy among
individuals possessing this style is something like "Everybody is
out to get me." The reality of the past, when such experiences
might have occurred, seems to be reintroduced into the present,
creating deviations from rational decision making. What will the
strategy and structure look like, and what kind of organizational culture exists in these firms? First, there is likely to be a
good deal of vigilance, caused by distrust of subordinates and
competitors alike. This may lead to the development of many
control and information systems and a CIA-like fascination with
gathering intelligence from inside and outside the firm. Second,
paranoid thinking will lead to much centralization of power as
the top executive acts on his distrust by trying to control everything himself. Third, the strategy is likely to emphasize "protection" and reducing dependencies on particular markets or customers. There is likely to be a good deal of diversification with
tight control over divisions and much analytical activity. There
are many other links, but the message is clear—the personality
of the leader driven by intrapsychic fantasies centering on distrust can set the tone for strategy, structure, and organizational
culture.

The objection might be raised that this example is loaded
—that the relation between neurotic style and organizational behavior will hold only when power is centralized in the organization, such that the leader gets her way and has the most impact.
Otherwise, a variety of top-executive personalities will cancel
one another out, resulting in a neutral (or mixed) orientation.
Certainly there are merits to this argument, and it sometimes
holds true, particularly in healthy firms. But it does not invali-
date our framework. First, there is a tendency in many patho-

logical organizations for one or two top executives to set the tone for the firm—to guide its strategy and create a particular structural climate. Second, many decentralized organizations that do not have a very powerful leader show uniformity or at least complementarity in neurotic styles among organizational participants. Organizational politics and the selection and socialization processes have a strong molding effect, enhancing uniformity. Senior executives tend to ensure compatibility and similarity of personnel in their selection, reward/punishment, and promotion procedures. For example, the conservative, insecure, depressive top executive often ensures that others reporting to him share his orientation. Indeed, the organizational culture in some firms strongly determines the nature of the personalities of those who will be attracted to them and will rise to power.

This similarity in outlook can be reinforced by organizational myths, legends, and stories, enabling organization members to identify common symbols, attain a sense of community, and create *shared* fantasies. These fantasies deal with the firm's origin, development, hardships encountered, and rites of passage, covering all intra- and extraorganizational relationships. According to Mitroff and Kilmann, "The corporate myth is the 'spirit' of the organization and is infused into all levels of policy and decision making."[14] Larçon and Reitter[15] make the same argument about the uniformity and complementarity of fantasies in organizations. They introduce the notions of corporate imagery and corporate identity, shared ways of viewing the organization, be they overtly codified or unconscious.

This brings us to a second reason for examining the link between neurotic styles and organizational functioning. Use of a rich set of neurotic styles will allow us to use each to predict *many* aspects of each organization. Once we have determined that a paranoid style, for example, prevails among the dominant coalition in an organization, we will find that it is manifested in many ways. Indications of paranoia will appear in strategy, structure, and organizational culture, and there may even be factors in the environment that feed or result from the paranoia. In other words, a set of mutually complementary elements may exist that appear to be consistent and integral aspects of the same constellations—constellations that have been identified by several independently derived typologies and taxonomies.

At this point we must qualify our arguments. Our framework will apply mainly to sick organizations and poor performers in which a good deal of decision-making power is centralized in the hands of one top-level executive officer. Healthy firms typically manifest too broad a variety of executive personality styles for any one of them to pervasively determine strategy and structure. Organizations in which power is broadly dispersed may have their orientations determined by too large and diverse an array of personalities for our framework to apply. But our experiences with poor performers run by dominant chief executives indicate that the personal styles of these managers often have a strong impact on strategy, structure, and even environment. Any elements of neurotic pathology in the executive's style are likely to be extensively mirrored in the way the firm is run.

Of course, not all failing organizations are run by neurotic executives. Those that are will be the most centralized and will be those in which strategies and structures seem particularly extreme or inappropriate to the environment. A still more important indicator that the personality of the top executive may be the source of the problem is that the symptoms will be thematically related. They will collectively form a gestalt, or configuration of signs, all of which seem to be direct manifestations of one particular neurotic style.

Five Dysfunctional Types

We have identified five very common neurotic styles, well established in the psychoanalytic and psychiatric literature: paranoid, compulsive, dramatic, depressive, and schizoid.[16] Each style has its specific characteristics, its predominant motivating fantasy, and its associated dangers. Table 2 presents an overview of the salient characteristics of each neurotic style.

In the following descriptions of organizational pathology we shall see how each of these styles strongly parallels the strategic behavior, culture, structure, and environment of a number of failing or borderline companies. Some of the firms are still successful, but their rigidity seems to contain at least the seeds of failure.[17] To reiterate a major point: Each of these organizational types has many characteristics that stem from its dominant neurotic style—that is, the shared inner world of the organization's dominant coalition. These characteristics not only appear to derive from the same source but are mutually supportive. They reveal a set of internal interdependencies that demonstrate the utility of deriving typologies of organizations and their problems, strengths, and weaknesses using individual neurotic styles as organizing constructs. It was only recently, however, that as a result of our consulting experiences we realized that the most common unsuccessful types seemed to manifest a broad array of attributes that mirrored one or another particular neurotic style and its related shared fantasy.

The Paranoid Organization. In the paranoid organization, managerial suspicions (see Table 2) translate into a primary *emphasis on organizational intelligence* and controls. Management information systems are very sophisticated in their methods of scanning the environment and controlling internal processes. The environment is studied to identify threats and challenges that may be leveled by government, competitors, and customers. Controls take the form of budgets, cost centers, profit centers, cost-accounting procedures, and other methods of monitoring the performance of internal operations. Top managers are suspicious and wary about people and events both inside and outside the firm. The elaborate information-processing apparatus is a product of their desire for perpetual vigilance and preparedness for emergencies.

The paranoia of the top-management group also takes another form: It influences the decision-making behavior of executives. Frequently, key decision makers, instead of withholding information from one another as part of their defensive mobilization, decide that it may be safer to direct their distrust externally. To protect against competitors, they share information. Moreover, in order to ensure an adequate response to threats, a good deal of *analysis* accompanies decision making. Concerted

Table 2. Summary of the Five Neurotic Styles.

Key Factor	Neurotic Style				
	Paranoid	Compulsive	Dramatic	Depressive	Schizoid
Characteristics	Suspiciousness and mistrust of others; hypersensitivity and hyperalertness; readiness to counter perceived threats; overconcern with hidden motives and special meanings; intense attention span; cold, rational, unemotional	Perfectionism; preoccupation with trivial details; insistence that others submit to own way of doing things; relationships seen in terms of dominance and submission; lack of spontaneity; inability to relax; meticulousness, dogmatism, obstinacy	Self-dramatization, excessive expression of emotions; incessant drawing of attention to self; narcissistic preoccupation; a craving for activity and excitement; alternating between idealization and devaluation of others; exploitativeness; incapacity for concentration or sharply focused attention	Feelings of guilt, worthlessness, self-reproach, inadequacy; sense of helplessness and hopelessness—of being at the mercy of events; diminished ability to think clearly; loss of interest and motivation; inability to experience pleasure	Detachment, noninvolvement, withdrawnness; sense of estrangement; lack of excitement or enthusiasm; indifference to praise or criticism; lack of interest in present or future; appearance cold, unemotional
Fantasy	I cannot really trust anybody; a menacing superior force exists that is out to get me; I had better be on my guard	I don't want to be at the mercy of events; I have to master and control all the things affecting me	I want to get attention from and impress the people who count in my life	It is hopeless to change the course of events in my life; I am just not good enough	The world of reality does not offer any satisfaction to me; my interactions with others will eventually fail and cause harm, so it is safer to remain distant

| *Dangers* | Distortion of reality due to a preoccupation with confirmation of suspicions; loss of capacity for spontaneous action because of defensive attitudes | Inward orientation; indecisiveness and postponement; avoidance due to the fear of making mistakes; inability to deviate from planned activity; excessive reliance on rules and regulations; difficulties in seeing "the big picture" | Superficiality, suggestibility; the risk of operating in a non-factual world—action based on "hunches"; overreaction to minor events; others may feel used and abused | Overly pessimistic outlook; difficulties in concentration and performance; inhibition of action, indecisiveness | Emotional isolation causes frustration of dependency needs of others; bewilderment and aggressiveness may result |

efforts are made to discover organizational problems and to generate and select alternative solutions for dealing with them. Decision making also tends to be consultative so that a large number of factors can be taken into consideration and thus many aspects of each problem or threat can be addressed. However, decision making can become overly consultative in that different people are asked for similar information. This "institutionalization of suspicion" ensures that the most accurate information will get to the top of the firm, but it may also lower organizational morale and trust (besides wasting valuable time and energy).

Another organizational characteristic that conforms to the paranoid style is the tendency to *centralize power* in the hands of those top executives and their consultants who design control and information systems. Those who feel threatened generally like to have a good deal of control over their subordinates. They use subordinates to find out what is going on, but they want to reserve the ultimate decision-making power for themselves. So the locus of power is high up in the organization.

Much use is made of coordination and planning committees, sales meetings, sessions with regional managers, and so forth. The information elicited at these sessions is taken into account in making decisions. But most of the key decisions come from the top of the organization, leaving out other tiers of management that are affected.

The *strategies* of paranoid firms tend to be more reactive than proactive. External challenges "get through" to managers, who do their very best to cope with them. If competitors lower prices, the firm may study this challenge and react to it. If other firms introduce and are successful with a new product, the paranoid firm will probably imitate. But strategic paranoia carries with it a sizable element of *conservatism*. Fear can take many guises, and it often entails being afraid to overinnovate, to overextend resources, or to take bold risks. So a reactive strategy dominates. The level of risk taking will be held to a minimum, "safe" incremental and piecemeal moves being favored. The level of product-market innovation will lag slightly behind that of competitors. But the paranoid firm will, in general, be quite responsive to its environment.

A potential problem with the reactive orientation is that it can impede development of a concerted, integrated, and consistent strategy. The firm's direction is too much a function of external forces and not enough one of consistent goals, strategic plans, or unifying themes and traditions. A *"muddling through"* or "meandering" strategy can result, under which no forceful, distinctive competences are developed. The firm tries alternately to wear too many hats.

One strategy that may be used quite frequently by paranoid firms is product-market *diversification.* Here the attempt is to reduce the risk of exposure to, or reliance on, any one environment. The firm enters into a number of often unrelated businesses, each run by a separate divisional manager who is responsible for day-to-day operations. The managers, however, are kept in line by developing more sophisticated management information systems and narrowly focused controls. The desire to reduce risk can lead to diversification, which requires more elaborate control and information-processing mechanisms, which in turn reinforce the paranoid potential.

. What is the etiology of the paranoid configuration? Corporate paranoia may stem from a period of traumatic challenge. The environment may cause the firm to suddenly experience a crisis. A strong market might dry up, a powerful new competitor might enter the market, or a very damaging piece of legislation might be passed. The damage done by these forces may cause managers to become very distrustful and fearful, to lose their nerve, to recognize the need for better intelligence. We would therefore expect many paranoid firms to be facing or to have faced a very hostile and *dynamic environment.*

The following example of a paranoid firm is taken from our consulting experience. Paratech, Inc.,[18] was a semiconductor manufacturer run by its two founders, who had originally worked for a much larger electronics firm that did a good deal of top-secret defense contracting. Three factors contributed to the founders' paranoid behavior. The first was an episode at the defense contractor in which Soviet spies had made off with designs of great value. The second was a competitor that regularly beat Paratech to the marketplace with products that Paratech had first conceived. Finally, there was a high rate of bankruptcy in the industry.

The founders took all kinds of precautions to prevent their ideas from being stolen. They fragmented jobs and processes so that only a few key persons in the company really understood the products. They very rarely subcontracted any work. They also paid employees very high salaries to give them an incentive to stay with the firm. All three of these precautions acted to make Paratech's costs among the highest in the industry.

The founders also pursued other dysfunctional strategies that reflected their paranoia. First, the cyclicality of the markets made them financially conservative in an industry known for its rewards to risk takers. For example, Paratech spent too little on R&D relative to the competition and hence was slow to develop new products. As a result, the paucity of "innovator profits" made Paratech's margins among the lowest in the industry. Second, the founders carefully scanned the environment to see what the competition was up to. Unfortunately, they waited too long for the market's reaction to the competitor's products before making the decision to imitate. The delay was very costly, as markets for high-technology products saturate very quickly. Third, Paratech did not want to be left out of any segment of the market or to be overly dependent on any one sector. Therefore it diversified. But this spread it a bit too thin. The firm was unable to develop sufficient distinctive competences to stay on the leading edge of any one market. All these tendencies squeezed Paratech's profit margins. Paratech became one of the least successful firms, even when the industry was booming.

The Compulsive Organization. The compulsive firm is wed to ritual. Every last detail of operation is planned out in advance and carried on in a routinized and preprogrammed fashion. Thoroughness, completeness, and conformity to standard and established procedures are emphasized. These are central tendencies manifested by the organization structure, decision-making processes, and strategies of the compulsive firm.

The organization of the compulsive firm is a bit like that

of the paranoid firm. There is an emphasis on *formal controls* and information systems to ensure that the organizational machine is operating properly. However, a crucial difference between paranoid and compulsive organizations is that, in the latter, controls are really designed to monitor internal operations, production efficiency, costs, and scheduling and performance of projects. The paranoid firm, in contrast, places more emphasis on monitoring *external* environmental conditions.

Operations are *standardized* as much as possible, and an elaborate set of *formal policies,* rules, and procedures is evolved. These have a very wide range and extend not merely to the programming of production or marketing procedures but to dress codes, frequent sales meetings, and a corporate credo that includes suggested employee attitudes. All is prescribed. All is systematized and formally inscribed.

The organization is exceedingly *hierarchal.* Much status is accorded individuals simply because of their position. This may be because the leader personally has many compulsive characteristics, generally manifested by a strong concern with control. The compulsive person is always worried about the next move and how she is going to make it (see Table 2). This constant preoccupation with domination and submission has been reinforced by periods in the firm's history when it actually lost control and was at the mercy of the other organizations or constituencies. Consequently, compulsive executives try to *reduce uncertainty* at all costs and to attain a clearly specified objective in a determined manner. Surprises must be avoided. The structural attributes that ensure this state are, of course, tight controls, standardization of procedures (and, where possible, of personnel and attitudes), and centralization of power through the emphasis on hierarchy.

The *strategy-making* style of the compulsive firm shows the same preoccupation with detail and established procedures. First, every move is very carefully *planned.* There are generally a large number of action plans, budgets, and capital expenditure plans. Each project is very carefully designed, with many checkpoints, exhaustive performance evaluation procedures, and extremely detailed schedules. There is often a substantial planning department, which has representatives from many areas of functional expertise.

Another emphasis in strategy making is the long-run reliance on an *established theme*. The firm has a particular orientation and *distinctive competence,* and its plans reflect this. This orientation, rather than what is going on in the environment, serves as the major guide for the firm's strategy. For example, some organizations take pride in being the leading innovator in the marketplace. They focus their strategy on being the first out with new products, whether these are called for by customers or not. Other organizations try to be the most efficient low-cost producers and are careful to obtain the best equipment, good cost controls, and so on. Still other organizations place great emphasis on product quality. Thus, unlike paranoid firms, which often lack a theme for their strategies, compulsive firms have clear and very well-established themes. They also tend to focus in on a carefully circumscribed target market. There are no conglomerates here. Unfortunately, the theme may lose its relevance or appropriateness in the light of new market conditions, but the emphasis on traditional methods and the strong inward focus prevent any realization of this fact. Change is difficult. The *fixation* on a particular line of thought makes a new strategic orientation hard to push through. Usually, a changeover is preceded by a protracted period of doubt and ambivalence because of the difficulty of relaxing existing decision rules.

The external environment has to be fairly *stable* and cannot pose any great challenges. Otherwise, the programmed compulsive firm will rapidly perish. Usually, the firm is quite dominant—being somewhat bigger and stronger than its major competitors. If there is some dynamism in the environment because of, say, product-market changes, the firm is sufficiently well positioned and powerful to ignore it, at least for a while. In fact, more often than not, where the compulsive firm *is* found in a dynamic environment, the source of the dynamism is the firm itself.

The Minutiae Corporation was a classically compulsive firm. It was dominated by David Richardson, its founder and its chief executive officer for the past twenty years. The firm manufactured roller bearings for railroad cars. It was generally accepted that Minutiae's bearings, though costlier than the competitors', were easily the best available. They had been designed by Richardson himself, a mechanical engineer of great ability. He made sure that the bearings were manufactured to extremely precise specifications. Minutiae's quality control procedures were the tightest and most sophisticated in the industry. The machines were always kept in excellent repair. The firm's strategy strongly emphasized selling a very durable, high-quality product, and for many years this strategy paid off well. Indeed, Minutiae became the largest firm in the industry.

Over the past five years, however, smaller firms in the industry had begun to pioneer the use of new materials in their bearings. They were able to produce rather high-quality bearings for a fraction of the cost of the old products and thus could lower their prices. Richardson steadfastly refused to adopt the new material and its related technology, having found out about its somewhat inferior wearing qualities. The new material's softness made it easy to machine and therefore extremely economical for use in manufacturing, but this softness reduced bearing durability by 20 percent compared with the old material. Minutiae's product now became *twice* as expensive as the competition's, and it lost market share as result. Richardson's obsessive attention to a few elements of product quality caused him to ignore his product's overall attractiveness relative to the competition. Minutiae's strategy was focused too narrowly to allow it to survive in a changing environment.

The Dramatic Firm. Dramatic firms live up to their name in many respects: They are hyperactive, impulsive, dramatically venturesome, and dangerously uninhibited. Their decision makers live in a world of hunches and impressions rather than facts (see Table 2) as they address a broad array of widely disparate projects, products, and markets in desultory fashion. Their flair for the dramatic causes top echelons to centralize power, reserving their prerogative to independently initiate bold ventures.

We begin our discussion of the dramatic firm by examining corporate *strategy*, for everything else seems to follow from the strategy as well as the decision-making style used to formulate it. *Boldness, risk taking,* and *diversification* are the themes. Instead of reacting to the environment, the top decision maker, often an entrepreneur, attempts to enact his own environment. He enters some markets and industries and leaves others—initiates some new products while abandoning older ones. Generally, these are major and bold actions. A sizable proportion of the firm's capital is placed at risk. Often the strategic moves are so major that they require the firm to become highly levered financially. Most of these strategic moves are made in the service of grandiosity. Unbridled growth is the goal. The organization's strategy is a function of its top manager's considerable narcissistic needs, his desire for attention and visibility. It appears that the chief executive officer wants to be at center stage, putting on a show. He likes to be noticed, to finally show "the others over there" how great an executive he really is. (This may have been true of John DeLorean, the General Motors executive who quit to form his own automobile firm in Northern Ireland.)

Though dramatic, strategy is by no means consistent or integrated. The ventures undertaken are almost never complementary and sometimes are downright *conflicting*. The goal becomes action for action's sake—to have a dramatic impact, to be noticed. It is not uncommon to see such a firm entering a new market one year and then abandoning it for another the next as radically different ventures seize the fancy of the person at the top. A multiplicity of market niches are approached, and a great deal of organizational resources are squandered in the process. The level of risk taking can be enormously high.

As might be expected, the decision-making style is quite *unreflective*. Decisions are made impulsively by someone who really does not have the time to look into things very carefully. Hunches and superficial impressions guide actions more than facts do. The greater the number of complex ventures addressed, and the more extensive the range of diversification, the more the demands on the chief executive's time and the less attention the executive can pay to handling complex decisions and the operating problems that they produce. To aggravate the situation, the CEO rarely consults subordinates or staff experts in making key decisions. Participative decision making and consultation are alien to the dramatic organization. Analysis rarely takes place, and major ventures are initiated on the basis of only one point of view.

The *structure* of the dramatic organization is far *too primitive* for its broad product-market scope. The firm typically has grown and diversified quickly and haphazardly, and structure has failed to adapt to the new conditions. First, too much *power* is concentrated in the entrepreneurial chief executive. Such CEOs meddle even in routine divisional and departmental operating matters because they want to put their personal stamp on (and take credit for) everything. Alternating between a broad range of strategic and operating matters contributes to the lack of continuity in the corporate orientation. A second key characteristic of structure follows from this overcentralization—namely, the *absence of an effective information system.* The top executives do too little scanning of the environment because they have too little time and prefer to act on intuition rather than facts. Even where lower-level managers gather information, they have too little influence on decisions for it to matter. Because the firm has grown so rapidly, the controls of yesterday are no longer adequate. Operating problems develop quickly because of impulsive ventures and acquisitions but are very slow to be recognized. Finally, the striving for dominance by the leader obstructs effective internal communication, which is mostly in a top-down direction. Upward and lateral communication is scanty.

All these inadequacies of information processing are, of course, aggravated by the diversified nature of the organization and the *high levels of differentiation* in the goals, methods, and interpersonal orientations of subunits.[19]

We can take another disguised example from our consulting experience. Ken Lane, with the help of several investment-banker friends, bought a faltering fire equipment company and converted it into Lane Corporation. Lane's first task was to turn the failing company around. This he did brilliantly by reorienting the marketing strategy to take advantage of several growing markets. He pruned away the less attractive product lines, fired many of the less promising managers, and was left with a fairly profitable company after eighteen months. The bankers were impressed, and Lane was exhilarated by his successes. It was time, he thought, to go on to bigger and better things.

With his newly acquired capital he began to buy up firms in related industries, using the same methods as before to turn them around and improve their performance. His continued success motivated him to move still further afield, to acquire companies in unrelated industries. Because his past growth record had boosted the price-earnings multiple of his firm's stock, he could, by exchanging shares, purchase new firms at a fairly reasonable price. Lane's past record as a turnaround specialist made him eager to purchase cheap companies that were in a lot of trouble.

The pace of acquisition soon quickened, and Lane began to buy firms in industries he was not very familiar with, firms that were much sicker than he realized. He now found himself the leader of a large, diversified, complex, and rapidly expanding company. Still, he continued to make all the key decisions himself. It was *his* company and *his* strategy, so he would take the credit for its achievements. The group of staff experts he had recruited were there only to iron out the details. He felt free to ignore their advice and usually did. Time pressures, resulting from Lane's wish to boldly run the firm by himself, forced him to make decisions quickly and impulsively. As he did so, his errors multiplied. His constant quest for new acquisitions forced him to neglect the problems of existing operations. Profits began to fall precipitously. Eventually, the investment bankers, weary of Lane's grandiose pursuits, forced him to leave the scene. They had to sell off many of the firm's new divisions at a loss just to keep Lane Corporation afloat.

The Depressive Organization. Inactivity, lack of confidence, extreme conservatism, and a bureaucratically motivated insularity characterize the depressive organization. There is an atmosphere of extreme passivity and purposelessness. Whatever does get done is that which has been programmed and routinized and requires no special initiative. The organization thus acquires a character of automaticity.

Most depressive firms are found in *stable environments*—the only setting in which they can survive for any length of time. Typically, these firms are well established and serve a mature market, one that has had the same technology, customer preferences, and competitive patterns for many years. "Negotiated environments" characterized by trade agreements, collusion, restrictive trade practices, and substantial tariffs to limit foreign competition are the rule. The primary steel industry and the agricultural or industrial chemical businesses are representative of the markets in which depressive firms can be found. The low level of change and the absence of serious competition make the administrative task fairly simple, as does the homogeneity of the customers being served. Generally, depressive firms address only one narrowly defined market, a market that is almost never redefined or broadened.

Predictably enough, the orientation is very *bureaucratic*. Technologies are fairly automated, and the same administrative procedures have been used for decades. The firm almost runs itself. Everything functions automatically, according to plan—or, rather, according to policy and program. The organization operates like a machine; its gears and energy are formal procedures, routines, and prescribed methods. In fact, the depressive organization shows great similarities to the Weberian bureaucracy.

Although the organization is *hierarchal* in the sense that formal authority is centralized and position-based rather than expertise-based, the issue of intraorganizational power is not very salient. The firm is not guided by any real leader and does not show evidence of making major decisions. Control and coordination are really exercised by formalized programs and policies rather than by managerial initiatives. Suggestions for change are resisted; inhibition of action seems to prevail. It is almost as if the top executive group shared a feeling of impotence and incapacity. It is thought that there is no way to change the course of events in the organization. Managers just do not feel they have what it takes to revitalize their firm (see Table 2).

In such firms there is a *leadership vacuum*. The firm drifts aimlessly, without direction. It floats along on a river of ritual without explicit goals or targets. The top managers have become caretakers who have given up trying to direct the enterprise. They merely serve as passive functionaries, operating at low levels of performance and maintaining the status quo. Their dominant feeling is one of powerlessness, of sensing that the course of events is unalterable. The political vacuum at the top sometimes induces second-tier executives to engage in political gamesmanship. This usually fails to materialize, however, since "gamesmen" tend to be more attracted to more dynamic enterprises.[20]

The final element of organizational structure is the *internal focus of the information system.* Organizations that function automatically, mechanically, and passively and are content with the status quo rarely make major decisions. As a result, they do not engage in much information gathering to discover the key threats and weaknesses in markets. They do not open up internal communication channels to supply decision makers with the best information or to foster the collaboration of functional specialists. It is difficult to say whether a stagnant orientation induces inattention to (or a disinclination toward) information processing or whether the opposite causal direction holds. In either event, the two aspects seem to go hand in hand in the depressive firm.

This brings us to the issues of *strategy* and decision making. If any type of organization lacks all semblance of conscious strategy, it is the depressive firm. The sense of *aimlessness,* purposelessness, and apathy among top managers seems to preclude any attempts to give the firm any clear direction, orientation, or goals. Strategic issues are never explicitly considered, so meaningful *change does not occur.* The general outlook is one of pessimism. Yesterday's products and markets become today's, not so much because of an explicit policy of risk avoidance or conservatism as from a lethargy or blindness to strategic matters. Managers are focused inward. They do not receive or process much information about the external environment. Most of their time is spent working out minor details and handling routine operating matters. Decisions are avoided and much procrastination occurs. In fact, any outside observer would say that the firm seems to be in a catatonic state. Instead of an effort to adapt, to grow, or to become more effective, we see mainly inactivity and passivity.

The authors have observed a number of instances of this kind of behavior in organizations, particularly in certain firms taken over by conglomerates. In one case, after the departure of the previous top decision maker, an executive with entrepreneurial inclinations, the firm was subjected to a new style of management. The parent company introduced detailed new control procedures, many of which were irrelevant to that type of business. A new marketing strategy was forced on the company, which might have been appropriate for the parent firm but was totally out of place in the market served by the subsidiary. This lack of understanding on the part of the parent eventually stifled initiative and induced apathy among the key executives, who felt that they had very little control over the firm. A number of the most capable eventually left to take up more challenging positions in less restrictive firms. After a lengthy period of stagnation and financial losses, the parent sold off the crippled subsidiary.

Another depressive firm we dealt with was run by Roderick Kent, who was in his early sixties. He had taken over his father's dairy company at thirty-five and had been running it ever since. Very little had changed in the Sealed Fresh Company since the early days. The same production techniques were being used, very similar products were being sold, and the identical geographical area was being served—in the same way. For the last few years Kent had been given to working a twenty-five-hour week. He focused only on minor details such as revising product labels, raising prices to keep up with costs, and presiding over the retirement ceremonies of his employees. Kent's health was not very good, and of late he had been looking for someone to buy the business. Few firms were interested, as the Sealed Fresh Company was behind the times: It had old equipment, served a declining market, and had an undistinguished product line. Sales had been growing very slowly; profit margins were below average and falling, and losses were becoming much more frequent.

The vice-president of marketing had been urging Kent to change the product mix to emphasize products with growing popularity, such as "all natural" ice cream and fruit-flavored yogurts. She also thought it would be wise to go after more rapidly growing segments of the market and to make greater efforts to land more lucrative wholesale sales contracts. Kent discouraged all these projects as too costly or risky. In reality, he just did not want to make his job or his life any more complicated. The firm just continued to amble along, functioning like a poorly maintained machine and sustained mainly by momentum. Gradually competitors took more and more good business away from Sealed Fresh, leaving it with a doubtful group of customers.

The Schizoid Organization. The schizoid organization, like the depressive one, is characterized by a *leadership vacuum.* Its top executive discourages interaction because of a fear of involvement. Schizoid leaders experience the world as an unhappy place, populated by frustrating individuals (see Table 2). Perhaps because of past disappointments, they believe most contacts may end painfully for them. Consequently, they are inclined to daydream to compensate for a lack of fulfillment. In some organizations the second tier of executives will make up for what is missing from the leader with their own warmth and extroversion. This complementarity among executive personalities can sometimes overcome certain deficiencies of the leader.[21] Frequently, however, the schizoid organization can become a political battlefield. Members of the second tier see in the withdrawn nature of the top executive an opportunity to pursue their own needs.

A key repercussion of this behavior is that the second tier becomes a *political playground* for "gamesmen" who try to win favor from the unresponsive leader. The leadership vacuum and the political infighting caused by the schizoid leader have some interesting strategic and structural implications. Perhaps the most important is that no concerted and integrated product-market strategy develops. The leader is insecure, withdrawn, and noncommittal. He seems to have no interest in the organization and refuses to adopt any consistent position, vacillating between the proposals of one favored subordinate and another. No clear sense of direction emerges. The effective power for strategy making resides in a *shifting coalition* of careerist second-tier managers who try to influence the indecisive leader and simultaneously to advance their pet projects and their little empires. As a result, the firm muddles through and drifts, making incremental changes in one area and then reversing them when a new group of managers becomes ascendant.

Strategy becomes more a product of individual goals, power, and politicking than any perceived key threats or opportunities in the external environment. The strategy also *may* be a product of the executive's intrapsychic fantasies, but not usually, as the CEO's emotional apathy and inactivity thwart translation of his ideas into actions. Moreover, a conservatism accompanies the organization's aimlessness. The initiatives of one group of managers are often neutralized or severely blunted by those of a politically opposing group. The result is that only small, incremental, and *piecemeal changes* occur.

We have already hinted at the structure of the schizoid firm. Its main characteristic is the dispersal of some power and almost all decision-making initiative to the tier of managers just below the top executive. The political and gamesmanlike style of these second-tier managers stems in large part from the characteristics of the leader, whose indecisiveness and withdrawal alienate well-adjusted managers and provide a fertile breeding ground for opportunists who are adept at catering to the leader's insecurities. These second-tier managers very rarely collaborate effectively, and so the structure takes the form of a series of warring or at least uncooperative and *independent fiefdoms* —of alienated departments and divisions.

The divided nature of the organization thwarts effective cross-functional (and, where relevant, interdivisional) coordination and communication. Information is used more as a power resource than as a vehicle for effective adaptation. Very real *barriers* are erected *to prevent the free flow of information*. But this is not the only shortcoming of the information system. Another is the absence of environmental scanning. The focus is internal—on personal political ambitions and catering to the top manager's desires. Second-tier managers find it more useful to ignore objective environmental phenomena that might reflect poorly on their own past behavior or might conflict with the wishes of the detached leader.

The Cornish Corporation was a political battlefield for two of its second-tier managers. It was a ladies' apparel manufacturer run by Selma Gitnick. Gitnick had been a very successful manager, but the suicide of her daughter and her recent divorce had turned an already withdrawn individual into a recluse. She rarely left her office or had other managers visit her there. Instead, everything was done through written memos. In a firm that required rapid adaptation to a dynamic and uncertain fashion market, this slowdown in communications caused serious difficulties.

Gitnick reserved the right to make all important final decisions herself; but she was very difficult to reach, and she had been very imprecise in allocating responsibilities and authority to the second-tier managers. These factors required the managers to make most decisions. But because they were unclear about their own and everyone else's decision-making authority and responsibilities, each decision involved a power struggle.

The design people believed they could make the final choice of designs. They began to clash frequently with the head of the marketing department, who accused the design personnel of incompetence and claimed he could veto any of their design decisions. Each department head had written to Gitnick, complaining about the other and asking for a final decision. Gitnick was ambiguous in her reply, essentially instructing the managers to give each other full cooperation. As a result, the bickering (and vetoing) continued, and the consequent delays allowed competitors to purchase the best designs. Moreover, Cornish was two months late with its new line—which was to prove disastrous for sales.

Table 3 gives an overview of the strengths and weaknesses of each organizational neurotic style. Should our framework possess predictive power, this list can serve as a preliminary tool for the diagnosis of organizational problems.

Table 3. Strengths and Weaknesses of the Five Organizational Styles.

Style	Potential Strengths	Potential Weaknesses
Paranoid	Good knowledge of threats and opportunities inside and outside the firm Reduced market risk from diversification	Lack of a concerted and consistent strategy—few distinctive competences Insecurity and disenchantment among second-tier managers and their subordinates because of the atmosphere of distrust
Compulsive	Fine internal controls and efficient operation Well-integrated and focused product-market strategy	Traditions embraced so firmly that strategy and structure become anachronistic Things so programmed that bureaucratic dysfunctions, inflexibility, and inappropriate responses become common Managers discontent owing to their lack of influence and discretion; stifling of initiative
Dramatic	Creates the momentum for passing through the start-up phase of a firm Some good ideas for revitalizing tired firms	Inconsistent strategies that have a very high element of risk and cause resources to be needlessly squandered Problems in controlling widespread operations and in restoring their profitability Rash and dangerous expansion policies Inadequate role played by second tier of managers
Depressive	Efficiency of internal processes Focused strategy	Anachronistic strategies and organizational stagnation Confinement to dying markets Weak competitive posture due to poor product lines Apathetic and inactive managers

(continued on next page)

Table 3. Strengths and Weaknesses of the Five Organizational Styles,
Cont'd.

Style	Potential Strengths	Potential Weaknesses
Schizoid	Second-tier managers share in strategy formulation; a variety of points of view may be brought to bear	Inconsistent or vacillating strategy Issues decided by political negotiations more than facts Lack of leadership Climate of suspicion and distrust, which prevents collaboration

Deciphering the Signifiers

In studying organizations we are really engaged in deciphering structures of signification.[22] Order is sought where chaos once reigned. As researchers of organizations, we are curious about why certain decisions are made and certain strategies chosen. Why does the organization end up with a particular kind of structure? Why is a certain individual selected for a particular job? What we are trying to do is to recognize the "signifiers" that constitute the organizational configurations, the cues that will give us insight into formal and informal structure, the occurrences that take place at the shared-fantasy level of the organization. We are also, in some sense, looking for the meaning behind these "signifiers"—that which gives rise to them and is "signified."

We believe that many aspects of strategy, structure, and organizational culture are signifiers (that is, are a function) of the neurotic styles and fantasies of the top echelon of managers. More specifically, the "neurotic" characteristics of executives—the peculiarities of their styles—seem to give rise to uniformities of organizational culture, in the form of myths, stories, and shared beliefs. These are long-lived and self-perpetuating and can, in turn, foster common *organizational* neurotic styles as manifested by certain strategies, structures, and organizational cultures.

Indeed, our argument seems to have some predictive importance. On the basis of five common neurotic styles and their associated fantasies, we believe it is possible to erect a predictively useful taxonomy of organizational dysfunction. Once the predominant neurotic style of the top executives has been identified, we feel that many aspects of the strategy and structure of the organization may be predicted, as well as its predominant culture and shared fantasies. We believe that these psychodynamic and organizational phenomena together form integral gestalts, or configurations. Given some aspects of each configuration, one can predict many of its other aspects by making reference to the taxonomy. These gestalts demonstrate mutual complementarities among their elements. They reveal the genesis of particular organizational weaknesses and the way these are tied to strategy, structure, organizational culture, and managerial personality. Our framework can be used to generate a set of hypotheses linking the neurotic style and shared fantasies for each type.

Should the framework we have outlined be borne out by subsequent empirical research, there will be a number of practical implications for management. The first is that organizational problems are often deeply ingrained, having as their etiology the deep-seated neurotic styles and intrapsychic fantasies of top executives. They are manifested by a broad array of structural, strategic, and "mythical" (shared fantasy) aspects. These are mutually reinforcing and pervasive and therefore resistant to change. Organizational change agents will be effective only if they get at the roots of dysfunctions—but this might be very difficult if problems are so deeply ingrained and so broadly manifested. Piecemeal changes will not do much good, and revolutionary ones are expensive, hard to implement, and politically inexpedient. Since our five common pathologies seem to be so multifaceted and thematically unified, it is unlikely that they can be adequately addressed by management consultants with a standard bag of tools. Implementation of information systems, use of strategic business units, committees, and matrix structures, or creation of organization development and quality-of-worklife programs will be of little help as long as an organization's executives cling to their dysfunctional fantasies and shared organizational ideologies. The new programs will have little effect unless they are complemented by more realistic views of the business and its environment or, failing that, by more adaptive executives. We are not suggesting that neurotic styles always require changing. They may sometimes be quite compatible with a firm's environment. But in general they foster a kind of rigidity that inhibits adaptation. In the long run, only a fluidity of styles and a healthy mixture of them can ensure corporate success.

Our framework also implies that executives must be on the lookout for the five pathological styles. Since it is hard to recognize these in one's own attitudes, it might be easier to examine the organization to see whether its concrete structure, strategy, or culture conforms across the board to one of our pathological types. If so, it might be time for an open discussion of shared fantasies—to the extent that they can be articulated—in order to scrutinize them. This discussion may lead to changes in the company's mission and structure. The stimulus for such dialogue usually has to come from a knowledgeable outsider, and the dialogue needs a considerable investment in time and effort. It might also be useful to examine the degree of similarity of these fantasies among top executives. The more uniform they are, the greater the dangers of being out of touch with reality and falling into the trap of insularity. Perhaps the time will have come to open up the organization to those with different personalities and fantasies to create a climate of healthy diversity.

Recruitment and promotion policies might benefit from the attempt to ensure substantial differences in the personalities of key executives. Executives tend to select and promote in their own image. There are also socialization processes that occur in a very subtle way in organizations and that tend to have a molding effect on character. Since organizations can easily become gathering stations for managers with similar styles, there will always be a danger that the lack of diversity may give rise to organizational pathology.

Having discussed the organizationwide dysfunctions that can stem from the neurotic style of the top executive, we next shift our focus down to the departmental or group level of organizations. We will proceed to examine the impact that members have on one another in developing irrational fantasies.

2

Shared Fantasies
and Group Processes

A group is extraordinarily credulous and open to influence,
it has no critical faculty, and the improbable does not exist
for it. It thinks in images, which call one another up by
association (just as they arise within individuals in states of
free imagination), and whose agreement with reality is
never checked by any reasonable agency. The feelings of a
group are always very simple and very exaggerated. So that
a group knows neither doubt nor uncertainty.
                    —Sigmund Freud, *Group Psychology and*
                                    the Analysis of the Ego

When individuals gather as a group, some form of collective mental activity takes place, resulting in common perceptions and desires that often lead to shared fantasies. In Chapter
One we concentrated on the neurotic styles of individual key
managers and the impact these might have on entire organizations. Now we shall focus on the shared fantasies of *groups*
within the firm and the impact of such fantasies on group functioning. We shall also show how these shared fantasies will influence organizational decision making, structure, strategy, and
culture. Of course, where the group is the dominant coalition and
the firm is small, the findings of the two chapters will overlap.

Psychiatrists, psychologists, and psychoanalysts interested in group work have made many observations about the organizing function of shared fantasies.[1] They have noted how such fantasies create a symbolic reality, how they influence the behavior of group members. In a classic study, Wilfred Bion has postulated the existence of a group mentality, a phenomenon that he views as the "pool" of members' wishes, opinions, thoughts, and emotions "to which the anonymous contributions are made, and through which the impulses and desires implicit in these contributions are gratified. Any contribution to this group mentality must enlist the support of, or be in conformity with, the other anonymous contributions of the group."[2] Bion expects "the group mentality to be distinguished by a uniformity that contrasts with the diversity of thought in the mentality of the individuals who have contributed to its formation."[3]

Another scholar of group behavior, Robert Bales, also stresses the importance of a group mentality. He describes a chain-reaction process engendering unified fantasies in groups, which occurs "when one or some of the participants presents in his communication symbols which have unconscious meanings for one or some of the other participants."[4] Bales breaks down the development of the group fantasy as follows: "(1) Elements are *selected* for more extended discussion; (2) accidents are *taken advantage* of for the creation of symbolic meaning; (3) the selected elements and chance combinations are *elaborated*; (4) the elaboration is performed *cooperatively* as an interpersonal process; and (5) the group process has the qualities of a '*chain reaction*'—a process which reinforces itself increasingly in an accelerated growth curve of interest, excitement, and involvement."[5]

Foundations of Organizational Culture

This chain reaction of shared fantasy creates a symbolic reality that resembles what is often described as organizational ideology, organizational culture, organizational imagery, or organizational identity. In spite of the frequent use of these terms in the literature, however, little effort has been made to explore these concepts. Very little analysis has been devoted to understanding common group fantasies and their implications for organizational culture and functioning. Thus we might ask ourselves: What will very basic shared fantasies look like? What beliefs and behaviors do the participants in an organizational culture have in common? To what extent do these basic shared fantasies influence and manifest themselves in organizational functioning?

It may be useful to start with an example. One of the authors recently witnessed a simple manifestation of a group fantasy. It took place at a succession planning meeting at a subsidiary of a large conglomerate. The meeting was to be chaired by the parent company's senior vice-president of human resources.

While waiting for the senior VP's arrival, one of the vice-presidents of the subsidiary recounted his experiences during a recent flight in a small private airplane. To allow the plane to regain altitude, the VP had been asked to change seats to improve the weight distribution. He emphasized how anxious he had been—and how vulnerable we all so often are without realizing it. One of the other vice-presidents of the subsidiary then joined in, telling how one of the engines of a plane he was taking to Chicago had caught fire just before takeoff. He described the panic among the passengers that had ensued as they were marshaled out of the plane. This story, in turn, prompted still another executive to tell about his visit to Beirut. He told of how he had been greeted by sniper fire as he left his hotel. The conversation continued in the same vein until the senior vice-president finally made his appearance.

Our long experience with this subsidiary revealed that its top managers were becoming increasingly worried about their positions. They had felt "under attack" by the parent ever since the takeover. Many feared losing their jobs or expected a demotion or some other threat to their status and self-esteem. A siege mentality developed, which was continually being manifested in discussions such as the one just reported. In general, however, the opinions expressed specific job- or organization-related worries. The airplane discussion (and many others in a similar vein) showed how widespread and pervasive the persecutory group fantasy really was.

The context of this fantasy is revealing. Until the take-over, the subsidiary had been one of the most prosperous firms in the industry. But it had recently been suffering from declining sales and profits. In fact, some of the more able executives had left the company, making it plain that they were disgusted at the lack of flexibility, understanding, and tolerance of the executives at the parent. Ruthless cost cutting, managerial lay-offs, and pernicious interference in the subsidiary's decision-making process had created an anxiety-ridden milieu. Many managers believed, with considerable justification, that their security was being threatened—that their careers might be unpleasantly disrupted. The airplane discussion and the fear-laden "group culture" seemed to make sense in light of all this.

Our search for the most basic shared fantasies has been aided by the seminal work of Bion.[6] On the basis of his research, Bion noted two common aspects of group behavior. First, groups have an overt, specific task to perform that necessitates cooperation and effort from the group members, a task that requires contact with reality and the ability to tolerate frustrations and control emotions. Bion believed, however, that, quite apart from this "work group" behavior, all groups are also dominated by a second characteristic—namely, their "basic assumptions." These operate at a more primitive level and are of a regressive nature. Basic assumptions can be viewed as determinants of an individual's manner of coping with the anxiety occasioned by different life situations. Whereas the work group is more oriented toward reality, the "basic-assumption group" operates at a more primitive fantasy level. These basic-assumption groups are expected to color and influence any rational task that the work group has to undertake.

Although the "basic assumptions" have been discovered through work with small therapeutic groups, it has been argued that they also characterize the groups that make up coalitions in organizations, groups that determine organization strategy, structure, and process.[7] These basic assumptions are, we think, the principal organizing units that create organizational culture and commonly shared organizational myths, legends, and stories. They operate at the social-fantasy level of organizations. After Bion, we have named the assumptions and their groups *fight/ flight, dependency,* and pairing, or *utopian.* These three types of groups have surfaced repeatedly in the clinical group work done by Bion and his followers at the Tavistock Institute in England during the last thirty years.

The basic fantasy found among members of the fight/ flight group is that there is somewhere an enemy against whom one has to defend or from whom one has to escape. In contrast, the dependency group seems to have met in order to be nourished or protected by a leader. Among Bion's pairing group, which we call utopian, the preoccupation is with the thought that somewhere in the future a person or idea will surface that will provide ultimate salvation.

Groups whose behavior is determined by these three basic fantasies can be recognized by particular defensive mechanisms and accompanying emotions. Fight/flight cultures resort to very primitive defenses to manage anxiety. Members of these groups see the environment as extremely dangerous. People are not believed to be trustworthy. The world and the people inhabiting it are "split" into "good" and "bad" parts—those that act in accordance with the group members' needs or against them. There is too little integration or balance here.[8] Fight/flight group members deny that any misfortune could be the result of their own actions. Self-reflection and insight are remarkably lacking. Only "the others" are to blame. Because hostile impulses are externalized and attributed, or projected, to others, the leader's primary role is seen to be the mobilization of the group for immediate action—be it flight or attack. The leader must set the example of valor and possess the ability to recognize dangers or enemies. The predominant emotions that originate from this group culture are anger, hate, fear, and suspicion.

Dependency group members want to be sustained by a revered, omnipotent leader, a person who is dependable. The main dynamic in these groups is the need for idealization. Members wish to merge with the all-powerful leader and thereby share in his power. They wish to believe that the leader's actions are all-good, and they deny any evidence to the contrary. The primary emotion of the group in such a situation is elation, a feeling of oneness and security with the good and protective leader. But elation actually conceals depressive feelings concerning the member's own sense of inadequacy, envy of the prerogatives of the leader and her protégés, and guilt over feeling these emotions. For some members of the group, the leader will eventually fail to live up to their excessive expectations. An attitude reversal then takes place, transforming idealization into devaluation. In some instances overthrow and replacement of the leader may result.[9] More often, however, the "rebels" are expelled.

When the leader retires or dies and there is no one to take his place, the dependency group may draw its strength from a "bible," a symbolic codification of policies and rules rooted in the history and traditions of the group and originally derived from the revered leader. The group engages in the "exegesis" of his works. In other instances the group may resort to an external entity, asking another department, a parent firm, a bank, or some other body for help, and thus fulfill its dependency needs.

The utopian culture is characterized by the messianic hope that in the future everything will finally work out and members will be delivered from their anxieties and fears. It almost appears as if participants in such cultures could do without an actual leader. Instead, the group nourishes the illusion that in the future a new leader or new idea will eventually solve all its problems. We can observe a sense of anticipation and a tendency to use fantasy in the form of daydreams to resolve conflict and obtain gratification. The predominant affects are hope and faith. This emotional state can persist, however, only as long as the idea or leader remains "unborn" and unmaterialized. Given the excessive expectations of the group, it will be impossible for the idea or person ever to live up to its wants. Eventually, when members' hopes and faith are shattered, the door is opened to despair and disillusionment. In the meantime these dynamics and emotions may stimulate enthusiasm, optimism, and some tentative goal-oriented creative gestures.

Table 4 summarizes the elements of the three basic cultures.

Quite often, one of these basic assumptions or shared fan-

Table 4. Main Features of the Three Organizational Cultures.

Basic Shared Fantasy	Feature		
	Assumption	Principal Dynamics	Predominant Affects
Fight/flight	There is an enemy inside or outside; defense or escape is necessary	Projection of own hostile feelings onto others; split world into good and bad	Anger, hate, fear, suspicion
Dependency	There is a desire to be nourished and protected by a leader	Idealization (sometimes devaluation) of "leader" or of leader's bible	Depression, envy, guilt, reverence
Utopian	There is an idea or person, still unborn, that will deliver the group from hatred, destructiveness, and despair	Anticipation and fantasy concerning utopian ideals	Hope, faith, utopianism, enthusiasm, despair, disillusionment

tasies will prevail among the dominant coalition or departments of the organization. Elements of the other shared fantasies are also likely to be present. Susceptibility to each basic fantasy will vary somewhat among the members of the group. A single assumption may correspond to a particular period in the group's life cycle and facilitate effective functioning, but tenacious adherence to one shared basic fantasy may have serious dysfunctional consequences, as it tends to exaggerate the importance of some realities at the expense of other, perhaps more pressing ones. Moreover, although one basic shared fantasy may be operative, remnants of other fantasies will take over in different circumstances. For example, the fight/flight fantasy may replace the utopian fantasy in times of crisis.

Organizational Culture and Dynamics

A fantasy shared by a dominant coalition most likely will permeate throughout the organization and determine its culture. More often, perhaps, a fantasy comes to characterize a department or division within an organization. Intensive and frequent interactions and face-to-face contacts are usually required before one of the basic shared fantasies can arise to produce a uniform culture. These conditions are most likely to be met in small groups. Cultures are, of course, likely to change as the organization changes its leadership or faces different challenges from the environment.

For the past decade we have worked with groups of top managers as general consultants, and time after time we have noted the frequency with which one of the three basic shared fantasies seemed to surface within departments of the firm and often within its dominant coalition. Given our backgrounds and interests, this observation, in and of itself, seemed most fascinating. But far more important, particularly for this book, was that both authors consistently observed certain departmental or organizational characteristics that were very commonly linked with each of the three basic-assumption cultures. We shall summarize our observations in the form of speculations about how these organizational cultures and their related basic shared fantasies might influence organizational functioning. We shall also show how each organizational culture will generate and perhaps, in turn, be nurtured by particular organizational scenarios that each carry with them performance consequences.

Fight/Flight Culture. Past experiences have caused lasting fears within the group and a tendency for the group members to "split" the world sharply into camps of friends and enemies. This process is the fight/flight group's primary defensive mechanism. Intense fears or antipathies rigidify perceptions and behavior, so that fight/flight groups have avoidance or attack goals that are not subject to change or discussion. General strategic goals are vague. There is simply a desire for protection from or conquest over the enemy. Only the means for accomplishing these goals are open to discussion and can be freely dealt with. Another factor prompting the focus on means instead of goals is the short time horizon of fight/flight groups. Attention is devoted to the current ongoing battle with a particular foe. All attitudes have been frozen by a past trauma involving the enemy.

All these aspects of the fight/flight culture make for a

very insular management style. More specifically, there is a closed, narrow, and rigid way of viewing the world, one that never changes or develops and has no real inspiration or vision. The members of the group act on impulse (prior categories and fears or anger) rather than deliberation. The antagonism toward "the other" and the desire for safety from "the other" dominate actions—even when there is no longer any basis for the beliefs that give rise to these actions. Behavior is rigid because all concepts are based on deeply ingrained fears. Table 5 summarizes these dimensions of the fight/flight culture (as well as the dependency and utopian cultures).

Two possible scenarios are associated with the fight/flight culture. The first relates to the group's paranoid mode, the second to its avoidance nature. *Paranoia* can result in very sharp or exaggerated responses to perceived enemies inside or outside the organization. We have already seen this in the paranoid firm of Chapter One, but in fight/flight cultures fears can be especially intense, as *everyone* shares them. The search for the enemy results in a great mobilization of energy and a strong conviction among the organization members of the correctness of their actions. It may lead to courageous action, but much of this activity will be wasted because of stereotyping, which leads to rigidity in decision making. Such departments exhibit a strong competitive posture. "Enemies" are vigorously sought out, tracked down, and responded to. For example, competitor's product-market strategies are imitated or countered by the firm. Employees suspected of disloyalty are fired. Power is centralized in the hands of the paranoid group of leaders, since "no one can be trusted."

This scenario of the fight/flight culture is quite reminiscent of Paratech, the paranoid firm of Chapter One. It may also become common in schizoid firms, as there too a theme of suspicion and distrust prevails. But the focus here is different from that of Chapter One in that our level of analysis is the group (*small* firm or department) and its basic shared fantasies, rather than the organization and the neurotic style of its top managers. This difference is the source of one potentially major difference between fight/flight groups and paranoid organizations. In the

Table 5. Dimensions of the Cultures Corresponding to the Three Group Fantasies.

Group Fantasy	Dimension				
	Time Perspective/ Horizon	Impulsivity/ Deliberation	Flexibility/ Rigidity	Means/Goals Specificity	Pervasive Style
Fight/flight	Past Short-term	Impulsive	Rigid	Means explicit, goals poorly defined	Insular
Dependency					
With strong leader	Present and future	Some deliberation by leader only	Flexible	Means and goals	Charismatic/auto-cratic
After leader	Past and present Short-term	No deliberation	Rigid	Neither	Bureaucratic
Utopian	Future Long-term	Highly deliberative	Flexible	Goals, no means	Democratic/partici-pative

former, there is a uniformity of simplistic thinking among members, who are convinced of the hostile intentions and ill effects of the enemy and the need to avoid or attack him. An unreflective, impulsive approach to decision making results. The paranoid organization is quite different in this regard. There the paranoid leader places a premium on information gathering and analysis. He is not in a panic, as the members of the fight/flight culture often are. The paranoid executive is concerned mainly with protecting himself and his firm by discovering what the major threats really are (the enemy may not even have been identified) and countering them in the most effective manner.

The second type of scenario associated with the fight/flight culture might be typed as *avoidance-based*. Fear creates the need to reduce uncertainty, to erect barriers and isolate oneself from one's enemies. This can take the form of a preoccupation with internal operating matters, efficiency, and smooth and economical production. Detailed and elaborate rules, controls, and programs are created to buffer the unit and regularize operations. As in depressive and compulsive firms, the focus is internal as the group tries to insulate itself from the hostile environment. The attitude is "If it seems impossible to beat competitors, at least block out their influence." Cartels and trade associations are sought to avoid industry competition. Departmental regulations and formalities are established to insulate the group from "rival" departments. Although the preoccupation with internal buffering and government protection can have its beneficial effects, the group's insularity, the inadequacy of analysis, and the lack of broadly focused attention to the environment may give the competition an advantage.

These organizational dynamics of the fight/flight culture (and the others) are summarized in Table 6.

The Lance Corporation's marketing department had long been a dominant force in setting the strategy of the firm. In fact, the department was in the habit of strongly influencing its production, R&D, and finance counterparts. Alice Marston, the director of marketing, invariably had the ear of the president, an ex-marketing man himself and the one responsible for training and promoting her.

Table 6. Organizational Dynamics Under the Three Cultures.

Organizational Culture	Organizational Scenario	Organizational Consequences	
		Positive	Negative
Fight/flight			
	Paranoid	Mobilization of energy	Poorly conceived strategy
	Search for an enemy	Sense of conviction	Factionalism
	Competitive posture is aggressive		Suspicion and fighting among departments, divisions, parent/subsidiary, outside constituencies
			Stereotyping
	Avoidance	Excellent internal operations and processes	Insularity
	Internally oriented	Efficiency	Inadequate environmental analysis
		Buffering of group through trade barriers, cartels, or departmental bureaucracy	Ignorance of competitive threats
Dependency			
	Charismatic	Goal-directedness	Passivity and lack of critical judgment of subordinates
	Centralization of power and decision making	Cohesiveness	Lack of moderation in decision making by the leader
		Focused strategy	
	Bureaucratic	Focused strategy	Excessive reliance on rules and regulations
	Rule- and procedure-oriented	Clarity of roles	Lack of adaptation
			Resistance to change

Takeover			
	Shift in power base and decision-making latitude	Revitalization	Upheaval Passivity among executive group Apathy Maintenance role Exodus of capable executives
	Technological innovation		
	R&D orientation	Creativity New technology	Drain of resources Much risk taking Lack of realistic analysis
Utopian	*Organizational innovation*		
	Utopian structures	Harmony Collaboration Democratization Great adaptive capacity	Excessive idealism Denial of present-day reality Floundering from one panacea to the next

The fight/flight nature of the marketing department quickly became apparent to the consultants who had been called in. Almost all the product development, advertising, and pricing strategies were explicitly aimed at counteracting the moves of competitors. For example, very rarely was a new product or product modification initiated without its being a direct response to a perceived threat from the key competitor. Further, advertising campaigns emphasized comparisons with the competitor's products. Indeed, one such campaign had resulted in a lawsuit by the competitor. Finally, price wars with the competitor were numerous. Thus, the managers in charge of pricing, promotion, and product development all enthusiastically shared Marston's notion that the firm was being viciously attacked by a particular competitor and therefore had to be vigorously defended.

The director of marketing, as well as all her managers, seemed to operate under a siege mentality. They believed that they, specifically, were the principal targets of one competitor in particular. Hence, their totally monolithic strategy was aimed at evading, attacking, and besting that competitor, while paying scant attention to what the customers really wanted. This strategy led to some major problems. For example, an entrepreneur with a background in engineering and design was in charge of the "threatening" competitor. He had a proclivity for introducing too many new products, a practice that vastly increased his firm's production costs and gave it a high level of R&D overhead. Marston did, at least in one sense, recognize her competitor's mistake. She articulated the problem very clearly to one of the consultants on several occasions, claiming quite correctly that the customers did not appreciate and did not require many product innovations but, instead, preferred low prices. Nonetheless, she continued to imitate the competitor's practices, incurring substantial costs while reaping very few benefits. Her rationale was that the competitor was trying to "get the jump" on them, and she "just couldn't risk falling behind."

Of course, the R&D and production directors began to quarrel with the marketing director, accusing her of putting too much emphasis on new-product development, in the first place, and blaming her for many production-line retooling interruptions and inefficiencies, in the second. The finance director complained that the frequent price wars and excessive product line variety were beginning to cause losses. The siege mentality now intensified. Marston could legitimately point to the other departments' overt hostility to her ideas. She now began to identify enemies within as well as outside the firm and was able to convince her key managers, who also were beginning to receive hostile responses from other departments, that their fears were justified. The paranoia fed on itself, so that all issues involving other departments were decided by political battles and conflicts. An "us versus them" attitude was created.

The marketing strategy conformed to fight/flight tendencies in every respect. The time horizon was short-term in the extreme: As soon as the key competitor changed his pricing, promotion, or product line, the marketing director reacted immediately. The focus was on short-term reactions to short-term feedback rather than on long-term goals. Decisions were made quickly and impulsively—out of fear. All the marketing managers had the same knee-jerk reactions to the tactics of the competition. When they met, these managers would discuss the means for coping with a new competitive threat, ignoring whether their response was appropriate in the broader market context. They operated without encompassing long-term goals and treated each threat as an emergency. The result was an impulsive, muddling-through approach to decision making, as different goals and issues surfaced according to the crisis in question. A disjointed, incremental strategy resulted.

Dependency Culture. The dependency culture is quite different from the fight/flight culture. It is characterized by three phases, each with similar underlying emotions but quite different behavior patterns. One phase associated with the dependency culture revolves around the worship of the *charismatic leader.* This leader-dominated phase may occur during the early period of corporate history, when the firm is dominated by a powerful founder or entrepreneur. This may be a charismatic figure who surrounds himself with compliant, subservient second-tier executives who believe strongly in his goals, talents, and strategies. Such a culture recalls some of the characteristics of the dramatic firm.

A company or department influenced by this type of dependency culture tends to have a short-term time horizon; it is preoccupied with the current ideology being proposed by the leader and its immediate action implications. The charismatic leader is often oriented toward action, trying to implement a desired state of affairs, and his followers go along with this, striving to serve his current desires. Although the dependency group does not appear quite so impulsive as the fight/flight group, neither does it engage in much deliberation in making decisions. The leader is charismatic—what he says goes. There is thus an unquestioning, trustful climate of subordinacy among group members. Zealous followers place too much faith in the leader to foster a reflective, analytical atmosphere. Although most deliberation is done by the leader, he himself is not usually motivated to do a great deal of it. Because his power gives him much latitude in which to act, he is free to consider both goals and means in making decisions. Both are subject to change and engender some flexibility in the group's pattern of behavior. The members of the group are tied to the leader personally—not to any deeply held fears, as in the fight/flight situation. The leader can therefore act boldly and change fundamental parameters without losing his basis of support. (This is by no means true of the fight/flight group, in which the leader is elected only because he happens to mirror and articulate the preexisting concerns and fears of the group. As soon as he stops doing this, he loses his power.) Indeed, leadership in the dependency group can be both charismatic and autocratic as long as the strong leader remains in charge.

The charismatic figure induces much goal-directedness and cohesiveness, strengths derived from the feeling that there is someone to depend on. These benefits are counterbalanced, however, by the passivity and lack of critical judgment of the subordinates. The leader sets the tone for the unit, while the other managers serve only to carry out his directives. Only the leader does the thinking and decision making. Deliberation and action are centralized as well as power. One of the negative consequences of the compliance of the second-tier executives may be a lack of moderation in decision making. The leader is free to pursue poorly conceptualized and risky strategic moves.

The nature of the dependency group can change a great deal, however, once the strong leader leaves and the "bible" of his or her legacy takes over. In this second phase a set of rigid policies and rules may replace the leader. Consequently, the group engages in less reflection and responds only to codified rules, becoming as rigid as the fight/flight culture. Flexibility is lost, time horizons shorten, and deliberation ceases altogether as an autocratic, charismatic style gives way to a *bureaucratic* one. Table 5 summarizes these dimensions. Adaptive decisions are no longer being made; the primary effort is to extend past practices, resulting in great resistance to change. The entrepreneur is replaced by caretakers who extrapolate but do not lead. This might have temporary benefits in terms of the clarity of roles and a focused strategy. Structures may, however, become mechanistic, formal, and bureaucratic, while strategies can become anachronistic and rigid.

A third and final dependency phase can involve the *takeover* of a firm (rather than a department) by a powerful parent company or even by a key customer or supplier, so that much latitude for decision making is lost. Occasionally, if a firm is stagnating and floundering, a takeover may be the catalyst for its revitalization. In many instances, however, the draining of power as well as the imposition of resource dependency can make an active executive group passive, apathetic, and docile. The executives' function changes from direction to maintenance, their position from leadership to subordinacy. Strong personalities leave the organization, while weaker managers pander passively to the powerful interests, much as second-tier executives served the charismatic entrepreneur. A typical example of such a culture is found in the depressive firm. Table 6 summarizes these scenarios.

On rare occasions, the dependency culture is associated with an internal rebellion, which may motivate replacement of the charismatic leader. In such instances some of the more capable second-tier executives may have become disenchanted with the leadership of the top executive, feeling that she has not been able to live up to their expectations. Such reactions may culminate in an attempt at overthrow. Usually these actions fail. They have, however, a destabilizing effect and may result in the exodus of some of the more capable executives.

Although Nouveau Shoe Manufacturing Corporation was over twenty-five years old, for twenty-three of those years its marketing department had been dominated by its aggressive and charismatic first employee, Vice-President John Aaron. Aaron regarded his department as an extension of himself. He personally made all the marketing decisions of any consequence, and the product lines closely reflected his particular tastes and interests (the president was a retiring "figurehead" manager whose health was rather frail). Aaron surrounded himself with managers who were content to play a secondary role in decision making. He granted very little authority to his subordinates and was accustomed to meddling with day-to-day operating matters at the lowest level of the department. So closely did Mr. Aaron embody and strive to represent his department that he even appeared in the company's television advertisements. In the eyes of the customers and the public, Mr. Aaron *was* Nouveau Corporation. Many wrote directly to him if they had any complaints, and, in fact, he encouraged it.

About five years after the firm was founded, there had been several important clashes between Mr. Aaron and his product development manager. Both men were strong-willed. Aaron wanted to continue to sell the more traditional lines of shoes, and although this guaranteed higher quality, it was both restrictive and expensive. The product manager strongly believed that the time had come to sell cheaper, more stylish lines, as most of Nouveau's competitors were already doing. Although the two men had got along well until then, after the product manager openly declared his opposition to the vice-president's policy, he became *persona nongrata* in the latter's eyes. Six weeks after this rebellion, Mr. Aaron hired a styling expert who shared his views. The new man was given authority that overlapped with that of the product manager. He also had a tendency to end-run the product manager by taking his designs directly to the vice-president. Since these were in line with his preferences, Mr.

Aaron usually approved them without consulting the product manager. It was not long before the latter tendered his resignation, and the new designer replaced him.

After this episode, the evidence seemed to indicate that other managers had learned their lesson. Many of the independent, thoughtful managers who liked to exercise some initiative in decision making decided that the department's style of management was too paternalistic and authoritarian. They left the company. The former director of advertising fell into this camp and quit six months after the product manager. Those who opted to remain with the firm were the more dependent and conforming managers. They decided to toe the line, to endorse all the VP's ideas, and to put up with his meddling. Many of those who found it easiest to adopt the second attitude were already strong admirers of the VP, looking on him as an idealized father figure. It was, of course, very easy to follow a leader who was held in such high esteem. And so the dependency culture developed. The remaining second tier of docile and cooperative managers recruited others who shared their adulation of Mr. Aaron and his ways of doing things. Of the new employees recruited, most of the strong personalities quit the firm, while the dependent, subservient types remained.

For many years the marketing department continued to function in pretty much the same way, with Mr. Aaron very clearly in charge. Because he knew the industry so well, his policies and strategies were most responsive to the high-quality, high-fashion niche of the men's shoe market, and all within the department strongly supported and believed in these orientations. The explicitly articulated strategy was to cater to this market, and the vice-president kept sufficiently abreast of current styles to adapt the product line continually and sensibly, within the guidelines imposed by the overall strategy. In other words, there was room for tactical flexibility within an established product-market strategy. Means and goals alike were explicit, as they all derived from a central notion of the VP of marketing. It is easiest to make policies specific when there is no political reason for concealing them. A powerful leader can articulate his intentions with impunity.

Suddenly, two years before our study, Mr. Aaron had a

heart attack and was forced to retire. At about the same time, the firm was sold to a conglomerate whose managers knew nothing about the shoe industry. As the firm had been performing well, the parent company interfered hardly at all. All major marketing decisions were left to the new vice-president—the previous styling chief, who had become the product manager. But this individual had very little managerial experience. He had been adept at following Mr. Aaron's orders and implementing his decisions but had almost no experience in, or aptitude for, making decisions on his own. His major preoccupation as vice-president was to formalize Mr. Aaron's strategies: to encode them in written policies and procedures, assorted quality control programs, pricing and advertising guidelines, and hopelessly confining product policies. At about that time, the market began to change more rapidly—new styles arrived and perished more quickly. But the rigid policies did not allow the department to adapt to the new conditions. To aggravate the problem, the department was staffed with followers but had very few capable leaders or decision makers. They had all relied on Mr. Aaron for guidance and had not developed their managerial potential. In the end, the parent company replaced the vice-president with the former top marketing executive of a competitor. This man eventually brought in several of his second-tier executives to help him modernize and reorient the product line.

Utopian Culture. We come finally to the utopian culture, which, as its name indicates, is quite future-oriented. So much emotional energy is invested in the anticipation of future meliorative events that pressing problems of the present and important lessons from the past are often ignored. We have observed that the focus is on goals themselves, much more than the means necessary for their achievement. Group tensions appear to be reduced by the shared anticipation of the utopian future, a future that members are willing to conceptualize, deliberate on, and work toward tirelessly. But the means of attaining the desired future do not seem well articulated by any powerful leader or any rigidly codified "bible." This fact lends considerable flexibility to the group's methods. The goals may not be subject to change, but there appears to be no commitment to particular means, procedures, programs, or plans. The climate of the group is participative and democratic. There are not the paranoid attitudes of the fight/flight culture or the charismatic leaders or "bibles" of the dependency culture to predetermine action. Therefore, an excellent climate evolves for participative decision making: There is enough consensus about goals to make collaboration meaningful and enough uncertainty about means to make it necessary (see Table 5).

The utopian culture is often manifested in future-oriented *high-technology* units or *R&D* groups. Often these have split off from more established and conservative parent organizations. Many such groups are found in companies on Boston's Route 128 or in California's "Silicon Valley." These are settings permeated by creativity. A key episode is the development of very futuristic and complex products in such industries as aerospace, semiconductors, or genetic engineering. Often it takes many years and very substantial resources to develop these products, many of which never produce any revenues or perhaps even fail to become functional. Great risks are taken as teams of visionary scientists and managers collaborate intensively to produce the product of the future or to establish new industries. Sometimes an entire organization pursues these dramatic novelties; sometimes it is only a single department, usually the one responsible for engineering or research and development. A critical aspect of the pursuit of innovations by utopian cultures is that the novelties are sought, to a large extent, as ends in themselves, rather than as means of making profits or responding to the threats of competing firms. Innovations are expected to revolutionize things, to improve the world, to strengthen society, and to place the firm in a paramount position in the industry. There is a striving for grandiosity, a form of optimism that seeks to improve and to inspire, often with little attention paid to present-day reality. We find an attitude that fosters intensive collaboration and participative, democratic decision making among groups of technical experts, scientists, and managers. These organizations will have a great adaptive capacity. Burns and Stalker's organic forms are recalled, in which power and authority are based on expertise rather than position.[10] The dangers of this scenario are that there may be too much risk taking, too little heed paid to existing resource restrictions or market constraints, and, in general, an unrealistic appraisal of the prospects of the venturesome projects.

A second scenario that characterizes a utopian culture is the quest for the *ideal structural environment* and organizational climate. Organizational experimentation takes place through matrix structures, parallel organizations, management information systems, organization development programs, participative decision making, industrial democracy, quality-of-worklife programs, Theory Z management, and other rescue missions. Large consulting firms, with their emphasis on packaged, ready-to-use techniques, will find a bountiful market among firms that seek out utopian structures. Whereas the more sophisticated firms are mindful about matching structural improvements to their operating and administrative needs, the more idealistic and primitive organizations are in danger of grafting inappropriate elements or techniques onto their established structures. In such instances we see companies drifting from one panacea to the next, paving the way for floundering and failure. Table 6 summarizes these scenarios.

The authors were present at the initiation of a prime example of a utopian culture. Bill Cohen and Art Jeffries worked in the research and development department of a large aerospace firm. Both were highly talented design engineers who had made substantial contributions to their company. But both felt that many of their better, more ambitious ideas and designs had been shelved without good reason by the manager of R&D. They believed that their most valuable contributions were not being recognized. Knowledge of their dissatisfaction spread to others within the industry.

One day, at a professional meeting, they were approached by a wealthy industrialist who had been very successful as an entrepreneur in the electronics and semiconductor industry. The industrialist agreed to finance Bill and Art in their own firm. They were to be given a large fraction of ownership and complete control over product strategy. The firm would specialize in the manufacture of aerospace component parts, very similar to the ones made by their large former employer. The two designers were elated. Now, at long last, they could pursue their most futuristic and grandiose ideas to come up with products that would revolutionize the industry.

Bill and Art realized that it might take quite a while to come up with a finished product. They were convinced, however, that once they did, it would be enormously profitable and would soon come to dominate the market. The wait, they felt, would be well worth it. The financier/industrialist agreed to play according to these rules on the basis of the stellar design reputations of his newfound partners.

The first task was to recruit some promising design engineers, scientists, and product development experts. There was a fairly successful campaign to hire only those whose experience and past accomplishments showed them to be at the forefront of the field.

The group was organized into three project teams of fifteen to twenty engineers and scientists, each working on one phase of the new design. Participative management was the order of the day, particularly as the founding designers wished to avoid the more authoritarian, hierarchal managerial climate that had stifled their own creativity at the large aerospace firm. Communications were intense and open, interaction among workers, scientists, and managers was frequent and enjoyable, and a very high level of *esprit de corps* prevailed. The firm functioned more like a university research group than like an industrial development department.

After three and a half years of effort, the firm had almost nothing to show for it. The reasons could be found in a number of characteristics common to the utopian group. First, although the overall goal of developing a range of sophisticated aerospace products existed, no means were clearly articulated for achieving this objective. Goals were of a long-term, futuristic nature, but there were no efforts to carefully plot out a course or to establish plans and time schedules for attaining the goals. This situation was aggravated by the loose organization structure and the absence of controls, clear reporting relationships, and carefully delineated responsibilities. Project managers tended to go their separate ways, sometimes duplicating one another's efforts, at other times developing in opposite directions. No consistent theme for the product strategy emerged. First one product was emphasized, then another, and finally still another. The hopelessly futuristic and ambitious nature of each caused its abandonment, and it was inevitably replaced by an even more grandiose venture. Much analysis was devoted to product design and technological features, but almost no attention was paid to market parameters, potential production or logistics problems, or even financial constraints. A major reason for this neglect was that the firm was really just one big R&D group. There were no marketing, finance, or production people on hand to force the principals to become more pragmatic about means. Today, two years later, the firm has yet to market its first product.

Culture and Leadership

We have tried in this chapter to highlight the importance of basic fantasies that exist within groups in organizations. Just as fantasies correspond to different psychic moments in the history of an individual's development, so basic shared group fantasies develop at different times of the organization's life. Basic shared group fantasies can be points of departure for understanding organizational culture; they mold culture and affect its accompanying dynamics. They thereby facilitate making predictions about emerging organizational scenarios, enabling us to appreciate the opportunities and dangers of each.

A key influence on the evolution of organizational cultures is the quality of leadership. The leader with a substantial degree of critical judgment, self-knowledge, and maturity can limit group regression. The extent to which groups deviate from their critical tasks and are swept away by shared fantasies depends largely on the susceptibility of the leader and his or her followers to rigid and dysfunctional fantasies. The maturity of the leader and of subordinates will also determine the feasibility of changing from one shared group fantasy to the next in response to the exigencies of the situation. The most severe dysfunctions develop when the group adheres to one shared fantasy too intensely or after its time has passed.

One way of helping managers to distance themselves and obtain a better perspective on their respective group cultures may be through participation in "Balint groups."[11] Such groups provide a nonthreatening environment in which executives can discuss their work experiences with professionals who have a broad knowledge of different organizational cultures and basic shared fantasies. These exchanges may help managers to recognize dysfunctional patterns in their way of dealing with their work environment. Although this orientation has hitherto been used mainly by health professionals, one can easily envision a similar approach for executives. Such groups will also help to identify transference reactions—the topic of our next chapter.

In this chapter we have moved from the organizational to the group level of firms. Now we shall focus our attention on a still smaller aggregation—the very crucial relationship between two persons.

3

Confused Interpersonal Relationships

A leader is best
When people barely know that he exists,
Not so good when people obey and acclaim him,
Worst when they despise him.
Fail to honor people,
They fail to honor you;
But of a good leader, who talks little,
When his work is done, his aim fulfilled,
They will all say, "We did this ourselves."
—Lao-tzu, *The Way of Life*

In his search for ways to treat hysteria, Freud came across what he called a "false connection" between his patients' feelings toward him and their feelings toward past figures in their lives.[1] Initially, Freud saw this "false connection" as an obstacle to treatment. He became particularly aware of it when one of his patients, a young woman named Dora, prematurely ended her analysis. Further reflection led Freud to believe that her termination was a revenge "transferred" to him but intended for her lover and, at the same time, at a much deeper level, for her father.[2] This setback made Freud aware that transference could, if detected in time, be a powerful aid to diagnosis and change.

We can roughly define transference as a reaction in which one perceives and responds to someone as if that person were an important figure from the past. If one is promptly made aware of the nature of such transference reactions, they can become the source of valuable insights into behavior. In the clinical setting, it has been argued, the only meliorative, change-evoking interpretation a therapist can give is the transference interpretation.[3] In fact, on meeting Jung for the first time, in 1907, Freud asked him his opinion about transference. Jung replied, "It is the alpha and omega of treatment," to which Freud responded, "You have understood."[4]

Since transference occupies such a central position in psychotherapy, we can readily explain the wealth of related literature in psychiatry, psychoanalysis, and clinical psychology.[5] Much less comprehensible, however, is that, despite the universal nature of transference, its significance and even its existence have been virtually ignored in the management literature. Given its importance as an influence in leadership and decision-making situations, this omission seems rather remarkable. Accordingly, this chapter will derive a tentative, pragmatically oriented classification of the types of transferences and will generate speculations about how these manifest themselves in, and help to explain, leadership and decision-making processes in organizations.

Roots and Scope of Transference

Transference is present in all meaningful relationships. It is a universal phenomenon applicable to any interpersonal situation, "a general human trait [of interpreting] one's experiences in the light of the past."[6] The essence of a transference expression is an unconscious intrapsychic fantasy that distorts an individual's perceptions and interactions. As Anthony Storr remarks, "We do not approach new people as blank sheets but transfer what we have already experienced from the past into the present."[7] Individuals tend to repeat in current situations attitudes developed in early family life. This pattern becomes particularly exaggerated in the psychoanalytic setting, where, induced by an unstructured atmosphere of deprivation, a patient will respond to the therapist *as if* he or she were mother, father, sibling, or another important figure in life. In such instances we speak of transference *neurosis,* in which there is a "concentration of the patient's conflicts, wishes, fantasies, and the like onto the person of the analyst, with a relative elimination of their manifestations elsewhere."[8] In less artificial settings we will usually not see the same degree of intensity in transference and, instead, might say that a relationship contains transference *elements* that, only in certain situations, may be transformed into a full-blown transference neurosis.

According to Ralph Greenson, "By transference we refer to a special kind of relationship toward a person . . . the main characteristic is the experience of feelings to a person which do not befit that person and which actually apply to another. . . . Transference is a repetition, a new edition of an old object relationship. . . . It is an anachronism, an error in time. A displacement has taken place; impulses, feelings, and defenses pertaining to a person in the past have been shifted onto a person in the present. It is primarily an unconscious phenomenon, and the person reacting with transference feeling is in the main unaware of the distortion."[9] As Greenson indicates, the actors in this process do not recognize the repetitive nature of their actions. Instead of remembering the past, the person misunderstands the present in terms of the past and relives it through his or her actions. In an effort to cope with conflict-laden relationships from the past, one falls back on stereotyped behavior patterns, reviving irrational and unsuitable archaic structures of personality. Thus, transference reactions come across as *overreaction* or *underreaction* or as *bizarre* responses. A careful observer might notice that the subject is responding to people as if they were mother, father, sibling, or another key figure from the past.

All human relationships contain a mixture of realistic and transference reactions;[10] what characterizes the latter is their *inappropriateness* to the current situation. Greenson calls attention to the intensity of the transference reaction, one factor contributing to its inappropriateness.[11] Transference reactions are also ambivalent. They may, for example, demonstrate conflicting feelings toward the same person. At first, transference feelings are often capricious—that is, fluctuating and inconsistent. But in the long run, they have a tenacious quality, the same person being seen in a similar light throughout the relationship.

Pernicious transferential patterns may arise from understimulation or unresponsiveness by the central figure(s) in childhood when, for example, parents ignore their children. Or these patterns may be the product of felt fragmentation caused by too few consoling or consistent parental responses to the growing, developing child. Finally, overstimulation and overburdening may occur owing to age-inappropriate responses.[12] For example, parents may goad their children toward achievements that are clearly beyond their reach. We must keep in mind that these transference patterns are not really due to single incidents in an individual's early life but are based on enduring patterns of interaction in childhood, which are reinforced later on and color all subsequent relationships.

A typical example of a transference reaction in a clinical setting was experienced by one of the authors. A demonstrative, lively patient suddenly mentioned that he must be boring the therapist. This perception was quite contrary to the therapist's feelings at the time. Further discussion showed that the patient was convinced that he had always been very boring and dull to everybody and that, as a result, people tried to avoid him. The consequences of the analysand's suspicions and sense of inferiority were unsatisfactory, prematurely concluded relationships: He would shun others before they could shun him. Further investigation revealed that at the source of all this behavior was the patient's inability to keep his parents' attention when he was growing up. The parents' jobs or other preoccupations may have left them little time to spend with their children. The patient's inability to get his parents' attention led to feelings of inadequacy, to a sense that he had nothing to offer and that his parents did not take pleasure in him. Only through exaggeration was he able to induce his parents to stay a little bit longer, to devote more time to him. Exaggeration and overdramatization became habits that he still indulged in.

Transference is a universal phenomenon and applies broadly to an organizational setting. We relate the following episode from our consulting experiences.

To many of his peers at Triad Corporation, Brian Pelman was an enigma. Although he was generally considered an outstanding manager, people often found it hard to cope with some of his more peculiar behavior. In spite of his considerable charm, there seemed to be a darker side to him. Colleagues were often at a loss to explain his actions. His suspiciousness was especially bothersome. Contrary to organizational norms, Pelman had the habit of locking his office door and desk every time he left. It was common knowledge that he kept a duplicate set of letters and memos at home. "You never know when it will come in handy; I'm not going to be the one caught cold," he had been overheard to say. This puzzled other executives, since the atmosphere at Triad had always been rather convivial. Corporate politicking had been minimal and scapegoating highly unusual. Whatever conflict did occur was almost always handled justly and amicably. To behave defensively—as if some kind of retaliatory action were in the making—was both rare and inappropriate at Triad.

One of Pelman's most irritating traits, especially to his secretary and subordinates, was his need to constantly check and recheck their work. His juniors felt that there were no reasons for Pelman's apparent distrust, since they had never been incompetent. What brought his behavior to the attention of the president was his reluctance to share information with other executives. This began to cause serious communication problems with other subunits of the firm. Soon Pelman's department became more and more isolated. The president of Triad began to exhibit concern over Pelman's effect on the overall functioning of the organization.

There was another matter that bothered the president. Whenever he was dealing with Pelman, the latter seemed extraordinarily apprehensive, always on the defensive. Yet the president was anything but coercive. He had rightly prided himself on his friendliness, fairness, and interpersonal sensitivity. Nevertheless, Pelman seemed to be waiting for the boss to catch him in a mistake and punish him. He would go through superfluous and tedious elaborations to justify even his most trivial decisions, apparently trying to ensure that he would not be blamed if something went wrong.

The president brought the matter to the attention of an organizational consultant (one of the authors) who had been working for Triad for a long time. The consultant, who already knew Pelman, tried to spend more time with him, at first talking about various concrete technical issues. Eventually the consultant was able to gain Pelman's tentative and tenuous confidence and could then probe into the motives behind his interpersonal relationships, especially with his subordinates.

In these conversations, the consultant learned more about Pelman's background. It turned out that Pelman had been the youngest child in a large family. Since both parents were working, not much time was available for the children. There seemed to have been a lot of competition for their attention. Since the parents regarded Pelman as the "baby," the other children came to feel that he was receiving preferential treatment, particularly from their father. It aroused the jealousy of the siblings. The result was that when Brian's parents left the house, his brothers and sisters would pester him and play threatening games. Sometimes they broke his toys, took his pocket money, or blamed him for various acts of mischief for which he was not responsible. When he complained, his brothers and sisters would call him a liar and emphasize to their mother how irresponsible "the baby" really was. It put him continually on guard. He would lock his bedroom door and hide his toys, always prepared to prove his innocence.

In the light of his background, Pelman's bizarre behavior at Triad seemed a bit more comprehensible. The consultant was able to draw logical connections and build up a more complete understanding of his personality. The relations between his childhood and his present behavior were pointed out to Pelman. He was shown that his previous behavior—so necessary for survival in the context of his excessively competitive family—was completely inappropriate in the context of his job. After repeated discussions on this theme with the consultant, a practicing psychoanalyst, Pelman's behavior began very gradually, almost imperceptibly, to change. As he slowly dropped his guard, he discovered that many of his elaborate precautions were really unnecessary. Nothing untoward happened when he relaxed his defenses. Punishments and disappointments were not forthcoming. These experiences made him more venturesome in trusting others. His changed behavior led to a much-improved atmosphere within his department and revitalized its relationships with the other working units. These improvements reinforced Pelman's insights into his earlier defensiveness, revealing to him how much things had been colored by his past experiences. They led him to still greater efforts to change his style of interaction.

Three Major Patterns of Transference

It was only in 1912 that Freud made an attempt to distinguish different types of transference. He differentiated between positive and negative transferences, the first characterized by affectionate feelings, the second by hostile ones. Psychoanalytic conceptualizing did not stop here, and a proliferation of transference classifications are now to be found.[13]

In our own analysis of transference we will take a rather pragmatic approach, because we intend to use transference patterns to understand the context of *leadership* and *decision making*. Thus we will distinguish among three general reaction patterns that are found in superior/subordinate interactions and that are transference-based. From our clinical and consulting experience and our review of the literature, we have arrived at the following three categories of transference: *idealizing* transference, *mirror* transference, and *persecutory* transference. As is often true in classification schemes, there will be elements of overlap, in part owing to differences among the schools of thought in the clinical literature from which these classifications derive. Naturally, any one individual is usually not confined to one transference pattern only. Transferences have a protean character and may alter depending on the situation or the individual toward which they are directed. Generally, however, for any given long-term relationship a single transference pattern will predominate. All three of our patterns are very basic and originate in early developmental problems or failures. Our discussion of each pattern will first address the nature and sources of the transference. It will then show how leadership and decision-making behavior are influenced by the transference.

Idealizing Transference. The first type of transference is a revival of an early phase of psychic development. One attempts to recapture an original state of bliss by fostering a sense of union with one who is "omnipotent and perfect." All satisfaction is derived from this idealized person, so that one feels empty and powerless without her. The idealized figure may be admired for her power, beauty, intelligence, or moral stance. There is a strong tendency, in the process of idealization, to ignore this figure's bad features and exaggerate the good ones. The idealization is motivated by the fact that some people feel lost and unworthy unless they have someone they can admire.[14] They thus become highly dependent on the idealized person. As a result, they feel a need to appeal to, support, and ingratiate themselves with her. Take, for example, the comments made to one of the authors by an idealizing manager of an agricultural products manufacturer:

> Our president, Mr. Myers. What can I say. He is incredible. I have now been working with him for over three years, yet he never ceases to amaze me. I don't know how he does it. Take his capacity for work. No matter what kind of pressure we are under, Mr. Myers seems to keep on top of things. Without him, we would never have done as well as we did.
>
> I still remember the day Mr. Myers hired me. The moment I met him, I knew we would hit it off. He taught me all that I know about this business. And still—I'm a long way from matching him. I would be lost without him. Sometimes I'm at my wit's end trying to grapple with a problem. Mr. Myers just walks in and in no time finds the answer.

The same holds true for meetings. He has a knack for getting at the crux of the issue and resolving things.

I once made a trip with Mr. Myers to South America. How he did it, I don't know. But he sure managed to bring in the orders. He simply over-powered all opposition. He got the largest order from someone I could *never* get through to. No, there is no one like him. Working for him is the greatest break I've ever gotten in life.

It is interesting that the executive quoted here came from a broken family. His father, an engineer in the merchant marine, was rarely home. After the marriage dissolved, family get-togethers became extremely infrequent. Not surprisingly, this executive had been looking for father substitutes all his life, first at school, later at college, and now at work. This quest was clearly reflected in his relationship to his boss.

Subordinates who idealize their superior are generally quite content at their jobs. They have faith and confidence in the leader, whom they do their very best to please. They are highly motivated and study the boss very carefully to see what they can learn in order to improve their own performance. Such subordinates are also likely to vie with one another for the boss's attention. They are prone to be very flattered by a few words of praise from the leader and devastated by the mildest of reprimands. They thus become extremely dependent on the leader and very easy to control and manipulate.

Although such subordinates can be excellent workers, there is a sense in which they are lost as an independent re-source to the company. They may conform to such a degree that their capacity for independent judgment vanishes. They become perfect followers but poor leaders, having no strong ini-tiatives or opinions of their own. Their suitability for manager-ial positions is thereby diminished.

Another potentially serious shortcoming of the idealizing transference arises because such subordinates have too high ex-pectations of their leaders. Any figure who is revered and held in awe engenders unrealistic appraisals by his or her worshipers. These appraisals can be quite fragile, as they are bound ultimately to cause disappointment. When the idealized leader has an all-too-human lapse of courtesy or character, the subordinates' image of him may be shattered, causing painful disillusionment and perhaps even outright rebellion and hostility. In some cases, however, the leader is held in such high esteem that all his apparent lapses and faults go unnoticed or are rationalized away. Subordinates have so much invested in the image they hold of the leader that they are completely blind to his faults or actually view them as strengths. In both forms of idealization, the subordinates' judgment is greatly impaired, and their utility is therefore restricted to following established routines rather than devising new ones or solving problems.

In a decision-making context, "perfect subordinates" may not contribute much. They will echo the views of the idealized leader and try to base any decisions they make on what the leader would do under those conditions. In fact, they will be very reluctant to make decisions until they discover just what it is that the leader wants. They are very hesitant to use their authority or to innovate. Moreover, even when it becomes obvious that the course being proposed by the leader is hazardous and poorly conceived, idealizing subordinates are unlikely to offer any resistance. Only the leader's perspective will be brought to bear in decision making, no matter how inadequate it may be. An advantage of idealization comes in the implementation phase, when malleable subordinates offer no resistance to the changes being implemented and do their best to make the project a success. Where the leader is idealized by numerous subordinates, much team spirit and enthusiasm exist in the group, so that major changes can take place quickly and problems of resistance to change are minimized.

The most common organizational example of idealization is, perhaps, the entrepreneurial, charismatic leaders who have established their own businesses. Often their companies tend toward the dramatic type and are permeated by the dependency culture of Chapter Two. The individuals in charge are frequently powerful visionaries who insist on a loyal and highly cooperative staff, a staff that is somewhat passive and willing to carry out the entrepreneur's bold programs unquestioningly. Those most likely to be attracted to such a position will probably be dependent, idealizing types—people who are more comfortable taking orders than initiating them. Thus, when the strong leader leaves the firm, there will be a leadership vacuum. None of the individuals who were compatible with the leader's bold and domineering style could be sufficiently independent to run the organization decisively. As a result, the firm must search for a leader from outside to replace the departing entrepreneur, or it faces the prospect of stagnation. The idealizing subordinates may attempt to formally codify the entrepreneur's philosophy of management so that a "bible" of prescribed procedures rules the firm instead of an individual. The "bible" becomes sacrosanct, so that meaningful change is exceedingly difficult to achieve, as we saw in the discussion of dependency cultures in Chapter Two.

Occasionally the leader will idealize subordinates, causing her to place unrealistic hopes on them. They may be asked to go on impossibly ambitious rescue missions—perhaps to bring in an extremely major account, to develop a complex new product, or to take a devastated division out of the red. Placing such excessive expectations on a few subordinates will make these projects impossible to realize. We should not view this transferential pattern completely negatively, however, because in some instances the elevated hopes placed on these executives may stimulate them to attain outstanding results.

It is possible to distinguish two types of idealization, which we shall call "normal idealization" and "clinging behavior." These are progressively more extreme in the amount of passivity and dependence shown by the followers. In "normal" idealization, the follower respects the leader and tries to emulate many of her general characteristics. But it is still possible for him to maintain a reasonable amount of initiative (especially if the leader is independent and strong) as he strives to be like the boss. In a more extreme type of transference, respect gives way to deification, and emulation is replaced by slavish subservience and ritualistic imitation. Here much initiative is lost as the subordinate becomes suitable only for simple and routine functions, with obvious impairment in his capacity for sound decision making.

Mirror Transference. In the mirror transference reaction, someone attempts to restore an original state of bliss by viewing himself as perfect and all-powerful. Such persons thereby create a grandiose sense of self,[15] demonstrating limited interest in the external world, to which they have ascribed all imperfections. There is a need for others who can "nourish" them through confirming and admiring responses. They need to display themselves to evoke the positive attention of others, as a way of counteracting a sense of worthlessness and a lack of self-esteem. Mirroring transferences are complementary to idealizing transferences—the former being the desire to be applauded, admired, and revered, the latter being the propensity to comply with such a desire. Mirroring superiors seek out idealizing subordinates. Whereas our discussion of idealizing transferences centered on subordinates, that of the mirroring transference will focus mainly on the leader.

Mirroring executives are narcissistic; they have a grandiose sense of self-importance and uniqueness and are desperately in search of praise.[16] Those with whom they interact are viewed, at a deeper level, as the parents who were never empathetic enough, who never recognized how the child really felt. These executives are still in search of mirroring parents; they crave constant attention and admiration. Unfortunately, because of their own overwhelming needs, they are unable to express empathy toward others. It is always "their turn now," and consequently they are likely to surround themselves with sycophants, obsequious yes-men who are all too willing to provide accolades and worship on a regular basis. Some of these subordinates will be prone to idealizing transferences, in which case their sentiments, though based on delusion, will be heartfelt. Others will be political climbers who knowingly flatter to get ahead in the organization or to curry favor with the boss so he will overlook poor performance. Strong and insightful subordinates will find the leadership climate established by the mirroring executive very difficult to tolerate. A colleague of a mirroring manager volunteered the following account:

Somehow it doesn't seem to matter to him whether we are here or not. Of course, he asks for our opinion. But he never seems to listen. We're expected to respond like a Greek chorus, anonymous, faceless, and impersonal. As long as we cheer him on, that's all that matters. Oh, at times he can be so charming—I hate myself when I fall for his manipulative tricks. I should really know better by now. But I must hand it to him, he really can get things out of people. In spite of all pretensions, however, he is anything but a team player.

Most of what he might say—all the plans, the promises—it's all phony. You feel used in the end. It is not only me. Others who deal with him have the same experience. He really only cares about himself and how much glory will be there in it for him. We are just part of the background, the furniture on a stage set for his success. And if he doesn't get his wish, he can be very vindictive.

The executive being discussed was the son of two successful professionals who were very actively involved in their respective careers. They had little time for their son, who was left in the care of a succession of uninterested housekeepers. This mirroring manager's craving to be noticed may have stemmed in large part from the neglect he experienced as a youth. The only way he could get attention was to do something spectacular.

A mirroring transference may have a number of serious drawbacks in a leadership context. The leader wants to take credit for everything, whether or not she deserves it; to receive all the applause so as to be able to demonstrate her talents to all and sundry. She will tend to be exploitative, taking advantage of others and disregarding their rights. The leader has a sense of entitlement and expects special favors. Criticisms or defeats are reacted to with outbursts of rage. Because of this emotional volatility, not much is needed for executives to change their opinions of their subordinates. Oscillations between idealization and devaluation are the order of the day. All these behavior patterns can be very damaging to the morale of subordinates who propose good ideas or attain important objectives but never get credit for their contributions.

Mirroring leaders are also likely to feel threatened by strong subordinates who might be able to upstage them. These employees pose the double threat of competing for the limelight and withholding their admiration when they are uncomfortable with the leader's proposals. Although they may be extremely valuable members of the organization, they will not last (or want to last) very long in their positions.

A final drawback of mirroring executives is their unrealistic assessment of themselves—their overvaluation of their own talents and abilities. This can produce arrogant leaders who are very confident of their position and therefore reluctant to take advice. They centralize power not only to make people recognize that they themselves are running things and to increase their visibility but also because they think that only they are capable of making the important decisions. Indeed, the dramatic firms of Chapter One, as well as the dependency cultures of Chapter Two, are often run by mirroring leaders.

A characteristic decision-making style follows from these mirroring traits. The leaders' overconfidence and their desire for recognition make them prone to undertake large and risky ventures. These can make heroes out of them, since their dramatic nature will capture the attention of a broad audience. But such ventures open the door to danger. They can entail a substantial drain on resources. Further, they do not benefit from the expertise of other organization members, since the grandiose leaders rarely consult others. Major errors may therefore go unchecked, particularly since such leaders surround themselves with those who are too politically motivated or too awed to give them any sound advice. So a bold, monolithically determined, inadequately balanced corporate strategy is devised and implemented. By the time the leaders find out they have made a blunder, they may already have gone too far to correct it.

Many examples of mirroring top executives can be found in the business-history literature. Sometimes these persons ascend to the leadership of a traditional, conservative organization and quickly try to transform it radically. New subsidiaries are acquired, new industries and markets are broached, and many top executives are replaced with the new leader's hand-picked choices. The firm grows rapidly, power is centralized, and the traditional methods of doing business are abandoned for the latest techniques of management information systems, strategic business units, and so on. But too little attention is given each decision by too few executives. Too many risks are taken, and too many resources (managerial and financial) are squandered in the pursuit of grandiosity. The chickens eventually come home to roost. Many conglomerates of the early 1960s went through periods of being run by mirroring leaders, and most of them paid the price. Or take the case of John DeLorean, the talented executive who left General Motors to establish his own sports-car company. DeLorean was unwilling to accept that his original dreams about a sportscar were no longer practical in a sagging market. His production methods and plant capacity were too ambitious. He was doing things on too grand a scale—and that led to his demise.

We have concentrated on the mirroring leader; we can also look briefly at the behavior of the mirroring subordinate. Such subordinates are likely to try to stand above their peers, to make themselves admirable and important in the eyes of the leader. They demand a great deal of attention and time from their superiors. They place much stock in formal rewards—salaries, size of office, promotions, and the like—and tend to pursue these rewards zealously. Rather than being motivated to achieve good results or to make substantial contributions to the firm, they are concerned mainly with the visible rewards that might accrue to them. It will therefore be necessary for the formal reward system to be directly tied to useful contributions in order to manage mirroring subordinates effectively. Their orientation toward achieving formal recognition might make these employees somewhat Machiavellian; they resemble Michael Maccoby's gamesman, playing games to get the boss's attention, wanting to be known as winners.[17] They will go as far as stealing their peers' ideas and engaging in end-running to directly approach higher levels of management (bypassing their immediate superiors if necessary). Mirroring subordinates might also try to call attention to themselves by undertaking some major projects on their own (often misguided) initiative.

Persecutory Transference. The persecutory transference pattern illustrates how one may use one's defenses to manage conflict—to defend against one's feelings of persecution in the manner of Brian Pelman. It is characterized by what we have earlier described as "splitting," the tendency to view the world as either ideal (all good) or persecutory (all bad). The origin of this tendency is excessive frustration in early childhood, which may lead to a high level of aggression, necessitating "splitting" as a defense—a way of managing anxiety.[18] If the good and bad parts of a person are experienced as separate individuals, guilt about one's hostility against the person will be reduced, since that hostility will be directed toward the "bad" person, who deserves it. Splitting preserves the sense that one is good. Feelings of guilt about one's rage are avoided by ascribing all unwanted thoughts and feelings onto others. All experiences, perceptions, and emotions will thus be allotted to unambiguously good and bad categories.

Persecutory transferences all tend to be negative. They manifest themselves in interpersonal relationships as attitudes of hostility, moral masochism, and envy. They are, like all episodes of transference, not reactions to current conditions but reenactments or reexperiencings of deep feelings derived from the past in the context of current situations for which they are inappropriate. The historical genesis, depth, consistency (longevity), and inappropriateness of these feelings must be borne in mind when interpreting the following examples of persecutory transference in interpersonal and decision-making contexts within organizations.

The main interaction pattern here is caused by the need to harm or attack the other person as a defensive reaction to one's feelings of persecution. The act of hostility stands central. Feelings of persecution can also cause moral masochistic behavior. One feels guilty about one's wishes to attack and feelings of hostility. One wants to redeem one's guilt about these feelings, so hostility is turned inward. There is a need to confirm one's sense of persecution. Suffering becomes regarded as a mode of ingratiation, as the payment one is prepared to endure to gain forgiveness for the hostile wishes toward key figure(s) in one's life. Another form this transferential pattern may take is envy. Envy is the desire to gain what the other has, be it an attribute or an attachment. Naturally, the original blueprint for envy is early sibling and oedipal rivalry.

Hostility: An attitude of hostility can characterize many leadership situations. It may be that the superior feels hostile to subordinates, or vice versa; the hostility may even characterize relationships among peers. Hostility may have its origins in early developmental failures leading to feelings of persecution and mistrust. Clearly, it is one of the most destructive attitudes of a leadership situation, making human relations almost intractable. The boss sees his subordinates as people who are out to ruin him, as malingerers and incompetents, or as those who are deliberately out to raise his ire. As a consequence, he is likely to gravitate toward one of two extremes in interpersonal relations with his workers. He might try to exert a tremendous amount of control through intensive personal supervision, formal controls and rules, and harsh punishments. This will take all initiative away from the workers, lower their self-esteem, and perhaps cause them to engage in a contest of wills with the boss, sabotaging the system whenever possible. The more promising and enthusiastic employees may leave the department altogether because they have so few opportunities to grow or to use their full repertoire of skills.

The second reaction of the hostile leader toward his subordinates may be overt aggression. He may be very reluctant to give them adequate salary increases, to recommend them for promotion, or to ensure that they receive adequate training on their jobs. He tries to give as little as possible, to come out on the better side of any trades. Obviously, morale can deteriorate substantially under these conditions. Subordinates may tend to hold back their contributions and to increase their "mistakes." Indeed, transference-based hostility by the leader often generates reality-based hostility among his workers as they try to even up the score and protect themselves from further exploitation. Work-to-rule practices, sporadic acts of sabotage, and deliberate "misinterpretations" of the rules become common. Such worker practices give the leader an even stronger sense that he has a worthless crew, and his hostility and attempts to control and punish become even more vigorous. This closes the vicious circle.

A subordinate experiencing transference hostility becomes uncooperative toward the boss and exhibits much the same characteristics as the workers whose hostility is based on a disturbing working environment. Mistrust, suspicion, and vindictiveness are likely and can cause subordinates to perceive all directives as attempts to manipulate or entrap them. Subordinates become uncooperative and assert their independence, trying to punish the parent represented by the person with authority. The leader then has firm grounds for reprimanding them, which aggravates the situation.

Hostility between superiors and subordinates can influence decision making in many ways. The first is that there may be a great tendency to decide things with a view toward protecting oneself and hurting one's enemies. In other words, affective rather than cognitive criteria are used in selecting among alternative courses of action. In addition, a selfish, narrow perspective is brought to bear in decision making. Parties look out for their own best interests and little else. The atmosphere of suspicion ensures that only those with the most power get to make the decisions; those to whom the powerful are hostile must make use of "informal" power to influence the course of events —they have to use group pressure, work-to-rule tactics, and organizational politicking in order to make themselves effective. In this atmosphere of conflict, "might is right." The dangers are that decision making may become a hopelessly parochial activity, mirroring the narrow and selfish objectives of the powerful. Alternatively, it can become characterized by toughly contested political infighting among equally powerful but very hostile, narrow, and selfish parties. In the first case, strategies will be too monolithic and simplistic because they reflect only one actor's personal ambitions. In the second case, a muddling-through orientation prevails as strategies shift with fluctuations in the power structure. No clear, consistent theme emerges; one orientation is soon countered by a very different one. The paranoid and schizoid firms of Chapter One and the fight/flight cultures of Chapter Two are often run by executives who are particularly prone to persecutory transferences.

Moral masochism: The moral masochistic transference pattern is almost the mirror image of the hostile one. One feels persecuted by others but at the same time feels guilty about one's wish to be the persecutor. Thus, instead of taking one's anger out on others, one blames oneself. Masochistic, self-defeating acts represent a flight from anxiety about expected punishment. The seeking of psychic pain is a redemptive act, a way of assuaging one's guilt over unacceptable wishes. Humiliation and defeat are thus pursued vigorously.[19]

In organizations we may find executives who engage in continual provocation through their own incompetence. Whatever the directives of their superiors, these "accident prone" managers always seem to go wrong. Frequently their failures result from their lack of information, energy, initiative, or imagination. Many of these managers fear success because they think it will make others envious and therefore hostile toward them. They therefore do their best to snatch mediocrity from the jaws of victory. Other, more masochistic managers really do wish to satisfy their guilt feelings by being punished. They unconsciously seek out failure, perhaps by taking excessive risks whose consequences might incur the wrath of powerful members of the organization. This invitation to be punished may attract individuals with the appropriate sadistic dispositions, particularly the transferential figure, making for sadomasochistic interplay. Such transferential patterns tend to be extremely destructive given the inclination of the subordinate to abdicate control over his or her life and place it in the hands of another.

This behavior may also lead to decision paralysis or extremely risky and inappropriate decisions. Executives may avoid making any decisions even when they know it could have dire repercussions for their careers. Their masochism might also prompt them to tempt fate in another way—by taking bold, unjustified risks that have a high probability of causing disaster.

Envy: A somewhat different interaction pattern resulting from a persecutory transference is that of envy. It is manifested by the unhappiness caused one by someone else's having something that one would like to have for oneself and feeling inferior for not having it. A need exists to emulate or surpass the other person, to acquire his or her coveted possessions. Envy thus has a destructive quality. It diminishes one's capacity for enjoyment.

Enviousness can be most destructive in leadership situations. It leads to conflicts and feelings of spite and selfishness. It will also obstruct cooperation and collaboration, since a great desire exists to spoil things for others. Envious subordinates see the leader as possessing all the power, acclaim, and resources. The attitude prevails that things are being handled unfairly in the organization, that one is being treated poorly.

A rarer form of envy in organizations is that of superiors toward subordinates. Leaders may believe that they are carrying the group by themselves, that they are doing all the important work and putting in the longest hours while those who work for them are getting away with doing very little. They may feel that their rewards are not sufficient relative to their contributions while the opposite is true for their workers. Another source of superior envy is the age difference between someone in her declining years and younger subordinates who are just reaching the prime of life. The boss who envies subordinates is likely to withhold praise and other rewards and to be hypercritical of their work. Severe motivational problems and demoralization may occur. We have named this phenomenon the "Laius complex" after the king of Thebes who tried to kill his son Oedipus, who, of course, eventually turned the tables. In such situations the superior sets up the subordinate for failure by deliberately giving him more than he can handle.

In decision making, envy results in the types of disputes, selfishness, and political maneuvering that render the effective interchange of information impossible and thwart the emergence of sufficiently encompassing goals and decision criteria. Everyone comes to have an ax to grind and a hidden agenda to follow.

Beyond Repetition

The transferential patterns we have identified seem to manifest themselves in many managerial situations. Leadership styles and decision-making behavior are frequently related to psychic developmental influences that are revealed in transference situations. We have only too often seen people concerned with changing organizations concentrate only on the external and current manifestations of the problems themselves. The autocratic leader, for example, is told to become more democratic and to develop a participative management style; or the impeded flow of information is addressed by constructing management information systems that disseminate better information to more appropriate individuals. We contend that such measures will very seldom be effective, simply because they fail to go to the root of the problem. What possible benefit could there be in telling an executive to become more responsive and to share her authority with her subordinates if she has a basic attitude of mistrust? Change requires cooperation from those who must change their own attitudes and beliefs. It is too much to expect those with power to alter their behavior voluntarily when that would run counter to their deep-seated nature. When the reasons for, or sources of, these patterns of behavior are found in early developmental experiences and are not known to the person herself, they become important and insidious determinants of behavior and of resistance to change.

The ability to use power effectively to promote change requires an understanding of its less overt manifestations, particularly in interpersonal and group dynamics.[20] In this context, identifying transferential patterns may be crucial. That is not to say that recognition and adjustment of transferential patterns are easy to achieve. But neglect or ignorance is not the answer. It invites resistance to change, sabotage, dissatisfaction, dismissals, and resignations.

It is important for both superior and subordinate to become aware of the existence of destructive interaction patterns, for awareness is the first step toward correction. Promoting this awareness requires the cooperation of both parties. It is the responsibility of senior executives to recognize the effect of their behavior on subordinates. They should never underestimate the symbolic role that they fulfill for the people with whom they interact. What may seem inconsequential behavior to them may easily be a catalyst for transference reactions by their subordinates. Subordinates should also be alert to their own symptomatic behavior. The inability to make decisions on one's own, the need to have each decision approved, an excessive need to be admired, a preoccupation with being taken advantage of—all are indications of trouble. Frequent mood shifts, sudden irritability, feelings of envy, a sense of being watched, excessive concern about what others think, and the continual need for an audience are other indications of possible transference distortions. Again, we wish to emphasize that it is the *excessive* quality of these feelings that can cause trouble.

A key message of this chapter and, indeed, of this book is that organizations are probably much less malleable and changeable than some organizational designers would like to think. Change may often require self-insight by those at the top of the firm. Organizational behavior is influenced by transference, which is a relatively subtle phenomenon. Only when one becomes aware of one's transference tendencies and experiences them in an emotion-laden situation are deep changes in attitude possible. This condition is by no means simple to achieve.

Two alternatives can be pursued to counteract the dysfunctional effects of transference patterns. The first is, as indicated earlier, that executives be given some motivation in an extraorganizational therapeutic setting to discuss their feelings about their subordinates, superiors, families, and so on. In this way the organizational consultants conducting the interviews can make a crude but relevant assessment of probable executive transference patterns, which can allow for better recommendations about job placement for the executive and perhaps about future therapeutic training groups. An alternative but more difficult strategy is to interview prospective executives to determine their transferential tendencies so that more appropriate recruitment, promotion, and placement decisions can be made.

4

Destructive
Superior/Subordinate
Interactions

"You should say what you mean," the March Hare went on.

"I do," Alice hastily replied; "at least—at least I mean what I say—that's the same thing, you know."

"Not the same thing a bit!" said the Hatter. "Why, you might just as well say that 'I see what I eat' is the same thing as 'I eat what I see'!"

     —Lewis Carroll, *Alice's Adventures in Wonderland*

In the previous chapter we illustrated how transferential patterns will color the way superiors and subordinates deal with each other. In this chapter we continue to look at this process, since the quality of superior/subordinate interaction is one of the cornerstones of successful organizational functioning. Short circuits in this interaction process will seriously impair organizational effectiveness.

Transference processes show the influence of early developmental experiences on leadership situations. But there are important *current* influences as well. Much of what has been written about dysfunctional family interaction and family communication patterns is directly relevant for providing insights into faulty superior/subordinate relationships in organizations. This chapter explores some of these relationships using ideas taken from the psychoanalytic, psychiatric, and systems literature on family processes.

Faulty Interaction in Families

The seminal work of Gregory Bateson and his associates[1] and Wynne and his collaborators[2] investigated the causes of schizophrenia. These researchers discovered that schizophrenics often experienced contradictory communication patterns within their family environment. Bateson was especially concerned with the damage done by "double bind" communications, in which no conceivable response or interpretation can be consistent with what is being demanded. The directive "Act spontaneously!" is an example, since the receiver of this message is damned no matter what his response. Common consequences of such communications are confusion, frustration, and hostility. In family life these communications may come to dominate interactions over a long period. Where treasured, intimate, and enduring dependency relationships are involved, double-bind communications and the interaction patterns that they typify can be especially pernicious.[3] Long-standing relationships can manifest and exacerbate their dysfunctions through distortive and manipulative patterns of communication.[4] Here irrationality may be transmitted and perpetuated by purposeful mystification and deliberate confusion.[5] These communication patterns play a key role in fostering mutually exploitative symbiotic relationships.[6] One party may send conflicting messages to another for purposes of manipulation, a process not always conducted consciously. For example, in Kenneth Loach's film *Family Life,* which tells the story of a young woman trying to leave home, we find the following interchange between the girl (Janice) and her parents after she has been placed in a mental hospital:

Father: [Talking to Janice about how she should feel] It's like falling and breaking your leg or having broken an arm. There is nothing to be ashamed of.

Janice: I am not ashamed.

Mother: This is just it. You are not ashamed. Even this would be understandable—but you are not, you're a law unto yourself, aren't you. You don't have to be ashamed.

Other disruptive communication patterns are intended to *bind* family members to one another in order to fulfill the dominance or dependency needs of parents and children.[7] For example, parents may suggest that they will suffer tremendous pain if a child asserts her own unique attitudes, beliefs, or values.[8] Some parents try to control their children because the latter are their principal means for vicarious wish fulfillment. The parents thus burden their children with unrealistic demands and expectations, which engender feelings of guilt and inadequacy. Another method of binding involves creation of family "myths" that help to maintain consensus and stability. Myths such as "All is well" or "I'm doing this for you" serve to rationalize family members' behavior while concealing their selfish motives. Myths keep relational patterns static. They defend against unpleasant realities and protect the family from potentially disruptive and "different" outsiders.[9] A final method of binding the family unit together is the "masking" of conflict.[10] Expressions of disagreement and of exclusively personal, idiosyncratic wants are not tolerated. Where this involves children, their identities become submerged in, indistinguishable from, and subsidiary to those of the dominating parents in a condition known as "pseudomutuality."[11]

It is possible to distinguish in the literature on family therapy a number of common types of relationships, all characterized by their degrees of connectedness. For example, researchers have contrasted the differentiated, or internally diverse, family from the undifferentiated, homogeneous family.[12] They have also compared the enmeshed, closely involved family with its opposite, the disengaged, fragmented one.[13] Finally, they have examined centripetal (binding) and centrifugal (dissolving) forces within families.[14] These patterns of interaction are all particularly germane in parent/child relationships because they characterize the extent to which parents thwart or support a child's growing cognitive and emotional individuality. The parents may have an all-or-nothing attitude—either never wanting to separate from their children or breaking the bonds with them completely.

We can discern from the literature three degrees of possessiveness or affiliation in parent/child interactions. These Stierlin has called the "binding," "expelling," and "delegating" modes.[15] He states that "where the *binding mode* prevails, the parents interact with their offspring in ways that keep the latter tied to the parental orbit and locked in the 'family ghetto.' "[16] An example is the mother who tries to give her child all the love that she herself had missed but who, in her persistent solicitousness, might not pay attention to the child's own needs. Through this overindulgence the mother encourages an infantile state, forestalling normal growth and development.

In the *expelling mode* "parents enduringly neglect and reject their children and consider them nuisances and hindrances to their own goals."[17] These parents constantly rebuff their children. They are so preoccupied with themselves that they let the children run loose. The parents fail to demonstrate their concern toward the children by setting and explaining behavioral boundaries.

In the *delegating mode* "the child may move out of the parental orbit but remains tied to his parents by a long leash of loyalty. The delegate must then fulfill missions for the parents . . . that embroil him in various forms of conflict."[18] In the delegating mode, the parents are torn between centripetal and centrifugal forces of seemingly equal strength. Delegating parents "need to bind their children, but also to send them out. . . . While sending [them out], they hold onto [them]. They entrust [them] with a mission, they make [them] into their proxy, their extended self."[19] It appears that the children become repositories of the parents' projected impulses.[20] For example, parents may enlist their children to help them in an ongoing battle with a hated mother-in-law or other "malevolent" figure.

Parallels can be drawn between these family interaction patterns and what happens in formal organizations between superiors and subordinates. Psychological binding can occur in organizations when personal initiatives are frowned on and conformity and dependency are encouraged. As in families, there are variations on these patterns, which can range all the way from allowing subordinates no freedom of action to completely abandoning them. Poor interactions manifest a lack of give-and-take in the relationship between superiors and subordinates. The latter are not given the opportunity to develop their unique potential in the organization. They become entangled in the superior's way of interacting and are no longer able to separate their needs from those of the boss.

Organizational Double Binds

Creation of "double bind" situations is quite common in organizations. In such instances inappropriate and contradictory signals are emitted, which create a state of confusion in the receiver.[21] For example, a superior may compliment her subordinate verbally while expressing disappointment through her facial expression and tone. Such contradictory messages will create a sense of entrapment and confusion and may evoke feelings of anger and insecurity.

The senior executive engaged in such actions often will attribute qualities of weakness and helplessness to the subordinate to justify her frequent interference. She will claim that the subordinate is "overworked," "nervous," or "not really suited for this kind of job," without trying to determine the actual state of affairs. To test her managers and reinforce her own position of control, the superior may even encourage the subordinate to express a courageous opinion and then attack it vehemently, making accusations of disloyalty and disobedience.

One is reminded of an incident in Joseph Heller's novel *Catch-22*.[22] Lieutenant Scheisskopf is encouraging a squadron of aviation cadets to tell him the reasons for their low morale and their inadequate marching performance in the parade competition. One of the aviation cadets, Clevinger, feels an urge to comply, disregarding the warnings of his friend Yossarian:

"I want someone to tell me," Lieutenant Scheisskopf beseeched them all prayerfully. "If any of it is my fault, I *want* to be told."

"He *wants* someone to tell him," Clevinger said.

"He wants everyone to keep still, idiot," Yossarian answered.

"Didn't you hear him?" Clevinger argued.

"I heard him," Yossarian replied. "I heard him say very loudly and very distinctly that he wants every one of us to keep our mouth shut if we know what's good for us."

"I won't punish you," Lieutenant Scheisskopf swore.

"He says he won't punish me," said Clevinger.

"He'll castrate you," said Yossarian.

"I swear I won't punish you," said Lieutenant Scheisskopf. "I'll be grateful to the man who tells me the truth."

"He'll hate you," said Yossarian. "To his dying day he'll hate you."[23]

But Clevinger does not listen and falls into the trap. He tries to be helpful to Lieutenant Scheisskopf and as a result is brought before the Action Board, accused of conspiring in an overthrow by the cadet officers.

As this story illustrates, double-bind communications thwart the emergence of mutual confidence and initiative. Anger is aroused, conflicts are suppressed, and an atmosphere of false consensus is encouraged. To subordinates, it seems easier just to give in. Paralysis of action becomes quite common. The activities of an overpowering, intrusive superior leave little room for personal growth, individuality, or action. On the rare occasions when a subordinate does act, mistakes and irresponsible behavior are that much more likely because of the confusing and frustrating relationship and his managerial inexperience.

The subordinate may therefore *in fact* confirm through his actions his superior's doubts about his capabilities.

But it takes two to make a dysfunctional relationship: Subordinates are not necessarily blameless in this regard. Maturation provides, among other things, the ability to think and act independently. But as we have described, many adults have highly frustrated and ungratified dependency needs. They still want to be cared for by others, and this renders them particularly susceptible to dysfunctional entanglements.

Given the importance of authority in organizations, superiors bear a heavy responsibility for the ways they deal with subordinates. Some managers are unable to let go of their managees, restricting all their moves. Others may push their subordinates toward premature autonomy, refusing to establish any form of meaningful relationship and essentially abandoning them. As in the family, somewhere between binding and expelling is another maladaptive compromise in which superiors hold their subordinates "on a long leash." These bosses are caught in a conflict between letting go and holding back, thereby sending out confusing signals to their workers, who react accordingly.

Binding, proxy, and expelling are three disruptive modes of interaction that operate in organizations. We shall describe some of the psychological processes associated with each, highlighting the dangers. One should keep in mind, however, that shifts can occur between these different modes, depending on circumstances, and that multiple patterns sometimes occur simultaneously.

The Binding Mode

Superiors operating in the binding mode view the environment as forbidding and hostile. Confidence is placed only in a few cherished subordinates. These executives feel that they live in a world where nobody can be trusted, where one must be on guard and in charge. This view of the world creates a need for the superior to protect and control the subordinates he is most attached to. Subordinates will be subtly discouraged from meddling in "dangerous" or "foreign" areas within and outside the organization. A clique of favored managers is created. In order to gain compliance from his managers, the senior executive caters lavishly to their demands. No material request seems too outrageous; no effort is spared in providing gratification. The price subordinates must pay for these rewards is extreme loyalty and devotion to their superior. They must back all his projects, act according to his wishes, and never disagree on matters of substance. They are locked into a golden cage.

The president and founder of a small chain of discount stores had become increasingly preoccupied with growth. Unfortunately, his desire for growth had been frustrated: The company had reached a plateau in sales for the past three years. The reason given for this stagnation was an inability to find capable middle managers to expand in new directions. As consultants, however, we perceived this explanation to be an oversimplification. The president was surrounded by executives who had been with him since the company was founded. This tightly knit group had become an extension of the president, blindly acting out his wishes while serving no critical function. The executives had rationalized this way of behaving as being in the best interests of the company. The rewards for their subservience were extravagant salaries, liberal expense accounts, lengthy vacations, and other perquisites. This group had no room for newcomers or new ideas. "Outsiders" would only disturb the existing equilibrium. Although lip service was given to attracting middle managers, new executives found themselves quickly isolated, without support, and eventually fired if they ever trespassed on the president's domain.

At first glance the senior executive's behavior might seem to have been altruistic, given his concern for his subordinates' welfare. On closer inspection, however, we realized that his behavior was actually preventing his subordinates from developing and learning by making their own mistakes. Under the pretense of being a helpful and benevolent boss, he was actually engaged in extremely selfish behavior. He did not allow his subordinates to "grow up," to act as responsible adults, or to reflect their separate identities. Instead, he reinforced their dependency needs and asserted his control.[24]

Some senior executives may subconsciously fear their subordinates' independence. Independent subordinates may be viewed as a threat because they arouse old memories of lost competitions, rivalry, and hostility. "Young Turks" can, in fact, be quite dangerous to their less adept superiors. To counter this threat, some superiors encourage and foster dependency relationships by preventing their subordinates from taking initiatives and by buying them off with their favors. Strangely enough, many subordinates do not complain. Instead, they view their relationship with their superior as excellent, praising him for his generosity and his attentions. Unfortunately, this is another example of a transactional mode that does not provide subordinates with growth opportunities.

Finally, there are those binding executives who have ambivalent feelings toward their subordinates. To overcome and counteract their subconscious feelings of hostility, these executives try to "overgratify" the wishes of their subordinates. To them, this seems the only way they can reduce their guilt about their repressed feelings of hostility.

These binding relationships are "symbiotic." The senior executive happily controls his subordinate's behavior, but at the same time he creates an insatiable employee. The exclusivity of the relationship with the senior executive leaves subordinates with very few alternative sources of gratification. Hence, they will tend to ask their boss for more and more attention and favors. The demands will become endless. To the outsider these subordinates come across as spoiled, childish, and demanding people who quickly become disappointed and angry if their requests are not met. The rest of the organization comes to view them as unreliable procrastinators, as people to be avoided, and so their isolation from others increases still further. Two specific binding strategies are discussed next.

Ambiguity of Responsibility. A common form of binding used by senior executives is the ambiguous diffusion of responsibility in an organization.[25] One of the results of such a confused situation is that when something goes wrong, nobody in particular can be blamed. The main outcome, however, is that because no specific responsibility is assigned to anyone, no one is able to be independent. Control remains with the executive.

We were recently called in by the president of a medium-sized family firm in retailing. His bank and a government funding agency had forced him to hire a consulting firm to review his operations. Only by being subjected to this scrutiny could the company qualify for debt restructuring, which was badly needed in the light of its first major financial loss. The consultant spent a considerable amount of time with the president and his four key executives, two of whom were family members. In conversations with the consultant, the president confessed to his fear of losing control. It appeared that the company had been growing rapidly over the past five years and had been very successful until recently. Now, however, the president found it increasingly difficult to oversee the operations. Too many mistakes were being made. Investigation by the consultant revealed that no one in the key executive group had any explicitly defined tasks. Executives could give only vague descriptions of their respective responsibilities. Comparison revealed an extraordinary degree of overlap and confusion.

It was obvious that, by leaving responsibilities vague, the president was able to tie each of his executives closely to himself, allowing them no room to maneuver. This binding pattern had originated when the company was small and the president alone was able to control the total operation. But now its dysfunctional effects had begun to show. Naturally, the president's binding strategy prevented the emergence of a creative, innovative, organizational culture. Instead, it resulted in a confused and depressed executive group.

Manipulation of Guilt. Manipulating the conscience of a subordinate by means of the incubation of guilt is another common binding strategy. The theme of sacrifice may underlie many of the superior's subtle communications. He may indicate that life consists of duties and that he has made many sacrifices to bring his subordinate into her present position. He now expects his subordinate to repay the debt and make some sacrifices of her own. Loyalty and support are demanded as a form of compensation.

The product manager of a brewery went to his vice-president and told him he was considering a job with an overseas competitor. After an initial reaction of shock, the vice-president reminded his product manager that he had been instrumental in bringing him into the company after he had obtained his M.B.A. Hiring him had not been easy. The vice-president recalled his fight with the director of personnel, who had expressed his preference for an M.B.A. with more business experience. The VP also explained how he had gone out of his way to initiate the product management concept in the company. He claimed that one main reason for advocating this idea had been to create more challenging management positions for people like the product manager, who had indeed been one of the principal beneficiaries. In addition, he mentioned that there was no worse time to bring him this news—that he was relying on the manager's assistance in introducing a new brand. He wondered aloud why he was being deserted after so many years of enjoyable collaboration. It did not take the product manager long to reverse his decision and promise the vice-president his future support.

Clearly, this interchange can be characterized as a form of blackmail. Pangs of conscience and guilt were aroused. The subordinate began to view breaking away, acting against the senior executive's wishes, almost as a type of treason. Many subordinates simply cannot withstand such pressure. They give in and accept the confinement that doing so entails.

The Proxy Mode

In some relationships both superior and subordinate seem to be torn between centripetal and centrifugal forces, between the "attraction" and "repulsion" associated with the binding and expelling modes.[26] The subordinate's main dilemma here is that he not only is supposed to be his own man and make decisions by himself but at the same time is expected to carry out his superior's wishes. He is trapped in a situation in which he is held on an invisible leash of varying and indeterminate length.

Superficially, it seems that the subordinate is supposed to act in the role of a proxy entrusted with a special mission. Although he is sent on such missions, however, the senior executive does not really relinquish control.

In many instances the subordinate is supposed to become the senior executive's "thrill provider," mainly through his participation in daring, often unacceptable organizational acts. He may be subtly encouraged to behave in various unorthodox ways—to do things his superior would have liked to do but was never bold enough to do. The subordinate is supposed to act as if these missions were his own ideas; but their real purpose is to serve the political interests, fantasies, or esteem needs of the superior. If the subordinate succeeds, the boss takes much of the credit. If he fails, he is later reprimanded for his indiscretion by his superior. The subordinate is placed in a guinea-pig role, acting out the wishes and fantasies that his senior executive does not dare to fulfill.

A product manager of an apparel company told her superior how she had surreptitiously entered the design department of a major competitor during a company visit. The purpose of the visit was ostensibly to explore the possibilities of a joint venture with the competitor. After her visit the following interchange took place between the product manager and her boss:

Director: [Laughs] How you have the nerve to do those kind of things, I'll never know. But I am glad you told me about the new products. I have been dying to know what they were bringing out.

Product Manager: [Laughs] You know, the whole thing was kind of funny. It took them a long time to realize that I had no business being there.

Director: [Amused] It is funny, but—

Product Manager: [Excited] Then I told R [competitor's design director] that I was sent by S [competitor's VP of merchandising] to check possible openings in the product line, and they

	believed me and showed me everything. I wish I could see their faces now.
Director:	[Suddenly very serious] But you left me out on a limb. This morning I got a very unpleasant phone call from S. Actually, I am quite upset about your behavior, and I told him so.

In this example we see how the director initially responded with a combination of restrained admiration and envy to the behavior of his product manager. Suddenly, after realizing what he was doing, he admonished her for her misbehavior. He made his proxy style pave the way for a classical double-bind relationship.

The need for provocation and thrills is only one way of explaining why proxy relationships occur. Another incentive for them is that they may provide superiors with a complete contrast to their own behavior, a vicarious outlet for repressed wishes. Subordinates come to represent what the superiors fear in themselves and are encouraged to embody the superiors' feared weaknesses. The superiors may thereby vicariously alleviate their guilt and appease their conscience by blaming the subordinates for the destructiveness that they themselves encourage. The superiors thus experience vicarious thrills *and* vicarious repentance—they obtain two benefits without having to pay the price.

Proxy relationships can also be engendered when a subordinate becomes burdened with a superior's exaggerated and frustrated vocational objectives. The superior may encourage the subordinate to initiate unrealistic ventures that can make the superior's own role in the organization more visible and more important. Even if such subordinates jeopardize their careers by supporting the new venture, they will be forced to take the blame if it fails and lose credit to their superiors if it succeeds. The superior must be seen as the more successful executive. Thus, the subordinate's scope for achievement is quite limited.

In other proxy situations the subordinate may become a flunkie, expected to be constantly prepared to aid the superior

in small tasks and projects. In one of our assignments we witnessed the case of a vice-president of administration of a
medium-sized chemical company who had risen to his present
position with the help of the president. During his time with
the company, his career had been closely tied to the upward
climb of the president. The vice-president was first the president's assistant, later his project manager, and eventually his director. Even in his elevated position, however, the vice-president
was expected to cater personally to the most trivial needs of his
boss. A series of rather demeaning situations followed.

A far more stressful proxy role develops when a subordinate is expected to support and protect the superior in his ongoing battles with colleagues. The subordinate becomes the
go-between, trying to mediate under impossible circumstances.
In such situations the subordinate frequently is torn between
the interests of the organization and those of the superior.
Sometimes the subordinate may even want for support from
the superior, since the latter may, for political reasons, wish to
avoid direct involvement in the conflict.

Subordinates operating in the proxy mode tend to become extremely confused and angry. The stresses of contradictory, impossible, and unacceptable demands often end in an
emotional crisis. At first glance, some individuals appear to cope
with the strain. Closer investigation, however, often reveals that
they suffer from excessive stress, which eventually takes its toll.

The Expelling Mode

Abandonment is at the "push" end of attachment behavior. Senior executives acting in this transactional mode view
their subordinates as expendable nuisances. There are various
reasons for this attitude. In a few rare cases, senior executives
have a personality characterized by a lack of interest in their
subordinates and in people in general. These "schizoid" executives, who for various reasons operate in an insular, self-con-
tained world, are unwilling to show the slightest consideration
for their subordinates. They will cooperate only with executives
who are politically important to them. More common expellers,

however, are senior executives who seem to be able to react only in extreme and inappropriate ways to the emotions aroused by their binding or proxy behavior. After years of an intimate working relationship, hidden feelings of rejection and hostility suddenly come to the fore. Expellers either love and bind the loyal employee or ruthlessly reject him forever because of a small slight. Dramatic changes in attitude may terminate earlier binding and proxy interactions as the offending subordinate is castigated and rejected. This may be a counterdependent reaction of superiors who fear their own dependency needs and the associated vulnerability. Seeing this dependence in others causes anxiety about what is feared in oneself, evoking rejection of the subordinates.

The artistic director of an opera company had been closely involved in the selection, by the board of directors, of a new administrative director, whose job was to handle the company's administrative affairs, a position complementary to that of artistic director. The artistic director, however, retained final responsibility for the opera company. It was noticeable to the other members of the company how pleased the artistic director seemed with the choice of the new administrative director, and this feeling seemed to be reciprocated. A relationship of close collaboration appeared to have been established. The artistic director spent considerable time explaining the functioning of the company to the new administrative director. Their meetings continued even after the administrative director had become quite familiar with the operations. At board meetings the two directors presented a united front to the other board members. At work they seemed to be inseparable, never differing in their recommendations. After two years that situation suddenly changed.

What had happened was that the administrative director had developed an interest in ballet and had become acquainted with the person in charge. When a new ballet was planned, he had given this man a provisory go-ahead without consulting the artistic director. When the latter found out what had happened, his attitude of congeniality and friendship changed abruptly. He withdrew completely from interaction with the administrative director and began to express his displeasure about the latter's performance to everyone who would listen. His support at board meetings was conspicuously absent. Naturally this situation was untenable in the long run, given the complementary nature of the functions of both men. Eventually, at a heated board meeting, the artistic director succeeded in persuading the other board members to terminate his colleague's contract.

The relationship between these two executives was probably not without conflict before the ballet incident occurred, but whatever negative feelings existed had long been suppressed. Excessive suppression seemed to give rise to a total attitude reversal. Dramatic action was taken to eliminate pent-up aggression as soon as there was reason to confirm the superior's suspicions about the unreliability of his subordinate. Such actions are often so extreme as to ensure that the abandonment becomes irreversible, making future reconciliation impossible. The subordinate will thereby be pushed into premature self-sufficiency. He must make it on his own, without any further support from his superior. Subordinates subjected to this situation will experience serious difficulties in their organizational activities and will probably fail to be effective at their jobs.

This transactional mode has other repercussions. The abruptness and callousness of the behavior of expelling superiors render subordinates themselves unable to perceive subtle feelings or to experience empathy. They tend to imitate their superiors and become callous in their own relations with others. Abandonment may be the only mode of organizational interaction with which they are familiar. Organizational life becomes viewed as a jungle where people do not really care for one another but merely manipulate and exploit. It is a world of power games, where relationships are shallow, superficial, and predatory.

Toward a Mature Separateness

The Asian proverb "He who rides a tiger cannot dismount" characterizes the problem of both parties in the situations described in this chapter. Superior and subordinate may be stuck in a debilitating transactional mode. This situation is not easy to change. But as we have illustrated, to keep things as they are jeopardizes both personal and organizational effectiveness. Leaders and followers alike must therefore embrace the responsibility for recognizing and combating the destructive nature of these transactional modes.

Breaking the Vicious Circle. Unfortunately, all too often the only choice open to the subordinate is to handle and control his anger toward his superior (given that he realizes what is happening to him) or to get out. Some suggestions can be made, however, to prevent or limit the destructive potential of these transactional modes. Since subordinates are usually on the receiving end of these dysfunctional interaction patterns, most of the guidelines are given from their point of view. It is they who will be more motivated to change the existing relationships.

It is important for both superior and subordinate to become aware of the existence of dysfunctional interaction patterns, for awareness is the first step toward dissolving them. Promoting this awareness requires the cooperation of both parties. It is the responsibility of senior executives to recognize the effect of their behavior on subordinates. They should never underestimate the coercive power of their requests. What may seem inconsequential to them can easily acquire dramatic importance in the eyes of their subordinates. For their part, subordinates should be alert to their own symptomatic behavior. Inability to make decisions on one's own, the need to have each decision approved, and obsessive concern about what the superior might think are all indications of trouble. The observation that a superior undergoes frequent shifts in mood also warrants closer scrutiny and may be symptomatic. Experiences of confusion, of feeling different from one's peers, of being locked in, of being blackmailed, or of a need to rebel or escape may also signal a dysfunctional climate for interaction.

In spite of all these possible danger signs, it is often very hard for subordinates to realize what is happening to them. The easiest response is to go along with the superior's actions. Similarly, senior executives may find it difficult to recognize the coercive effects of their behavior. But attention by both superior and subordinate to these forms of symptomatic behavior and regular joint appraisals of their relationship should have some preventive and corrective value.

Instead of having a direct discussion or even a confrontation between subordinate and superior, a third party may be employed to clarify things—to reveal the destructive nature of the existing transactional mode. If the party is from inside the organization, it will be useful for him or her to have a history of good working relationships and a solid power base. Occasionally, the senior executive may even have a "confidant" who can be used in this role. Such a third party can also intervene discretely, functioning as a blind to protect the subordinate in situations in which the superior might resent intervention.

Another way of improving interaction and avoiding entanglements is for the subordinate to refuse to play the superior's game. This refusal can take various forms. It may entail a strategy of active resistance, with all the obvious risks attached, or it may take a more passive form. In the latter case the subordinate goes through the motions without real commitment. He tries to maintain a certain distance from the superior, minimizing his involvement in the relationship. The risk, however, is that the subordinate's aloofness and lack of commitment may provoke the wrath of the senior executive.

The subordinate can also build coalitions with other employees working for the same superior. They may engage in concerted action to force a change in behavior or even to get the senior executive to leave the organization. Support may also be sought from executives in other departments to help create a broader awareness of the offender's destructive potential. Clearly, these actions are not without risk, since their effectiveness depends on the balance between the consensus generated by the dissenters and that which is ultimately marshaled by the offender. It is essential that the superior recognize the genesis of this dissension instead of simply retaliating. Otherwise, a situation of escalating conflict may result.

As a last resort, a subordinate may decide to ask for a transfer to another department. In extreme cases, when that is not feasible, the subordinate may look for a position in another organization. Such a step is usually taken when everything else has failed. An unusually high turnover in one department may be a signal for top executives to be on their guard and to investigate the prevailing mode of interaction.

Accepting Personal Responsibility. In any relationship the adage "One cannot not communicate" should be kept in mind. Communication is inevitable, but it does not have to be debilitating. Superior/subordinate interaction must take place in a balanced relationship. Although some degree of gamesmanship and manipulation is unavoidable in organizations, it is important to try to reduce dysfunctional entanglements that can cause submissiveness, lack of initiative, rebelliousness, and ineffectiveness. Effective organizational functioning is a question not only of leadership but of mature followership. Accordingly, executives have to arrive at some kind of trade-off between dominating and ignoring their subordinates. Superiors have the responsibility of giving their subordinates the opportunity to articulate differing needs and interests. Subordinates, in turn, have the responsibility of resisting when communication becomes coercive and exploitative. At the same time, recognition of individuality implies not abandonment but awareness of mutual obligations.

5

Life-Cycle Crises
and Individual
Career Satisfaction

All the world's a stage,
And all the men and women merely players:
They have their exits and their entrances;
And one man in his time plays many parts,
His acts being seven ages. At first the infant,
Mewling and puking in the nurse's arms.
And then the whining school-boy, with his satchel
And shining morning face, creeping like snail
Unwillingly to school. And then the lover,
Sighing like furnace, with a woeful ballad
Made to his mistress' eyebrow. Then a soldier,
Full of strange oaths and bearded like the pard,
Jealous in honor, sudden and quick in quarrel,
Seeking the bubble reputation
Even in the cannon's mouth. And then the justice,
In fair round belly with good capon lined,
With eyes severe and beard of formal cut,
Full of wise saws and modern instances;
And so he plays his part. The sixth age shifts
Into the lean and slipper'd pantaloon,
With spectacles on nose and pouch on side,
His youthful hose, well safed, a world too wide
For his shrunk shank; and his big manly voice,
Turning again toward childish treble, pipes

And whistles in his sound. Last scene of all,
That ends this strange eventful history,
Is second childishness and mere oblivion,
Sans teeth, sans eyes, sans taste, sans everything.
          —William Shakespeare, *As You Like It*

Throughout this book we have pursued themes largely unexplored in the management literature in order to provide insights into the impact of deeper psychological forces on organizational functioning. This chapter presents a different point of view. After examining the total organization, the group, and two-person relationships, we focus now on an *individual's* satisfaction with his or her job and organization. This topic has been much explored by the literature on organizations, but in a very narrow and confined way. Such factors as age, sex, education, and level in the hierarchy have been used to predict satisfaction. The search has usually been for simple, one-way relationships. This chapter, however, will examine the psychoanalytic, psychological, sociological, and management literature in an attempt to tease out broad themes that relate to overall satisfaction at different stages of the life cycle. This exercise, incidentally, led us to do an empirical study that strongly bore out the predicted systematic variations in job and organizational satisfaction across the phases of the life cycle. The empirical results are presented elsewhere.[1] Here we wish only to describe each stage and present a vivid case example of each, to show how extensive an array of experiences must be brought to bear in examining satisfaction and to show that the search for simple samplewide relationships is more likely to obscure than to uncover the truth.

Despite an extensive literature on the topic, there remain many questions surrounding the correlates of work satisfaction. Most research has been of a piecemeal nature, looking mainly at linear relationships between satisfaction with work and context characteristics. A number of scholars have been troubled by this state of affairs. Locke, for example, in his excellent review article, claims that "much of this literature is trivial, repetitive; and inconclusive."[2]

One possible reason for the absence of more conclusive

findings on job satisfaction is that most researchers have focused exclusively on the work environment without examining nonwork conditions that can vitally influence reactions to the job and organization. In particular, little has been made of the fact that perceptions, needs, levels of fulfillment, and, indeed, satisfaction with work and the firm change as one moves through the life cycle. The earliest working years for managerial employees may be characterized by disappointment as the constraints and routine nature of the job become felt for the first time. Subsequently, promotions, increased responsibility, and greater expertise may boost job satisfaction and organizational satisfaction until the middle years, when the "midlife crisis" strikes and lowers satisfaction. Finally, as older employees become reconciled with their lot and try to reduce any dissonance that might be experienced as a result of their career paths, satisfaction rises once again. These life-cycle effects seem very plausible. Ignoring them may account in part for the great confusion in the literature relating age, job longevity, and many other factors to job satisfaction.[3]

A few researchers have considered the influence of the overall life situation on the work environment.[4] They have discussed the possibility that frustrations not directly related to work can be displaced onto the job and the organization. Nonetheless, research that integrates job satisfaction studies with findings from life-cycle research has been rare. Indeed, until recently, most life-cycle research has been devoted to the study of the early stages of development.[5] Research into the adult stages began to emerge only with the work of Erikson,[6] White,[7] and Frenkel-Brunswik[8] and has come of age with the recent works by Levinson,[9] Gould,[10] and Vaillant.[11] These studies have identified the critical themes of each life period and the ways of coping that tend to be employed in each. Unfortunately, they do not devote much attention to career progress and organizational and job satisfaction.

Our previous research used a life-cycle approach in studying job and organizational satisfaction. It discovered important relationships between satisfaction and the life cycle (see Figure 1). This chapter will attempt to explain these life-cycle influ-

ences by making reference to the most common experiences of
each phase.

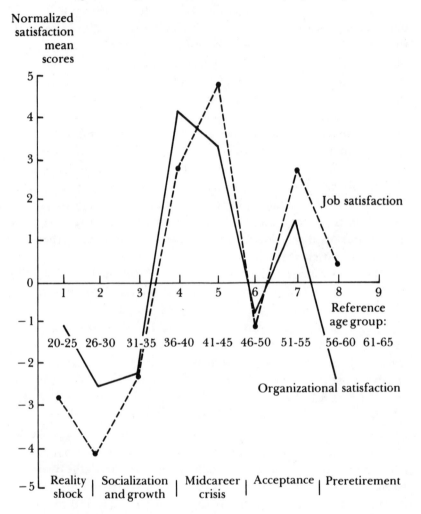

Figure 1. Adjusted Satisfaction Scores by Age Group.

From M. F. R. Kets de Vries, D. Miller, J.-M. Toulouse, P. Friesen,
M. Boivert, and R. Theriault, "Using the Life Cycle to Anticipate Satisfaction at Work," *Journal of Forecasting,* in press. Copyright 1984. Reprinted
by permission of John Wiley & Sons, Ltd.

Reality-Shock Phase

We can see from Figure 1 that, after entry into the organization, the level of job and organizational satisfaction declines. A number of reasons can be given to explain this occurrence. One common argument is that the young manager often enters the organization with highly unrealistic expectations about his job.[12] Moreover, even where expectations are more realistic, the organization may not be able to amply reward and train the new recruit.[13] It might also be difficult for the young manager to accept that satisfaction in the organization involves longer time horizons than those typically experienced at school. It tends to take quite a long time in organizations to see the results of one's endeavors, and frustration can follow. New members may feel that their responsibility does not match their capabilities and that the job offers too little challenge.[14]

The "rites of passage" associated with entry into an organization and the dependence on a senior manager are not always easy to accept. The actions of organizational participants may not be completely understood, and a state of confusion may result that leads to dissatisfaction with the organization. Often the situation is exacerbated by the fact that the organization does not use the recruit to his or her full potential. The new manager may not be able to cope with the ambiguity of the situation and the lack of guidance. In addition, the search for a "mentor" in the organization who can give the young manager a sense of direction and be a sounding board for the newcomer's frustrations is not always successful. As Schein[15] has noted, throughout this phase the organization tests its recruits. What happens here is perhaps best described by the tournament model of Rosenbaum.[16] According to this model, the organizational selection system fosters a social Darwinism in which only the fittest survive. Although this situation may threaten and demoralize a large fraction of new managers, others may rise to the occasion rather quickly, engendering sharp differences in reactions to the job and the organization among recruits.[17]

This stage of life is also often the period when the first

steps are being taken in finding a spouse and setting up a family, a time that is not without its upheavals. It is a time of exploration when an initial life structure is being developed and for the first time trade-offs are contemplated between public and private life. The stress and frustrations experienced in the nonwork environment, in combination with the lack of congruence between individual and organizational expectations immediately after entry into the firm, may explain the low levels of satisfaction and the declines observed in the plots of organizational and job satisfaction (Figure 1).

The reality-shock phase is illustrated by the early career history of one of our students in a management development program. Burton Philmore was a four-letter man at an Ivy League university who graduated with the highest academic honors. He had been president of the debating society and a prominent member of several other university clubs. He was the sort of "catch" that campus recruiters dream about: very bright, sociable, and highly ambitious. Philmore went to numerous job interviews and received offers from all the firms he visited. He decided to accept a job as a financial analyst for a large computer manufacturer, reasoning that he could immediately use many of the skills he possessed and that chances for advancement would be very good because he was joining a dynamic and rapidly growing industry.

Four weeks into his job, he began to have second thoughts. His dissatisfaction intensified over the next two and a half years and culminated in his leaving the company. He had a number of complaints. First, the work was not nearly as exciting or as important as the company recruiters had suggested it would be. A great deal of time had to be spent evaluating the potential of small, marginal projects. Philmore would complete his analyses, many of which took months to prepare, only to find that his recommendations would be ignored by his boss or someone further up the hierarchy. Second, he found he was not getting much exposure to top-level managers. He was not meeting many executives, as his boss undertook to sell his projects or deemphasize them (he was never sure which). Philmore felt a decided lack of control over the results of his efforts. Third, the boss was obviously intimidated by Philmore, so that relations between the two men became strained. A fifty-year-old graduate of a Midwestern state college, the superior had been put into a dead-end job. He realized that he was neither as bright nor as capable as Philmore and dreaded to see still another of his subordinates pass him in climbing up the hierarchy. So he kept his star subordinate out of the limelight.

After two years at the company, Philmore told one of the authors that he was "royally miffed" by his job. He claimed that at the university he had been intellectually challenged, had had an outlet for his competitive instincts in athletics, and could exercise his managerial and leadership abilities in club activities. But now he was stifled. He was not learning very much, he was not having a substantial impact on his organization, and his chances for rapid advancement seemed poor, especially in the light of his unsatisfactory relations with his boss. Moreover, he worked in a staff department where his peers were largely conservative and unambitious types. A few strongly resented his zeal and aggressiveness. Finally, after three years of marriage, he felt, perhaps erroneously, that his wife was losing some of her respect for him. Since he expected more of himself, he felt that his wife was also somewhat disappointed at his lack of career and economic progress. This seemed especially irksome, since a child was on the way and the costs of buying and furnishing a home were straining finances. His wife would soon have to quit her part-time job, and many of the little extras of life would vanish along with it.

Socialization and Growth Phase

We can see from Figure 1 that, after a number of years of decline in job and organizational satisfaction, the curves move upward. One explanation may be that the results of organizational socialization processes are beginning to bear fruit.[18] Alternatively, alignment may occur between one's personal orientation and the job and organization.[19] The individual is gradually adjusting to the organizational environment. In addition, reality testing is becoming more effective; the gap between aspirations and opportunities narrows, making it easier to settle down to a productive task. The young manager begins more fully to appreciate the realities of organizational life and to understand the limitations of his or her job. There are fewer illusions. Whether one learns what to expect from the organization or lowers one's expectations,[20] the result is the same: Satisfaction increases.

But this is also a period when managers will be able to experience their first positive achievements, thereby reinforcing their sense of competence and becoming more satisfied with their job and the organization. At this point in their career they are more capable of deciding whether the match between their contributions and rewards has been satisfactory. If not, they will take the necessary step of finding a more suitable position elsewhere. By now, one can assume that most of the individuals who remained highly dissatisfied with their jobs have left the organization.

The time horizon of the manager is beginning to change. A concept of long-term career goals and of an organizational identity is emerging. It is a period when a manager is becoming more his own person, moving away from his guiding mentor.[21] The manager finds a niche in the organization, and this adds to his peace of mind. He now knows how and where he "fits" in the organizational environment. There is a greater awareness of the realities of organizational politics, and it facilitates getting along with coworkers and superiors. All these factors can contribute to increasing satisfaction.

At home, the stress of courtship and setting up a family has subsided. Raising a family and educating one's children become more important issues. Helped by the stability that a family usually provides, the manager develops a more secure sense of identity, which may lead to an increased sense of well-being.

A more optimistic example can be used to illustrate the socialization and growth phase. Flora Carlson had been at her job with a pulp and paper company for eleven years. She had started as a production analyst soon after graduation from the university. After a few years Carlson began to find her job dull; she perceived it to present little opportunity for advancement. She asked to be transferred into the cost-accounting department, as she had begun to take accounting courses in the evening and found that these suited her aptitudes and interests. She began as a cost analyst and within three years had obtained sufficient course credits to qualify to sit for her exams to become a registered industrial accountant. Within two years of receiving her degree, she became assistant manager of the accounting department, her first managerial position.

Although Flora had hitherto occupied staff positions only, she soon became quite adept at handling her new responsibilities. Her professional expertise and easygoing manner earned her the respect and affection of her employees. Her enthusiasm and skill were much appreciated by her boss. In fact, it was not long before she received her first truly challenging assignment: to reorganize and modernize existing cost-accounting methods. This took about a year of very hard work, but it led to very tangible and visible results—so much so that Carlson began to have more contact with the vice-president of finance and the treasurer of the firm. But what pleased her most was that she had mastered a new field of expertise and had applied it skillfully in a project that was of major consequence to the company. Her role in the organization was becoming more and more important, her skills were growing, her talents were beginning to be recognized, and her future was starting to look much brighter.

Midcareer Crisis

The age range thirty-five to forty-five is a critical period in the manager's life. A sharp decline can be noted in job and organizational satisfaction. Many reasons can be given for this development. In the life-cycle literature, the concept of the midlife crisis stands out as a possible explanation. Jaques, who introduced this notion, discovered a sudden rise in death rates between the ages of thirty-five and thirty-nine among creative people.[22] He attributed this phenomenon to the realization at this life stage of the inevitability of one's death. The recognition of one's mortality seemed to foster depressive symptoms. Other researchers have further explored this changing perception of life. Neugarten mentions the different way in which time is considered at this age. She notes that "life is restructured in terms of time left to live rather than time-since-birth. Not only the reversal in directionality but the awareness that time is finite is a particularly conspicuous feature of middle age."[23] Erikson calls it a period when the conflict between generativity and stagnation comes to the fore, "generativity" referring to the capacity of the middle-aged individual to guide the next generation—in business, coaching and sponsoring the younger manager and assuming the role of mentor.[24] The other side of the coin is stagnation, the absence of growth. It gives rise to envy of others and the anger that accompanies missed opportunities.

Midlife is also a period when the effects of the organizational funnel are becoming more pronounced. The realization is dawning that opportunities for advancement in the occupational hierarchy are severely limited. At this stage, the career progress of managers will slow down or become arrested, contributing to a sense of entrapment. Middle-aged managers often do not dare to make changes because of felt psychological and financial constraints. Sofer found in his study of men at mid-career that the middle group of his sample (ages thirty-five to forty-four) were the least satisfied with their work of all ages studied.[25] Another factor adding to this state of dissatisfaction and anxiety is that professional obsolescence is becoming more noticeable at this stage of life. Thus, the crisis is not caused only by personal evolution but is also related to situational factors and social environment.[26]

This sense of crisis is compounded by such extraorganizational problems as the realization of one's physical decline, complaints about health, sexual problems, and the bewilderment surrounding the menopause. It is also a period when marital satisfaction reaches its lowest point.[27] Predictably enough, encouraged by the increasing self-sufficiency of the children, many belated divorces occur at this stage, adding to a state of depression and dissatisfaction. Overcoming disappointment about one's children and coping with one's sense of its being too late to remedy their faults also becomes an important issue. Midlife seems to involve the recognition of the limitations of life in general and of one's own life and abilities in particular. The disparity between ambitions and achievements becomes more noticeable. It is a period experienced with a sense that time is running out, often accompanied by disillusionment and various defensive reactions as ways of coping with disappointment.[28] New accommodations in the mix between organizational and private life have to be worked out, and this task adds to the overall experience of stress.

Given all these factors that play a role in this transitional phase, we can assume that dissatisfaction with the job and the organization is only one way of expressing one's overall dissatisfaction with one's fate in life. It is very likely that many stressful life experiences may be displaced onto the job and the organization.

The midlife crisis is a time when expectations falter in the light of a series of disappointments. Peter Quincy was forty-three years old when he reached the nadir of his midlife crisis. His early vocational background had been quite impressive. He joined the company without having finished high school and started work as a stockboy. Over the next six years he progressed through jobs in the mailroom, first as a clerk, later as an assistant manager, and finally as a manager with fourteen employees under him.

The next years of Quincy's career were also quite successful. He had acquired an interest in sales mainly because he liked dealing with the public and because salesmen made a good deal more money than he did as mailroom manager. The personnel manager, recognizing his potential and his ambition, decided to send him to several sales training courses. He joined the sales force as an industrial field representative, where he soon distinguished himself as one of the most successful salesmen in the company. In fact, he won the sales award for his division in his second year as a representative. His salary had more than doubled since he had been mailroom manager and had quintupled since his initial job. Within six years of joining the marketing department, he became regional sales manager, with eighteen salesmen reporting to him. He rather ingeniously devised a much improved sales compensation scheme. He also reorganized his districts to make the logistics of selling much easier for his salesmen. Finally, he reallocated sales territories so that the best salesmen got the best areas. Sales for his region rose rapidly. Only three years later, he was made divisional sales manager, at age thirty-five. Over the next two years he applied the improvements he had implemented in his old region to the entire division. He even helped other divisional sales managers to do likewise.

But then things began to slow down. In comparison with his early career, the next six years were really quite uneventful. Quincy settled down into the routine of his job. He watched as better-educated, younger, more socially adept managers climbed up the organization while his own progress seemed to have been arrested. Twinges of envy resulted, since Quincy was quite convinced that he was just as ambitious, talented, and hard-working as those receiving the promotions. He also saw his career stagnation as having been due to the inequities of organizational politics—to his distaste for playing the game and ingratiating himself with his superiors. Bitterness crept in with the realization that he would probably spend the rest of his working life at less exciting, challenging, and rewarding pursuits than his first twenty years with the company had provided. He saw that opportunities for advancement, both within and outside the firm, were beginning to close—that he would have to lower his vocational aspirations, since at this point it seemed very unlikely that he would ever become a top executive. It was difficult to avoid feeling dissatisfied with the organization that had stymied his progress and with his job, which itself symbolized something of a terminal point.

A final and significant unpleasantness for Quincy during this phase of his career was that his family life was deteriorating. His eldest teenaged daughter had embraced a set of values that were the polar opposites of his own. She had moved in with her boyfriend, an act that Quincy could never really forgive her for. His wife was somewhat more sympathetic with the daughter, and so a rift opened between Quincy and these two members of his immediate family. His growing sense of inadequacy was fed by his problems at work, so that he became defensive and irritable at home, prone to outbursts of temper and overreaction—which, of course, aggravated the family problems. It was at that point in his career that he sought help.

Acceptance Phase

The period of dissatisfaction at midlife seems to be followed by a gradual acceptance and/or rationalization of one's destiny. Levinson and his coworkers call it the "restabilization period," when a new life structure begins to provide a basis for living in middle age.[29] The "maintenance stage" of the manager's career has been attained, with its implication of having reached a plateau.[30] The disappointment at not having been able to realize one's fondest vocational fantasies has been worked through, leading to a rationalization and acceptance of one's position in life.[31] Managers come to terms with their probable future; they begin to accept their limitations. They are less concerned with "dreams" of the future and more with obtaining immediate gratification.

Many managers now begin to get more satisfaction from playing the role of mentor to the next generation of employees. Developing subordinates can provide much vicarious gratification. The turmoil of the midlife crisis has passed, and the choice between generativity and stagnation or self-absorption has been made. As a consequence, peace of mind generally increases.

Frequently, a shift occurs to activities outside the work environment, and these become new sources of satisfaction. A new equilibrium may be found in marriage, which is facilitated by the children's leaving home. New roles now become more of a possibility. Satisfaction with marriage tends to increase at this stage in life.[32] The more positive aspects of career and personal life and the reduction of midlife turmoil seem to be reflected in Figure 1, which shows an increase in job and organizational satisfaction in the acceptance phase.

We can continue with our case history of Mr. Quincy. He was quite a changed man after he had spent a few years going through the acceptance phase. Two major conditions revitalized his work life and boosted his level of satisfaction. The first was that he began to view his job very differently. Before, he had focused most of his energies and hopes on his work, trying to build his reputation in the organization by making major contributions. But now he began to modify this behavior. He started to put his job in proper perspective—viewing it mainly as a way of making a good living for his family and providing for his retirement years. No longer was he bent on being the hot shot or the star performer. He was now more concerned with developing two of his subordinates who showed the most promise. He sent them on training courses, gave them a variety of tasks to broaden their experiences and skills, and spent a good deal of his time with them, giving them pointers about their jobs and listening to their problems. In short, he began to play the role of mentor and started to derive a good deal of satisfaction therefrom.

Quincy's home life was the second major factor that contributed to his increased satisfaction. Because of his more relaxed and accepting view of his job, he now had more time and attention to devote to his family. He began once again to feel closer to his wife and daughter as his interactions with them became more frequent and more meaningful. This was facilitated by the more secure and mature outlook that he once again developed in the absence of vocational pressures. Another welcome addition to his extraorganizational activities derived from his decision to become involved in charitable work. His decision to broaden his life, to take it beyond the boundaries of his firm, led him to attempt to make a more concrete contribution to his community. He received a great deal of pleasure from coaching underprivileged children and working with the elderly. Quincy also began to devote more time to golf and fishing, two hobbies he had neglected since his teens.

Preretirement Phase

The midlife crisis is a precursor to the now-final realization that life is a one-time matter without any second chances. Managers become more introspective and reflective, seeking a new balance between activity and contemplation.[33] This is a time of reassessment, a time to integrate and resolve the unfinished business of the past. The older manager seems to undergo a new identity crisis symbolized by coming to terms with the retirement state. Erikson refers to the polarity between integrity and despair that begins to predominate in this phase of life.[34] One either discovers an integral pattern and meaning for one's past or despairs at its final, absurd, or painful nature. One looks back at one's life with a sense of pride or with regret and sorrow.

Many managers find it difficult to accept the reduced levels of power and responsibility that come with impending retirement. They may not find it easy to adjust to new roles or to find interesting extraorganizational pursuits. This problem is very well illustrated by entrepreneurs facing the problem of their succession.[35] The older manager begins to anticipate the loss of social and financial support that will accompany retirement. Coping with role and status changes and losing the secure and affirmative work environment are difficult, particularly since an important part of the manager's identity has been determined by the organization.

Other factors will contribute to one's general state of malaise. Learning to spend more time at home with one's spouse can lead to friction. New patterns of adjustment take time to develop. Poor health, financial problems, and a decline in social interaction will be other irritants. It is therefore not surprising that anger about one's fate may be displaced onto the organization, which is seen as rejecting or spurning the retiring manager in spite of his or her past contributions.

Fred Crane-Robertson was two years away from retirement. After thirty years in the personnel department he had been transferred to the profit-planning area. A large consulting firm had reorganized the personnel department, and there was no room for Fred in the consultants' plans. So he was placed in a dead-end staff job as a cost analyst, after having served in a line capacity for many years. Fred really enjoyed working with people and helping them with their careers. His new job left him with no opportunity to do either. He therefore became extremely disenchanted with the organization because of the rather inconsiderate and cavalier way in which he had been treated after so many years of valuable service.

Fred became lethargic at his new job and spent a good deal of his time taking long lunches, visiting his ex-cronies at personnel, and using up some of his sick leave. He was just counting off the days before he could retire and, in fact, was considering early retirement.

Matching Life Stages and the Work Environment

Though tentative, our findings suggest that satisfaction with one's job and one's organization is a function of a myriad of life-cycle influences. There seems to be a close match between the hedonic states suggested by the literature on the human life cycle and the levels of job and organizational satisfaction. Perhaps a conscious effort to control these life-cycle effects can explain some of the conflicts in the literature on the determinants of job satisfaction.

As consultants work to design more interesting jobs and to fill them with the right incumbents, they would do well to pay heed to the life-cycle influences we have discussed. Attention should be given not only to the life cycle of the company but also to the phase in which managers find themselves and the tasks and challenges associated with each. It would be useful for job designers to pay particular attention to designing interesting and supportive work environments during the reality-shock, midcareer-crisis, and preretirement phases. These periods pose the most severe morale problems and as a result probably require the most attention.

Part Two

Overcoming Resistance to Change

6

Identifying
Defense Mechanisms
and Sources of Resistance

O unhappy Oedipus! Why did you have to know? I did
what I could to stop you from tearing aside the veil that
protected our happiness. Now that you have repulsed me,
left me hideously exposed, how can I dare to reappear before you, before our children, before the people whom I
hear approaching?　　　　　　—André Gide, *Oedipus*

Having discussed in Part One various types of dysfunction
in organizations, in Part Two we now turn to the process of
change.

The purpose of this chapter is to link the clinical psychoanalytic concepts of resistance and defense to their counterparts in the organizational setting. In the framework of clinical
psychoanalysis, resistances to change are obstacles erected by
the patient to psychoanalytic work and insight. These are largely
resistances to recollection of relevant material or to free association. There are several common motives for resistances. First,
patients may be reluctant to change because they derive benefits such as care and attention from their symptoms. Second,
discovering the roots of one's difficulties can be very unpleasant,
and of course the tendency is usually to avoid pain. An interest-

ing reversal occurs when patients suffering from guilt welcome pain as a form of penitence. This may entail still a third motive for resistance—the patient embraces his symptoms because he feels he does not deserve relief. Errors in psychoanalytic technique may also call forth resistances. There are a myriad of other causes.

Another psychoanalytic concept closely allied to resistance is that of defense mechanisms. Whereas the term *resistance* refers to observable behavior, *defense mechanisms* refers to the hypothesized processes through which resistance is brought into being. In other words, defense mechanisms cause resistances. "Defenses" is a broader concept than "resistance" in that defenses are crucial to all normal functioning and play a part in behavior having nothing whatever to do with resistances.

Typically, in a clinical setting we encounter a large number of resistances that express themselves as hindrances to insight. This assortment of reactions is initiated to *defend* the individual against painful realizations, thereby maintaining in a homeostatic way a stable conception of the self. These defenses are employed to control impulses or affects that may cause conflict. Another perspective is that they represent a person's way of dealing with stress-evoking situations. One should realize that defenses are not of themselves pathological. We all need them to maintain a normal state of well-being. It is only the exaggerated development or overuse of certain defenses that should be considered problematic. Occasionally, defenses may fail altogether, resulting in an inability to control impulses and making it difficult to cope with the challenges of everyday life. Among the motives that give rise to resistances are feelings of anxiety, guilt, disgust, hate, envy, and shame; or a person may fear being exposed or rejected and hence may defend himself against being found inadequate, evil, or ugly. Irrespective of their etiology, defenses have the effect of restricting the accuracy of an individual's perceptions and the range and appropriateness of his behavioral repertoire. They engender resistances that manifest themselves in all aspects of life but particularly in emotion-laden situations involving long-standing interpersonal relationships. This is certainly true of scenarios that involve organizational change, particularly of the dramatic and far-reaching variety.

Organizational change can excite many fears among those most directly involved. Change often reallocates de facto, if not formally defined, authority. The managers concerned will have to reassess their position in the organization, adjust to a new and possibly inferior formal status, and learn to cope with the resulting sense of loss. Any proposal of changes in the hierarchal structure of the firm or in the incumbents occupying major positions will generate a broad range of emotional reactions among organization members. Those seemingly "passed over" are envious of those who are not. Some older managers may resent the "young Turks" who ascend to more powerful positions during the change. Still others might require lengthy periods of adjustment to become used to their new subordinates, bosses, and peers. At other times, organizational changes require a redefinition of tasks that may create major new vocational challenges. These challenges, when presented to insecure individuals, may induce fears about their ability to handle the new job requirements, particularly where employees have held the same job for many years. The fear of coming face to face with some new inadequacy can be a powerful incentive to resist change.

Administrative change can occasion destructive political behavior as factions compete for power. Problems in the form of wounded pride, lowered morale, and increased distrust, hostility, and suspicion may result.

Still another common motive for resisting change is that it may reflect poorly on one's past performance. This might be true, for example, when executives responsible for creating a particular structure or strategy must admit that it is no longer appropriate. They may feel that to accept changes in the ventures, policies, or procedures that they themselves have formulated entails an admission of past incompetence—that it lowers their status in the eyes of other members of the organization and somehow involves "losing face."

Obviously, then, organizational change is a disruptive and often traumatic phenomenon for those most directly involved. As such, it generates resistances within these persons. They will mobilize a broad array of defense mechanisms to try to protect themselves from the threat of change and to cope with the personal insecurities that change elicits. The patient undergoing therapy will typically strongly resist grappling with his or her innermost vulnerabilities and will utilize defense mechanisms and strategies of resistance to prevent any changes in awareness and personality. There is a great deal "invested," so to speak, in the psychological status quo, as a myriad of forces strive to maintain a homeostatic balance that holds primitive fears, aggressions, and desires in a state of adaptive equilibrium. As the therapeutic experience begins to unearth threats, fears, or unpleasant realizations, there is a natural tendency to defend against them by denying their existence, by repressing them, or by pretending that they exist in others but not oneself.[1] The same kinds of defenses and resistances may emerge during periods of organizational change, as again managers strive to preserve past states of affairs and the security, stability, protection, and blissful unawareness associated with them. In the following pages we shall discuss a number of these resistances and the ways they are usually manifested during periods of organizational change. The most common of these include the "defense mechanisms," the "secondary-gain resistances," and the "superego resistances."[2]

Defense Resistances

The *defense mechanisms* have as their general aim to ward off anxiety caused by intrapsychic conflict stemming from incompatible demands between an individual's wishes and external reality. They are motivated by anxiety and the desire for protection and typically involve some conscious pretense, emotional suppression, or cognitive unawareness concerning the factors that induce fear. A primary manifestation of this type of resistance is the belief in a crisis situation that there is no problem.

We shall identify six defense resistances in the literature[3] that, our experiences with organizations have revealed, play a major role in obstructing or inhibiting organizational change.

Examples of how these common mechanisms can thwart effective organizational change will be given. We do not wish to suggest that our list of defense resistances is exhaustive. In fact, there is considerable controversy in the literature about what actually constitutes a defense mechanism.

Repression. In repression, memories, desires, emotions, thoughts, and wishes are made unconscious and thereafter divorced from awareness. It is as if they did not exist in the individual's conscious life. Repression is a way of avoiding anxiety-provoking thoughts and feelings.[4] Memory gaps and forgetting are its most common manifestations.

We have seen vivid examples of repression while acting as consultants to large organizations. In one case, a firm's market share had been declining steadily under its product manager's rigid prestige pricing strategy. Profits suffered owing to the shrinkage in sales volume, as the competition sold a very competitive product at a much lower price. During our discussions with the product manager, he was able to list many defects of the competitors' products, knew many details about cost and profit margins going back for years, and in general had a good command of financial statistics. But he could never remember any market-share figures. Indeed, it became apparent that the manager could remember all the statistics that reflected favorably on his strategy but had a great deal of trouble recalling the figures that showed there were very severe problems with it. When the top marketing executives and the consultants decided that a change was necessary, the product manager, after some initial resistance, agreed. But his selective forgetting caused him to slow down the implementation of the new strategy. He forgot to show up for crucial meetings, raised the same points about product advantages based on his selectively incomplete arsenal of statistics, and monitored and remembered sales margins (which declined, pointing to the "superiority" of his old strategy), while neglecting to consider sales and market shares, which were rapidly increasing under the new strategy.

Regression. The resistance of regression consists in an attempt to revert to modes of adaptation and behavior more appropriate to an earlier stage of development.[5] Generally, regression occurs when self-esteem is seriously threatened. When one's habitual ways of dealing with stress are perceived to be inadequate, one resorts to actions that have provided some form of security on previous, seemingly simpler occasions. Behavior emanating from childhood may serve to reassure, since it is less complicated than that required by the responsibilities associated with adult living. Regression is to some extent a form of remembering and reenacting old ways of behavior.

One executive we worked with had for many years proposed entry into a new high-technology industry. Finally he was given the approval and resources he needed to proceed with his plans. After two and a half years, however, it became apparent to the top executives of the firm that as things stood, the costs of the new venture were likely to exceed the potential returns. The consultants who were called in recommended that the new venture be cut back dramatically or completely reoriented. The sponsoring manager realized that his prized project was in jeopardy and that his past competence was, at least implicitly, being called into question. He began to spend more time away from work, often going to a city park close to his firm. He also started to devote many hours to model airplane building, a hobby he had not pursued since childhood. During meetings with his superiors the executive often daydreamed and was much less alert than he had been. At one point, when questioned about the completion date of a certain prototype, he became extremely emotional and began to act childishly. Eventually a new manager had to be brought in to redirect the venture.

Projection. Projection ascribes to another person or group an attitude or quality that one possesses but rejects in oneself. It is an attempt to keep the self conflict-free by "projecting" good or evil intentions onto others. Whatever is painful or dangerous from within is projected onto another person or some part of reality.[6] Projection is a common defense among those who have paranoid tendencies. These persons reduce their guilt and anxiety by blaming other people or external circumstances for events that they themselves are directly responsible for. Projection causes managers to distort their view of reality. We have seen this mechanism in operation in our discussion of the fight/ flight culture in Chapter Two.

In a large paper company there was growing pressure from the engineering department to convert to electronically controlled monitoring of the quality of paper. This procedure had been successful in reducing scrap rates and boosting product quality at competing manufacturers, and it had reduced costs and increased profit margins. As soon as the technical consultants and engineers began to try to convince one of the plant managers and his superiors of the need for changes, the manager began to display paranoid personality traits. He was convinced that the head of the engineering department was after his job and therefore was out to make him look like a fool. He also believed that the technical consultants had been coopted by the head of engineering so that they too would be working to carry out the personal vendetta of the engineering head. Finally, he was worried that the top executives would have an excuse to sideline him if the new procedures were implemented. This would imply that the old method—for which he was at least implicitly responsible—was an indication of his backwardness.

It is interesting to note that the plant manager had an engineering background. A few years earlier, when the head of engineering had suddenly resigned, he had lobbied vigorously for the position, only to be disappointed that someone else had been chosen. At the time he had complained to many executives of foul play, indicating that the new engineering chief did not deserve the job. The suggested change in production monitoring brought these feelings back to the fore. The plant manager seemed to be projecting his feelings of hostility, attributing his own wishes to the head of engineering. He did everything in his power to resist change, and because he did so against all rational opposition, his career progress was arrested. At the same time, his opposition effectively delayed implementation of the new system for about nine months.

Identification. When identification occurs, a person thinks, feels, or acts as he conceives another person to think, feel, or act. The consequence is his adoption of the behavior patterns, values, or attitudes of the individual significant to him.[7] Identification can be a very constructive process, because it allows for adaptation to the social and cultural environment. It is a defensive pattern that rarely occurs in isolation—it is usually combined with one or more of the other defenses.

A special form of identification is identification with the aggressor, whereby the person, by "impersonating the aggressor, assuming his attributes, or imitating his aggressor . . . transforms himself from the person threatened into the person who makes the threat."[8] It is a defensive maneuver used to protect oneself from the severe anxiety caused by the person with whom one identifies.

In an organizational context identification with the aggressor can often generate a change-resistant uniformity, as subordinates begin to take on beliefs, values, attitudes, and behavior patterns of their feared superiors. We have seen how important a role these mechanisms can play in the idealizing transference reactions (Chapter Three). In one rather dramatic case of identification with the aggressor, we observed how, after a takeover, the frightened executives of the acquired firm began to pattern their behavior after that of the newly arrived president. They had many reasons to be scared, given the parent company's reputation for ruthless personnel practices. In spite of their better knowledge of the market, the executives, instead of challenging the new president's assumptions, agreed with almost all of his misinformed ideas. The president's new strategy was based on his experiences in a totally different industry and was completely inappropriate for the acquired company. None of the senior executives, however, was willing to tender any objections or even to think about them. Indeed, the executives' agreement extended to adopting the president's style of dress and imitating many of his mannerisms and expressions. This conformity eventually had serious consequences for the organization, as it led to a change-resistant, monolithic orientation totally inappropriate to the firm and its markets.

Reaction Formation. Reaction formation is a form of defense that can result in persistent, long-lived patterns of behavior that are fundamental in determining an individual's character and personality. In reaction formation, one of a pair of contradictory attitudes or traits is kept unconscious and hidden by emphasizing its dramatic opposite.[9] Thus, hate becomes replaced by solicitous love, messiness by compulsive neatness, selfishness by overgenerosity, stubbornness by compliance. The opposite, nonobservable attitude, however, persists unconsciously. Whenever an emotion or behavior is so excessive as to be unrealistic and abnormal, it may be an indication of reaction formation at work.

Frederick Taylor, the father of scientific management, is an archetypal example of someone who used reaction formation as a way of coping with aggressive impulses.[10] Taylor strongly believed that his system of work measurement, of time-and-motion studies, would make for enthusiastic cooperation, peace, and harmony between management and workers. Interestingly enough, Taylor was himself extremely ill at ease when witnessing hostile scenes. All his life he tried to play the role of peacemaker. In fact, his contemporaries commented about his *driven* need to make peace, even when a conflict had nothing to do with him. We might interpret this behavior to have been Taylor's way of turning his aggressive impulses into their opposite. Indeed, one of the paradoxes of scientific management was that it caused continual quarrels and led to violent behavior by both management and workers. Kakar, in his thoughtful analysis of Taylor's personality, states that "it was only for the cause of peace that he could let go of his hostility."[11]

In many situations reaction formation can cause behavior so extreme and uncritical that it greatly obstructs the adaptive capacities of the executive and therefore of the organization. As we have seen in our discussion of the idealizing transference in Chapter Three, extreme idealization of a subliminally hated superior blinds one to the superior's faults and thereby paralyzes one's critical faculties. Reaction formation against dependency can result in aggressiveness and hostility toward those in power, making sensible cooperation impossible. This dysfunctional narrowness of perception and the amplification of affect diminish the capacity for rational and responsive organizational change.

Denial. Perhaps one of the most common, basic defense

mechanisms to enter into situations of organizational change involves denying the existence of an external fact of reality. This can often occur after a manager has undergone a traumatic experience such as being demoted, being transferred to a less favorable department or function, or being passed over for a promotion that seemed "in the bag." Denial consists in an attempt to disavow the existence of an unpleasant or unwanted piece of external reality.[12] The truth has become too anxiety-provoking. Denial leads to the temporary delusion that nothing has changed, causing a rejection of all information that might conflict with this assessment. In the normal course, denial is a very short-lived phenomenon and is rapidly followed by confrontation of the painful facts. But sometimes denial, and the misunderstandings it engenders, can endure for a long time.

In one rather clear-cut case of denial, a senior administrator in a large hospital was in effect demoted by having the number of departments under his control cut in half. A new executive was assigned to take over several of the administrator's most promising departments. For months the first executive behaved as though nothing had changed. He continued to maintain contacts with and to advise managers who no longer reported to him. In speaking to peers inside the organization, as well as to the consultants, he constantly referred to the reassigned departments as though they were still under his control. In fact, it was not until three months after the reorganization that the executive told his wife and friends what had happened. This turned out to be his first step toward accepting the loss. Needless to say, the months of denial made things rather uncomfortable for the managers of the departments and their new boss.

Secondary-Gain Resistances

In secondary-gain resistances the underlying desire is to get the care and attention of others by remaining in an "invalid" state. The resistance is a way of gratifying dependency yearnings. Such behavior can be manifested by asking for help in changing when in fact one only wants attention (the secondary gain). The ability to adjust to change and stand on one's own would imply losing these gratifications.

Secondary-gain resistances often originate in those who feel unwanted and rejected. They crave attention, if not affection, in order to cope with their weaknesses and insecurities. Generally, these people will try to appear to cooperate with change agents just to receive attention, but they will resist actual change. They know that change would involve the loss of attention from the agent—that is, the loss of the "gain" that is a collateral or secondary benefit of the affliction or condition that requires changing. The advantages deriving from dysfunctioning, such as gratification of dependency needs and attention, are hard to give up.[13]

John Barron, the manager of the accounting department of a large firm, had seen his department undergo many changes in personnel. In just ten years he had lost as colleagues, through transfers or retirements, all the managers of his own generation. He was now left with subordinates and peers who were, on the average, twenty years his junior. As a result, he had become quite isolated, particularly over the previous two years. Even his relationship with his boss, the vice-president of administration, had become distant. They had had a very close working relationship. But over the last five years the vice-president, recognizing John's considerable talents, had left him very much on his own. John's competence had earned him his independence, so the vice-president began to devote his attention to his less capable subordinates. One day John called in sick. His complaints were drowsiness and nausea. The family doctor could not find anything physically wrong. He diagnosed general nervous fatigue and advised John to take a rest.

John Barron's absence from work had a number of repercussions. Almost immediately the vice-president called to express concern. The next day he came to visit John, and over the next few months he continued to visit once or twice a week. It became quite clear that John enjoyed these visits tremendously, as he would temporarily come out of his morose state. He really appreciated the attention his boss had suddenly begun to lavish on him. However, his condition did not improve. The vice-president of human resources asked one of the authors, who had done some consulting work for the firm, to look into the situation. The consultant had had a few brief meetings with

John in the past. From early conversations he had come to realize that John dreaded the loneliness he expected at work. John
preferred his invalid state. In spite of the confinement and dis-
comfort, it gave him the opportunity to have lengthy talks with
his boss, who needed his advice to run the department. Knowing this, the consultant suggested restructuring John's job to
allow him more interaction with his boss and other senior executives, thus reducing the "secondary gain" and reviving his motivation to come back to work.

Superego Resistances

Our final main category of resistances is characterized by
feelings of guilt and the wish to be punished for real or imagined sins. There is a felt need to placate the social and moral demands of the "superego." Superego resistances express themselves as checks on pleasures. They are frequently symptomized
by the making of errors so that one can be punished and, eventually, forgiven.

In corporate situations we have often observed managers
who become extraordinarily error-prone soon after being promoted. The reward initiates feelings of guilt, which can be re-
lieved only through punishment. One such case occurred after
the radical reorganization of the man-made fibers division of a
large chemical company, as a result of which one person was
promoted to the position of manufacturing director. The promotion increased his salary by over half and, for the first time,
elevated him to a position of sufficient prominence to attract
the attention of the firm's top executives. This executive had
hitherto been extremely competent, and his new job did not
pose any challenges that he had not already proved himself able
to handle. Now, however, he began to advocate new technologies that showed very little promise of success, making extremely large and risky capital expenditures in the process. Even
though he was warned by all his advisers, as well as his superiors, that he was heading in the wrong direction, the manager
stubbornly persisted in sponsoring one dramatically ill-fated
venture after another, until he was demoted and replaced by

someone else. In his new job, which, oddly enough, also involved manufacturing process development, the manager became his old competent self and within eight months was responsible for the initiation of two of the most successful manufacturing innovations in the history of the firm. Having been liberated from his sense of guilt by his demotion, the manager no longer felt the need to sabotage his own efforts, and his competence was thus restored.

Resistances involve all the mechanisms that protect one from experiences that one views as dangerous. Despite the original protective function of these defenses, however, they can take on a maladaptive quality. Excessive use or misapplication of resistances can lead to a restriction of freedom and may impair decision-making capacity.

The success of therapy as well as that of organizational intervention depends on managers' abilities to overcome their resistances. Resistances may sustain the maladaptive defenses that are symptoms of organizational dysfunctioning. An understanding of the resistances can help the consultant or therapist to remove obstacles to change. It can lead him or her to insights into the intrapsychic processes that have given rise to the symptoms.

As we shall see in the next chapter, resistances do not quickly disappear. Insight is not easily obtained. It takes time and much effort to work through and overcome resistances. Unfortunately, we often do not have these luxuries and must resort to manipulative, suggestive, or cathartic techniques that give only temporary symptomatic relief. No meaningful, lasting change is possible, however, without a certain amount of insight into the problems that caused the resistances to occur in the first place and a systematic effort to dismantle their most dysfunctional aspects.

7

Helping Managers
Gain Insight
to Facilitate Change

I know why there are so many people who love chopping
wood. In this activity one immediately sees the results.
—Albert Einstein

The word *intervention* is often used in organizational
studies. It evokes images of consultants and other "change
agents" trying to change organizations to improve their functioning. Many intervention strategies, however, focus on the isolated mechanics of a system, paying insufficient attention to the
human complexities of the total operation. For example, consultants will often suggest a change in an information system,
introduce a new marketing strategy, or design a new quality-of-
worklife program. Frequently, only perfunctory thought is
given to how these programs will influence the culture of the organization and the key individuals who constitute it. The emphasis is on overt, directly observable phenomena, and too little
attention is given to the more covert cognitive and emotive
forces that vitally influence the success of any program of change.

Managers have to concern themselves with the ways in
which organizational priorities must adapt to changing conditions. These adaptations have a pervasive influence throughout

the organization and take place on intrapersonal, interpersonal, group, and organizational levels. Effective organizational change requires that all these levels be taken into consideration. Organizational analysis and intervention take on particular importance when dysfunctions indicate the need for change. The contributing circumstances can range from inferior technology to competitive threats to shifting political forces within the organization.

As we shall see, the process of change follows a fixed pattern and is characterized by different, often problematic phases. We shall try to distinguish among these stages in the hope of displaying the key intra- and interpersonal challenges evoked by change and shall discuss how they can be overcome.

This chapter will focus on organizational changes from two perspectives. The first will dwell on the *role of the therapist* or consultant in generating insights into individual or organizational problems. The emphasis will be on the acts of confrontation, clarification, and interpretation as they can be used to generate the insights needed to effect lasting change-inducing attitudes. The second major section of the chapter looks at changes from the *point of view of the person* or organization undergoing the change. The focus is on the process of "working through," the various cognitive and emotional reactions that individuals must normally go through between the onset of a disruptive incident and the final change or adaptation resulting from the incident. Generating insight will be of no avail without the process of working through. Conversely, unless the working-through process is accompanied by change-evoking, realistic insights, it may be an exclusively disruptive, rather than a constructive, experience.

Stages in the Generation of Insight

As in medical practice, the first step in the managerial analysis of organizational dysfunction is the study of symptoms. By forming an integrated view of these various symptoms, one is able to arrive at a diagnosis.[1] Such an assessment should serve as the basis for designing an intervention program that is expected to lead to improved functioning. The organizational analyst becomes a change agent, helping the participants to arrive at a more satisfactory mode of functioning.

Change has become a popular topic both in organizational and in clinical literature. In order to make change effective, psychoanalysts pay considerable attention to the acquisition of *insight*. It is considered an essential precondition for change. Without insight into problems, relevant and appropriate change will be difficult. To facilitate its acquisition, a number of techniques may be used. These procedures can be called "confrontation/clarification," "interpretation," and "working through."[2] We shall discuss each as it applies to individual and organizational change and shall illustrate it with examples taken from our experiences of working with changing organizations.

Confrontation involves making problems or events explicit so that the persons involved will recognize what is happening. Attention is given to issues and behavior that the individual or organization has been avoiding. *Clarification* is an elaboration of this process whereby the problem is analyzed more closely and brought into sharper focus. Ambiguities are clarified. Usually these two processes complement each other.

We will take an example from our psychoanalytic work. Mark Fenton, an entrepreneur, had been talking at great length for a number of weeks about his job. He elaborately described how well things were going in his company. He gave detailed accounts of his excellent relationships with his subordinates, explaining how some measures he had recently taken had greatly improved the working climate. He told of how appreciative his managers were of his leadership. He said he experienced particular pleasure in the many invitations he had been receiving to speak at trade association meetings. Obviously his speeches had been popular. At that point the therapist, having become more and more struck by the one-sided, grandiose, and driven nature of his soliloquy, interrupted. He confronted Fenton with the fact that during all these weeks he had said very little about his relationship with his wife, one of the main issues that had motivated him to look for help. It seemed to the therapist that he was running away from something and that this *confrontation* might make him aware of the fact. After a long silence, Fenton admitted that he had refrained from talking about his wife for very good reasons. Everything, he said, was going extremely well in their relationship. In an attempt at *clarification,* the therapist asked Fenton to elaborate on this answer. Fenton commented on how much he and his wife had enjoyed themselves at a recent dinner, how this attested to the soundness of their relationship. At that point the therapist again confronted Fenton, pointing out that a few months ago he had been bitterly complaining that his wife never seemed to show any interest in his work. Actually, Fenton had even gone so far as to say that she always played the role of the "spoiler," the critic, the one who belittled his accomplishments. Fenton did not react directly to these comments by the therapist but continued with a series of associations regarding how much he could expand his business, the time it would take him away from home, and how it would affect his personal life, particularly his health. It appeared that there emerged from the therapist's confrontation elements of understanding, since the patient began to realize that things were not all well. However, it was not easy for Fenton to accept this suggestion from the "spoiler" therapist. Although he seemed to be a little less defensive, he still did not have sufficient insight into the causes of this problem, nor was he able to recognize any of his resistances.

We illustrate the process of confrontation and clarification with a clinical example because of the details it provides, but the process is quite similar in an organizational context, where an individual tends to hold onto his resistances, not wanting to deal with the pain and feelings of loss usually accompanying insight. The preceding example illustrates how, through confrontation and clarification, a problem that is being evaded is brought back into focus and how a foundation is laid that eventually may lead to insight. Additional work, however, has to be done before the person is ready to change some of his perceptions about himself and his way of relating to others.

The next stage in the process of insight and change can be called *interpretation.* Through interpretation we, as therapists or consultants, assign a meaning and a genesis to people's experiences, thereby going beyond what is directly observable. We investigate the dynamics contributing to the problems. We are trying to help them understand and experience the links between the different themes that evolve in the therapeutic session or the organizational consultation. Interpretation can take many forms,[3] but we can distinguish among three main types. *Transference* interpretations identify and elaborate transferential elements in interpersonal interaction. In such situations the clinician will indicate how patterns of relationships with significant persons from the individual's past are coloring present interaction patterns—how the person is repeating in the present a conflictual situation from the past. *Content* interpretation involves the reconstruction of an individual's developmental history in and outside the organization. An attempt is made to identify and clarify the influential forces during growth and maturation that made the person what he or she now is. Connections are formed between the past and the present. *Resistance* interpretation points out how an individual uses various defense mechanisms and under what conditions they tend to emerge. In all cases it is expected that the process of interpretation will lead to insight, which will make for constructive change.

Beginning with Freud,[4] clinicians soon realized that interpretation and insight, though preconditions for change, were not sufficient to bring it about. The existence of the various resistances to change had hitherto been ignored. Insight discloses new ways of looking at old phenomena. It is usually by no means pleasurable and causes disturbances of the status quo. These disturbances of the homeostatic state tend to be defended against. Our discussion of resistances in Chapter Six showed how persistent these can be. Only by dealing at length with such resistances can insight be transformed into action and change. This necessitates a lengthy, repetitive process of mulling over insights, of small experimentations and explorations, of exposing the resistances and considering alternative scenarios. Change is a painful process; it involves giving things up, losing what one has cherished in the past. This process of mastering loss, of changing one's inner representational world of fantasies, beliefs, attitudes, or values, is often called *working through*. It is comparable to mourning. Something has to be given up in order to be replaced by a new realization. Without the process of working through, insight—and therefore lasting and constructive change—is rarely achieved.

To illustrate the processes of interpretation, resistance, insight, and change, we will continue with our earlier example, Some time after the session reported earlier, Mark Fenton related a dream he had recently had in which a female employee had given him admiring glances. Reflecting on the dream, he began to describe his frustrations of childhood. His complaints centered on his inability to get a positive response from his mother. No matter how well he performed at school or how helpful he was around the house, he had never felt really appreciated. Instead, when he discussed his ambitions, his mother would tell him that his ideas were too grandiose, that he was aiming too high, and she warned him that his exploits would end in disgrace. Fenton's tone became quite bitter when he recounted that, in spite of all his success, his mother had *still* not complimented him on his achievements. On the contrary, the only things she would talk about were the recent business failures listed in the newspaper and all the dangers of the recession. At that point the therapist made the *content interpretation* that perhaps, given his past history, Fenton had always been trying to prove his mother wrong by creating a business and being successful. In spite of all his success, however, he behaved as though he were still very fearful, as though he thought calamity would strike at any moment. The therapist wondered aloud whether these fears might have been among the reasons Fenton had been bombarding him with all these stories about his business achievements. Continuing with his interpretation, the therapist noted that Fenton's behavior could be seen as a reactive action, a way of coping with insecurity. He inquired to what extent Fenton had been fishing for the compliments he had never received from his mother. (The dream in which the patient expressed a wish for an admiring woman seemed to corroborate this interpretation.) The therapist also suggested that perhaps Fenton had *transferred* the apprehension about his mother to his wife, the latter becoming the new "spoiler," the belittler of all his ambitious deeds. Maybe the same could be said about his relationship to the therapist. Perhaps the therapist was also a "spoiler" for not complimenting Fenton on his successes. On the contrary, with all his interpretations, the therapist was disturbing Fenton's defended perceptions of himself. Perhaps Fenton saw all his relationships as basically threatening; he always seemed to be on the defensive, ready for emergencies. The response to all these interpretations was a short silence followed by a few disconnected comments about a hockey game Fenton had seen the previous evening. It was as if he had not heard anything the therapist had said.

Two weeks later Fenton remarked what a terrible day it had been. He told how, for statutory reporting purposes, he had prepared an auditor's report. To his great surprise and consternation, he discovered that his company had incurred a loss for the fiscal year. It was quite a shock. He had thought his firm was extremely successful, and he was sorely disappointed. The therapist again pointed out Fenton's defensive need to believe that "without any doubt" everything was going beautifully, how he seemed inclined to ignore unpleasant information by changing topics. The therapist, in making this *resistance interpretation,* linked these tendencies to his ways of dealing with the frustrations of childhood. It must always have been so much easier to deny painful reality. This time Fenton did not switch to discussing the hockey game or any of his other diversions. He mentioned that only now did he realize how inadequate the management control system in his company was, how infrequently he had been getting reports. In fact, he soon admitted that reports would not have done him much good, since he had rarely examined those available. All the time he had been convinced that he was going to have a tremendously profitable year. Only now did he see how deliberately blind he had been.

A few weeks later Fenton told the therapist that he had contacted a management consulting firm with the explicit goal of having his management control system updated. Gradually he began to take a more active operating role in the management of his company, moving away from the more ceremonial function he had been assuming, and getting back into the stream of things. He now saw how much he had abdicated responsibility and to what extent his company had been floundering as a result. Fenton had been much more interested in the glamorous side of being president and had neglected internal operations. He now initiated a review of profitability by product line and discovered that the pricing strategy for many of his products had been completely inappropriate. He also decided to become more involved with the sales force. This involvement led to the discovery that many of the "specials" that made him so popular among customers had been largely responsible for the deteriorating profit picture. Apparently Fenton had been trying to gain the approval of his customers, as well as his mother. At the same time, he began to make more of an effort to talk about his business concerns with his wife. He was now much less afraid that she would be bored and criticize him. Instead, he discovered genuine concern on her part.

From this abbreviated case vignette we can discern the operation of various resistances against interpretation. Note that it took much time for Fenton to "work through" the therapist's various interpretations so as to be able to change his perceptions about himself, others, and the world in general. Granted, an outside event in the form of poor profits facilitated this process; but it is doubtful whether, without repeated interpretations in a supportive, contemplative atmosphere, Fenton would have been able to see the auditor's report in its proper light and assume responsibility for the financial problems. It would have been all too easy to blame other people or circumstances for the deteriorating profit picture.

The role of the consultant is not so different from that of a clinician. Like the clinician, the consultant is engaged in a continual dialogue with clients, an interactive process in which confrontation, clarification, and interpretation play major roles. As our clinical case example shows, acquisition of insight is a time-consuming process. As illustrated in the following pages, resistances need to be "worked through." This has important implications for the field of consultancy. It implies that effective organizational change is unlikely to be brought about by the traditional "quick fixes."

The Working-Through Process

There exists a considerable body of research and clinical literature that deals with the processes of loss and mourning. One mourns the passing of old attachments and prepares for new ones. Bowlby, in his monumental trilogy on attachment, separation, and loss, synthesized much of the existing literature related to this topic.[5] He was particularly interested in how people deal with losses stemming from the death or desertion of a loved one. Bowlby defines healthy mourning as "the successful effort of an individual to accept both that a change has occurred in the external world and that he is [thus] required to make corresponding changes in his internal, representational world and to reorganize, and perhaps to reorient, his attachment behavior accordingly."[6] In his review of the literature Bowlby was able to discern four general stages of mourning that seemed universal. He notes:

> Observations of how individuals respond to the loss of a close relative show that over the course of weeks and months their responses usually move through a succession of phases. Admittedly these phases are not clear-cut, and any one individual may oscillate for a time back and forth between any of them. Yet an overall sequence can be discerned.
> The four phases are as follows:
> 1. Phase of numbing that usually lasts from a few hours to a week and may be interrupted by outbursts of extremely intense distress and/or anger.
> 2. Phase of yearning and searching for the lost figure lasting some months and sometimes for years.
> 3. Phase of disorganization and despair.
> 4. Phase of greater or lesser degree of reorganization.[7]

There is considerable agreement in the literature that the process of dealing with the loss of a loved one is the model after which all other forms of loss are patterned.[8] And loss necessitates mourning. A disturbance of the organizational status quo precipitates a comparable process. It causes the loss of old and familiar patterns of functioning and administrative relationships as they are replaced with new ones. Working through, mourning, and change thus appear to be intimately connected.

A classic example of the working-through process of an *individual* in an organizational context is the reaction of an executive who has just been told he is being dismissed. For purposes of illustration we shall present a personal experience related to us during a series of interviews at one organization.

One Friday morning Henry Thurgood, an account executive working for a large advertising firm, was told by his boss that his services were no longer needed. He was given his last paycheck and told to take his personal belongings from his office. Thurgood had known that key personnel changes were in the works, owing to a major reorganization. But in spite of this knowledge his dismissal came as a major shock. It had really never crossed his mind that he would be affected by the changes. He recalled how after he had heard the word *dismissal,* he felt as though he were "walking in a daze." No other word in the message had got through to him. He did not even remember what he had said in response. He recalled only having ended up at a nearby bar and having a few drinks. It was there that he experienced his first attacks of panic, wondering how he would go about getting another job. The job market did not seem very promising. Thurgood's recollections about the weekend were not very clear either. The only thing he did remember was lying in bed, watching television.

He told the interviewers that on Monday morning his first impulse had been to get up to go to work, until it belatedly dawned on him that he no longer had a job to go to. It was then that he began to ask himself why he had been singled out for dismissal. Were others fired too, or was he the only one? These thoughts led to reflections about what he might have done wrong, about the mistakes he had made. Nagging thoughts about his performance continued to haunt him. He recalled that he had felt tempted to call one of the vice-presidents, whom he knew only vaguely, and ask for an explanation. Hindsight led him to believe that this idea had stemmed from the hope that the vice-president would tell him that it had all been a bad dream, that he was still working for the company. Afterward, it crossed his mind that the new project leader may have been at fault for his predicament. The latter was presumed to feel resentment because of Thurgood's criticisms of his leadership at a recent design meeting. Thurgood told the interviewers about the anger he had felt toward the project leader at the time. He toyed with the idea that if only he could explain all this to the vice-president, the whole matter would be resolved in his favor. He also mentioned to the interviewers how sorry he had been for himself and how helpless he had felt.

He had spent the next few days calling several executives in the company, who commiserated with him, and by talking to friends, who did likewise. What stood out in his memory was his strong feelings of anger at the time. It seemed as if everybody else had it so much easier. Thurgood also felt that most expressions of sympathy toward him were quite hollow. He recalled how he had burst out angrily when a friend suggested that he should get some kind of professional help from a career counselor. A few days later he apologized to his friend for his behavior, and the two had a long discussion exploring possible reasons for Thurgood's dismissal. He felt that the discussion had been quite helpful, though not always pleasant.

His friend had commented on his tendency to ignore organizational norms; perhaps his behavior had aroused the anger of other executives. The friend also mentioned that Thurgood's occasionally abrasive behavior may have acted as a red flag to people. Thurgood had heard similar comments at other times but had been very quick to discount them. This time, however, things were different. His incontrovertible dismissal made it possible for the comments to sink in. In retrospect, he gave his friend a lot of credit for getting him out of his state of malaise and lethargy.

After the talk, Thurgood began to feel motivated to look

beyond the classified pages in the newspaper and contact a career counseling service and a placement agency. He also made an appointment with a therapist, whom he began to see weekly. Thinking back to that period, he recalled how confused he had been, how much difficulty he had had in dealing with all the new information about himself. Several sessions with the therapist had been quite disconcerting, since they made him see things about himself that he did not find very pleasant at the time. It had been a period of intensive self-exploration.

Thurgood remembered how his confusion had affected the way he dealt with the job market. At times he would wonder about the right way to act during a particular job interview. He recounted his despair at not hearing from a prospective employer or at getting a noncommittal response from an interviewer. On such occasions he would ask himself whether anybody really valued his previous accomplishments. He questioned whether he really had anything to offer.

In retrospect, however, he felt that this had been a period of great personal growth. He had learned a lot about himself and believed he had become less cocky and more empathetic toward others. He told how he had gradually become more secure about his talents and limitations. Exciting opportunities in the marketplace now became apparent. Thurgood realized that his dismissal was not a major catastrophe after all. Four months after his departure, he joined his present company, and he has been quite successful ever since.

An example of the process of working through in an *organizational* context is based on the authors' consulting experience. This episode started when the vice-president of merchandising of a large consumer goods company was informed of a change in his reporting relationship. To improve coordination and complementarity among the sales, marketing, and merchandising functions, his department would in the future report to the senior vice-president of marketing, no longer to the president. Because we lack information, we can say very little about how the vice-president dealt with his sense of personal loss. During a visit to the firm at the time, however, we noticed the profound state of confusion experienced by the members of the merchandising department. This confusion was multifaceted but related mainly to feelings of uncertainty about the future, regarding the distribution of power, reporting relationships, task responsibilities, and even mundane matters such as parking spots and office allocations. The department's productivity declined sharply during this period. No new projects were undertaken. Operations were sluggish, and there was a general unresponsiveness to demands from other departments or from field personnel. Moreover, there began to emerge a considerable amount of hostility among members of the merchandising group, directed mainly against the ascendant marketing managers, which manifested itself in general belligerence, aggressive pranks, acts of subtle sabotage, and attempts to put certain members of the marketing group in a bad light.

A myth was formulated in which the "pushiness" of the vice-president of marketing, now the senior vice-president, was blamed for the unfavorable reorganization. The overall attitude was uncooperativeness. Managers were reluctant to take responsibility; instead, the sales and marketing groups were blamed for all merchandising mistakes. We were also struck by how much time the members of the merchandising department spent outside the company, going on field trips, courses, and long lunches.

As consultants we became aware of a good deal of "clinging" behavior. It became difficult for us to leave the merchandisers' offices; it was as if they wanted to talk to us forever. A persistent question was "Why do you think there was a reorganization?" What, they wondered, had they done to deserve this change? The unexpressed wish during many of these conversations was that the merchandisers wanted us to advocate their point of view to the president and thereby have him restore the status quo ante.

By the time of our next visit to the company, a few months later, the situation had changed markedly. A modest amount of collaboration could now be observed between a number of merchandisers and marketing managers. We were quite surprised to see how the "lunch situation" had changed. The two groups now intermingled and ate together in the company cafeteria. Conversations with the vice-president of mer-

chandising revealed that he was less bitter. He seemed less withdrawn, more outgoing. A task force made up of marketing,
sales, and merchandising managers had been set up with our
help. The new group proposed a product management organization. The idea was welcomed, albeit with some hesitation, by
many of the merchandisers. Even the vice-president of merchandising showed some enthusiasm. He realized that such an organization would allow him to devote more time to design and
R&D, always his first loves. When we visited the company five
months after the initial reorganization, the merchandising group
was proceeding full steam ahead, ready to face new challenges.

These two clinical vignettes illustrate the diverse emotions aroused during the process of working through and the
various stages involved. There appears to be much similarity between the way an individu il deals with the loss of a loved one
and the way organization members deal with change. We shall
now present a conceptual framework describing the various
phases an individual passes through in the mourning/working-
through process and how it can affect organizational life.[9]

As we saw from the two case vignettes, the first reaction
to a disturbance, which often involves a withdrawal of or
change in status, is *shock*. The person is reluctant to assimilate
new information, especially if it is damaging to self-esteem. A
short period of numbness often occurs, which may be interrupted by attacks of panic and outbursts of anger.[10] All these
processes could be observed very clearly both in the case of
Thurgood and in that of the merchandising department. During
this shock phase organization members give considerable attention to any threats to their position caused by the change. The
feelings of shock that they experience have many organizational
consequences. As we saw in the case of the merchandising department, a sense of bewilderment can spread throughout the
organization, making for a state of disarray. Vital organizational
processes may falter or continue to function only in a ritualistic, mechanical way.

The two case vignettes illustrate, however, that this situation will not usually continue very long. A change in behavior
will occur. Although the reality of the situation occasionally

surfaces in awareness, there is at first a great need to believe that what has happened is not really true, that the event can still be undone. Thurgood's thoughts of calling the vice-president to secure his reentry into the company and the merchandisers' belief that the consultants could make the president reestablish the previous reporting relationship can be seen in this light. In this second phase, *disbelief,* the individual or group will yearn and search for what is lost.[11] At the same time, people feel a great deal of frustration about the fact that the change-inducing event had to happen to them. Irrational outbursts of anger, alternating with periods of self-reproach, may result. People may blame themselves for minor acts of omission or commission that they may see as the cause of their predicament. Recall Thurgood's doubts about his performance in the company and the merchandisers' insistence that the consultants find out the causes of the redistribution in reporting relationships. Accompanying all these emotions is a pervasive sense of sadness.

During the disbelief phase we often see the emergence of the fight/flight and dependency cultures of Chapter Two. For example, fight behavior in the form of displacement of anger becomes common. Thurgood directed his anger against the project leader, the merchandisers toward the other departments, particularly marketing. Quite frequently this anger is directed toward those who try to be helpful but are blamed for the change even though they have nothing to do with it. Thurgood's eruption following his friend's advice is another example. One finds a great amount of irritability and bitterness. Flight behavior in the form of withdrawal reactions, such as staying away from the office, is also common. Dependency needs become manifest as well. There is an intense longing for the status quo ante, the good old days of status, esteem, power, and predictability. There is a search for the omnipotent leader who will make things right. In our case examples, this was a vice-president, consultant, or president. In the organization, dependency manifests itself in passivity—there are very few manifestations of initiative. All energy seems to be wasted on internal politics or is directed toward external agencies that are held responsible for the change. The behavior of the merchandising department in dealing with the other units in the company is an example.

The most prominent feature of the third phase in the working-through process is the *discarding* of old patterns of thinking, feeling, and acting.[12] This is the time when the manager or group of managers begin to accept that the change may be permanent. It gradually dawns on them that a redefinition of the situation is needed, making for the first tentative explorations of reality and adjustment strategies. It is a period of self-examination and disorganization. But with it comes a sense of despair over the loss of what once was valued. Despair gives rise to flight behavior, causing bouts of depression and apathy. Thurgood's confusion about who he really was, his attempts to find out more about himself, his despair about his first job interviews and about his ability to adjust are good illustrations of what happens in this phase. The same can be said about the merchandisers' suspension of disbelief manifested in their first tentative collaborations with members of the marketing department and their membership in a joint task force. The first attempts of the vice-president of merchandising to reappraise his strengths and weaknesses can be seen in a similar light.

The final phase is one of *realization*—the redefinition of oneself and the situation.[13] One's internal representational world is reshaped, leading to acceptance of new values, beliefs, and thoughts. One becomes willing to look at other realities. The focus on the past that characterized the other stages is abandoned for a more future-oriented, proactive stand. Note Thurgood's realization that he had something to offer, that there were many exciting opportunities in the future. The same pattern could be observed among the merchandising group when they began to see the mutual advantages of a joint approach, particularly through the vehicle of product management. Even the vice-president of merchandising realized how much more effective he would eventually be by focusing his creativity on design and R&D.

Table 7 summarizes the different phases of working through.

Table 7. Phases of the Working-Through Process.

| Phase | Manifestations | |
	Individual	Organizational
Phase 1: Shock	Numbing, interrupted by panic and outbursts of anger	State of disarray; organizational processes come to a halt or become ritualistic
Phase 2: Disbelief	Yearning and searching for what is lost; disbelief, denial of reality; irrational anger, self-reproach, sadness	Fight/flight and dependency assumptions; reactive posture; past orientation
Phase 3: Discarding	Discarding of old patterns of thinking, feeling, and acting; redefinition of oneself; self-examination, disorganization, despair	Acceptance of organizational situation; occasional flight behavior; redefinition of situation; tentative explorations
Phase 4: Realization	Reshaping of internal representational world; acceptance of new reality	Reorganization: proactive posture; future orientation

Arrests in the Process of Working Through

Executives who are capable of working through these four phases will arrive at some form of reorganization, both of their inner representational world and of their external situation. This sets the stage for change. In some instances, however, the change process will be less successful. An *arrest* may occur, an inability to proceed from one stage to the next, producing dysfunctional and painful symptomatology. Passage through these four phases will no longer be self-limiting. Defensive patterns may persist and begin to dominate organizational functioning completely.[14] Executives may deny the reality of the situation and cling to the past. They will continue to function as if nothing had happened and, of course, incur the associated adverse consequences. Or the perceived withdrawal of status or respect may lead to manic activity, often in the form of aggressive and destructive acts in the organization. Very prominent defensive maneuvers may be of a *displacement* nature or may cause a form of *cognitive disconnection*. In displacement the affected executives will redirect anger away from the responsible party and toward someone else, be it a person, department, institution, or object. When cognitive disconnection occurs, the emotional responses are uncoupled from the situation that elicited them, making for repression and splitting.

As discussed in the previous chapter, in repression unacceptable ideas or impulses are banished from direct awareness. For example, an executive who repeatedly promises to hand in a certain report or to make a decision but keeps forgetting may be engaging in repression. Splitting may also occur, creating a world divided into camps of friends and enemies. Toward the latter is directed all one's hostile energy. Chapter Three showed how splitting creates a paranoid view of the world, where "others" are always out to attack and calamities are always just around the corner.

Occasionally the troubled individuals or groups will themselves assume the *scapegoat* role, instead of looking for others to blame. They will continue to reproach themselves for some minor mishap. This behavior may be accompanied by accident-proneness, extreme helplessness, and passivity.

In some cases of failure in the working-through process we can observe the "Lone Ranger syndrome." The executive or department acts as if nobody else were needed. This can be viewed as a protective reaction based on the deep-seated wish to be taken care of. Since nobody else seems to be able to do this job satisfactorily, the Lone Ranger will do it all by himself. He will show everybody how self-reliant he really is. A variation on this pattern is found in the executive or group of managers who react to a sense of helplessness (perhaps incurred by a perceived loss of status) by taking a more active role and by boosting their attitude of independence.

Many of the defenses that arrest the working-through process may occur concurrently. We will take another example of "Lone Rangerism" from our consulting experience. In one organization, it was decided not to have the heir-apparent vice-president of sales succeed the president. Although the sales organization had always been relatively independent, its independence became even more dramatic after this decision. The sales organization began to act more and more as if the rest of the organization, rather than the chief competitor, were the enemy. A fight/flight culture prevailed. It seemed that nothing the other departments did was good enough. At sales conferences "everybody else" was held responsible for deviations from plan. Very little self-searching was done to locate the real source of difficulties. The finance department was blamed for its tardiness in reimbursing salesmen for their expenses and for its "nit-picking" way of handling customer credit. But these accusations paled in comparison with those leveled against the marketing department. No matter how well thought out the marketing plans were, the vice-president of sales spared no effort to find severe fault with them. We were present at some of the marketing presentations and were quite struck by the viciousness of the attacks. They led to a very destructive atmosphere. The sales group habitually ignored the marketing department's requests for customer information. When information was given at all, it tended to be inaccurate or incomplete. The other functional areas were also criticized. Even manufacturing was not immune from the attack of the sales managers. Their attitude was "We'll have to do it all alone, since we cannot really rely on anybody."

This internal warfare did not abate. It kept on festering, causing sales and profits to fall. Only the dismissal of the vice-president, the original catalyst of this destructive atmosphere, and the careful efforts of a new director of human resources brought an end to this stalemate.

In this example of arrest in the working-through process, the disappointment of the vice-president of sales reverberated throughout his department. It led to persistent manifestations of denial, "splitting," paranoid thinking, displacement behavior, repression, and the "Lone Ranger syndrome." We should keep in mind, however, that all these arrests in the working-through process may occur in the transformation toward *successful* change. What distinguishes their dysfunctional nature is simply their tenacity and persistence.

By using examples from our personal clinical and consulting experiences, we have tried to show how difficult it can be for managers to recognize the need for change and why they often fail to recognize that need. Organizational and personal "pain" becomes an important motivation behind change. We have tried to show how much work is required both by the therapist/consultant and by the manager working through the change in order to effect a satisfactory transition. This can be an involved, thankless, and time-consuming process. It would be much easier for a consultant to look at the "objective" problems and to make his or her "sensible" recommendations. But this simple approach fails to come to grips with the sources of the problems—it addresses symptoms more than causes. Any symptomatic relief will therefore be very temporary. It also assumes that the recommendations will be followed by those who are dead set against them. The only way to effect lasting change is to convince key managers of the need for it; to show them the desirability of the solution even though implementing and achieving it may cause them pain; and to help them to attain insight and to work through the intrapsychic barriers to change to arrive at a new set of mental representations of self and others.

8

Steps in Diagnosing, Overcoming, and Preventing Problems

Look beneath the surface: never let a thing's intrinsic quality or worth escape you.
—Marcus Aurelius, *Meditations*

Our analysis of organizational dynamics so far has been long on description and short on prescription. The nagging question remains: What can we do to combat organizational neuroses? How can we take some first steps to resolve their problems?

Certainly, the authors cannot at this stage provide any final answers. All we can do is offer tentative suggestions.

It may be useful to recap our conclusions about organizational problems of psychodynamic origin before making any prescriptions. First, many problems have deep roots that are not at all obvious. This circumstance places a great onus on diagnosis as an essential preliminary activity. Second, the roots of the problems are often to be found in the long-standing, deepseated personality characteristics of powerful executives. Character is by definition stable and resistant to change. Neurotic styles commandeer the victim's perceptual faculties in a manner that makes him blind to, or extremely defensive about, the very

167

insights that could provide the incentive for change. Third, when neurotic executives hold much power in the organization, an enduring impasse can result between the change agents and the client. The sensitive, threatened executive may simply get rid of the tormenting consultant. Even where the executive *wants* to change, doing so can involve a lengthy therapeutic process beyond the capacities of most consultants. Finally, many problems we have discussed are supported and propagated by a sort of "social synergy," "groupthink," or "folie à deux." That is, the problem is incorporated into, amplified by, and preserved by the organizational social system. For example, group fantasies evolve around emotion-laden issues and give rise to much conformity. There are group pressures and sanctions that can thwart the influence of the more realistic group members, who may, in fact, be chastised for their potentially sobering nonconformist comments. Similarly, in superior/subordinate dysfunctions, the superior's power can entrap the subordinate, initially provoking opportunistic conformity or compliance but eventually resulting in "folie à deux" as a subordinate's tentative rationalizations and compliance give way to conviction.

To summarize the difficulties, it can be said that the problems we have discussed have four properties that make them particularly difficult to address: They are deeply rooted and thus hard to diagnose; they are caused by long-standing personality characteristics that resist not only change but also recognition of the need to change; the problems center on emotionally sensitive issues, so that the consultant who probes these too vigorously or too high in the executive hierarchy is likely to find himself or herself without a client; and finally, the social system of the organization amplifies the problems.

These considerations give rise to three crucial but general prescriptions for those trying to promote healthy, adaptive organizations. First, a good deal of one's time and effort must be devoted to systematically *diagnosing* and addressing organizational problems to discover their roots and causal interconnections. Only in this way will it be possible to discover the leverage points that can be used to break the vicious circles and to circumvent the perceptual, political, and social resistances. Second, much more attention must be paid to changing key actors in organizations instead of simply trying to change what they do. Neurotic styles do not self-destruct when an information system is introduced; debilitating transferential interactions do not vanish when management by objectives appears. Much more emphasis is required to *change key people*—their insights, self-awareness, behavior, and, where necessary, their positions. Third, and perhaps most important, a great deal more must be done in the way of *preventive maintenance*. Because the problems are so difficult to deal with once fully established, it is doubly important that we try to anticipate them before they occur or at least catch them in their early stages.

We shall devote the next three sections of this chapter to a discussion of these prescriptive themes.

Four Steps in Intervention

There are four stages in analyzing complex organizational, group, or interpersonal problems. First a simple listing of symptoms and obvious problems is made from the facts available. Then one constructs a "model" of the problem by interrelating problems and symptoms in a manner that allows inferences about the underlying root causes of the syndrome. Next, a number of solution alternatives are generated, compared, and discussed. Finally, one devises a plan of implementation.

1. *Make a simple listing of the primary symptoms and problems.* Primary symptoms and problems are the most obvious of the firm's difficulties. For an entire organization these might include declines in market share, falling profit margins, morale problems, absenteeism and strikes, obsolete technologies, product quality problems, rapidly rising costs, or even such things as a total absence or superabundance of conflict in group and interpersonal relationships.

It might be helpful to make a list of symptoms and problems by looking at each functional area in sequence. This systematic approach ensures more thoroughness in eliciting the most important manifestations of the problems.

2. *Make conjectures about the syndrome, working back-ward from symptoms to discover the underlying roots of the problem.* At this stage of analysis, the objective should be to connect the symptoms and problems on the list with their causes, eventually working back to the root psychodynamic sources of the difficulties. It is relatively useless to alleviate symptoms if their underlying causes remain, since then relief will be only temporary. To obtain a lasting solution, it is neces-sary to uncover the *fundamental* source of the problems by con-structing a "model" of the syndrome. The source, or root, may have several independent components that must be addressed separately. Often, however, it represents a cohesively intercon-nected, thematically related set of basic difficulties. Only when these have been identified is the diagnosis complete.

The *only* thing that distinguishes a symptom from an underlying problem is that the latter causes the former. There may then be a chain of problem-to-symptom links so that the same phenomenon is both a symptom and a problem. However, symptoms often tend to be of a somewhat different nature from problems. Events such as declining profits, poor sales, and loss of market share are always symptoms. Improper allocation of authority, extreme risk averseness, vague or rigid strategies, and impeded flow of information are problems that may often underlie the symptoms. Finally, neurotic executives, dysfunc-tional group fantasies, or defective interaction modes may be the root situations behind the problems. It is these that must ultimately be addressed.

The problems in Table 8 are some of the more common ones that we have encountered in organizations. They often re-late quite closely to the root situations given on the left of the table. These are, of course, illustrative and not exhaustive—the relations with roots being suggestive only, not causally deter-mined.

A model of the failure syndrome can be constructed using a causal, or "arrow," diagram such as Figure 2, in the next chapter. The diagram serves to trace back the symptoms on the list to their underlying problems and, where possible, to trace problems back to their common roots. For example, to diagnose an organizationwide problem, one may start with obvious sur-

Table 8. Common Organizational Problems and Possible Roots.

Possible Root Situation	Common Problem
Depressive firm: Leaderlessness Paranoid firm: Suspiciousness Dramatic firm: Overcentralization Mirroring transference: Dangerous grandiosity Binding mode: No delegation	*Improper allocation of authority in the organization* Responsibilities are not commensurate with authority; those with the best information are not allowed to make decisions; those who make decisions have too broad and hectic a job to do it well; top managers exercise very little authority, so that there are problems of control
Dramatic firm: Excessive risk taking Depressive firm: Excessive conservatism Mirroring transference: Dangerous grandiosity	*Attitudes toward risk may be out of line* Too much or too little risk taking and innovation take place relative to marketplace demands; excessive risk taking and changes often threaten the firm's resources and may be costly; too little risk taking and innovation lead to traditions that cause methods and products to become obsolete
Dramatic firm: Undercontrol, overcentralization Depressive firm: Rigidity Utopian culture: Unsettledness	*The organization structures may be inadequate to the task* They may be too uncontrolled or bureaucratic, too flexible or too rigid, too unsettled or too formal, too monolithic or too fragmented, too centralized or too decentralized
Compulsive firm: Rigid, narrow focus Depressive firm: Vague strategy Utopian culture: Vague strategy	*Strategies may be too vague or too rigid* Strategies concentrate on too few considerations; they are too sketchy to serve as a guide or too rigid to allow for adaptation
Paranoid firm: No distribution of information Fight/flight culture: Factionalism, secretiveness Persecutory transference: Secretiveness	*The right information may not be going to the right decision makers* The necessary communication cannot take place between different levels of managers; there are too few or too many financial and managerial controls in place; information on the environment is not being gathered or disseminated

(continued on next page)

Table 8. Common Organizational Problems and Possible Roots, Cont'd.

Possible Root Situation	Common Problem
Binding, proxy, or expelling top executives: Incapacity for independent action	*The caliber of executive talent may be deficient*
	Many activities (for example, new-product development, capital budgeting) are being neglected because there are no executive skills available to carry them out well

face symptoms such as stagnating sales and ask why this occurred. Some of the other entries on the list may provide clues; for example, poor advertising and sales methods, ignorance of markets, and delays in delivery might be most directly responsible. We must study the situation carefully to make sure there is some justification for believing each inference. We must also ask whether we have omitted factors that might be relevant. We can represent the hypothesized causal connections between the symptom and its hypothesized causes by using arrows, as in Figure 2.

Such a process of inquiry is continued until we have worked backward in a like manner to discover the ultimate causes of all the symptoms on the list. We have usually reached the root causes when there is convergence on a very few central themes—that is, when a few basic roots explain almost all the symptoms and problems. It is at this stage that consultants must decide whether a clinician should be brought in to investigate whether the roots of the problem have a psychodynamic origin. The roots can then be explored through interviews, discussions, and further psychological probing until the result is something like Table 9, in the next chapter. Of course, there is generally no one simple model that describes a complex syndrome. Often several causal diagrams are equally plausible. Indeed, the development of alternative models can result in broader understanding and greater flexibility among those grappling with the problem.

It is worthwhile to stress that the ultimate source of many organizational problems may be simple ignorance—just the lack of knowledge and competence by key decision makers about the nature of their business—rather than any deep psycho-pathologies. That is why it is so important to try to implement a simple solution first—to address only the objective problems. Only if this approach fails will it be necessary to assess whether more deep-seated psychological factors are the basis of the intractability of the problem.

3. *Generate a set of alternative solutions and choose the one that best seems to address the roots of the syndrome.* A number of solution alternatives should be generated. The creative exercise required to derive and appraise these should result in a deeper, more balanced appreciation of remedial possibilities. The alternatives should each be relatively complete. That is, they should serve to eradicate all practical obstacles to recovery by getting at the most serious roots of the syndrome. Moreover, alternatives can fruitfully be quite different from one another. They should be extensively discussed by consultants and managers. Clients' responses reveal a great deal about their main underlying fears and aspirations and will be of use not only for improving the quality of solutions but also for better defining the parameters of the problem. Reframing the context of the problem might help avoid unpromising solutions.

In order to appraise the desirability of the different solutions, they should be compared along a variety of criteria:

- *Completeness.* Are there key symptoms that the proposed solution may not eradicate? List these for each alternative and compare their severity.
- *Side effects.* Might the alternative cause any other negative repercussions that would initiate a new pathology? Is the impact of the alternative foreseeable or highly uncertain?
- *Economy.* Which alternatives are the least costly? Does the firm have the resources necessary to carry out the alternative, or will it be risking more than it can afford? Does the alternative build on existing organizational strengths?
- *Depth of solution.* Does the alternative go far enough, or does it merely address symptoms? Would a more superficial solution work by creating a new acceptable equilibrium in the organization?
- *Timeliness.* Can the alternative be executed fast enough to

be effective, or will its complexity cause delays that may jeopardize the organization's survival?

- *Political feasibility*. Will it be possible to get the support of enough employees and managers to implement the solution?

It is difficult to balance these criteria to choose the one best alternative, because the importance of each factor depends on the nature of the firm and the problem it must face. For example, a firm hovering near bankruptcy with extremely scarce resources must devise an economical and timely stopgap solution. A complex bureaucracy that is financially strong may require a solution that is politically acceptable and complete. The particular nature of the situation must always be considered.

4. *Develop a plan of implementation*. The proposed solution or plan of action should be specific. It should make clear what should change, how, when, why, and by whom. No doubt must be left about exactly what must be accomplished, its expected costs and benefits (that is, its rationale), and the manner in which the change is to take place.

Implementation plans should include proposed methods for making the remedial measures acceptable. The persons who must be persuaded, the order in which they are to be contacted, and the arguments to be used to convince them of the soundness of the plan of action must all be decided on.

The timing of implementation should be such that the most severe and urgent issues are dealt with first to stem the erosion of the firm's resources. More costly and ambitious measures must often be postponed until the firm's resources have been amply strengthened. In all cases the time sequence of implementation should be carefully thought out so that premature and tardy acts are avoided.

Implementation must involve an iterative process whereby plans that meet with unexpected obstacles or negative side effects can be modified before too much time has elapsed. A firm and its challenges are very complex, and sometimes it is impossible to foresee weaknesses in a solution. It is therefore necessary to be flexible and modify plans where needed as part of the implementation process.

Organizations and their environments are constantly changing. It is therefore useful to reappraise the soundness of the firm's strategies from time to time in order to ensure that they remain relevant. Periodic appraisals will also help to detect unexpected and gradual side effects of the implementation plan.

People, Not Process

The analytical scheme delineated in the preceding section is not very different from those expounded by conventional scholars of organizations. The main differences are the explicit focus on interrelations among symptoms, problems, and roots and the quest for depth in diagnosis and flexibility and breadth in prescription. But what about content? Exactly what tools are there to deal with these deep, intrapsychic problems and their effects? This section will address this issue as it applies to *existing* severe problems. The next section will dwell on the prevention or early detection of such problems.

Our theme is that the problems caused by deep-seated personality characteristics cannot generally be combated by superimposing "rational" techniques on the organization. As we suggested earlier, a paranoid executive will not become less so just because he is given a better information system. Utopian groupthink does not cease because one is told to adopt more concrete objectives. "Rational solutions" work only with "rational people." Where defense mechanisms are active, transferential patterns intense, and neurotic styles pronounced, the perceptual, social, and power blockages discussed at the beginning of this chapter are enough to resist the traditional forms of organizational intervention. The question becomes: What is left?

Obviously, the answer depends on the precise nature of the problem. Our discussion must therefore be both general and cursory. Certainly, however, the focus must be on the people whose behavior, personality, and intrapsychic fantasies are the sources of the problem. We shall assume now that the problem has been traced back by competent clinicians to its psychodynamic roots. We shall assume also that the problem has proved resistant to "objective" changes in the work environment—measures such as strategic adjustments, better information systems, more appropriate reward and appraisal systems, or better structures.

Two possible "people" strategies can be used to combat psychodynamic problems. The first is to try to change the people; the second is to place them out of harm's way. We shall see in the case of the Diana Company in the next chapter that enduring patterns of dysfunctional interaction can be established that prove most onerous to change. Even lengthy psychoanalytic or alternative therapies do not necessarily promote successful change. Most organizations have neither the time nor the resources to make use of these elaborate forms of therapy. There is also the obvious barrier of resistance by the powerful client to undergo such treatment. In such cases, which can easily be flagged by a consultant with clinical training in the course of a few lengthy interviews with the parties, organizational therapy must differ from individual therapy. It becomes a matter of *changing the context* in which the individual is operating. For example, one can move the individual to a new, less conflict-laden position in order to sever permanently the most disturbing transferential or binding interpersonal relationships or to transfer an executive to a position where his or her problems will have minimal impact. In some cases it will be preferable to arrange for early retirement or even dismissal. Demotion is a measure that usually does not work. It tends to exacerbate personal problems and simply transfers difficulties to a lower level of the organization. Our reluctant conclusion is that even though the measures we have mentioned may have high short-term costs, present political obstacles, and cause suffering and temporary disorientation, they are sometimes very necessary. The organization as a whole can occasionally benefit a good deal by circumscribing the damaging influence of a few key persons. And in the longer run (after the to-be-expected angry reaction) it may even benefit the individuals concerned by finally forcing them to deal with their problems.

Often, however, it will not be necessary to resort to such dramatic measures. Neurotic styles, disruptive group fantasies, and dysfunctional interactive patterns can sometimes be overcome by the use of a number of assorted therapies, which we will describe in the following pages. In all instances, the need is to diagnose the sources of the difficulties and to gradually make the client aware of these; to give the client insights that will promote change.

A parallel can be drawn between intervention in a clinical situation and in an organizational setting. In both it is necessary that the patient or the organizational clients have at least a minimal capacity to establish a *working alliance* with the therapist or consultant. That is, the two parties must have the capacity to work together purposefully and cooperatively. But it is not enough simply for them to recognize the advantages of collaboration. To work together on a problem, it is also necessary to have a certain amount of basic trust, to tolerate at least some frustration, to have an adequate sense of reality testing, and to have a secure sense of self.[1] Only when a good working alliance exists can a therapist or consultant make change-evoking interventions in the face of their tendency to induce anxiety. It is mainly because of the positive working alliance that a client will hang on in spite of the angry, hostile, or distrustful feelings that frequently accompany negative transference reactions. Without a working alliance between the consultant and the organizational clients, most change efforts will fail. Fortunately, in most situations, the reason for bringing in a consultant is that the company is experiencing a certain amount of "pain," symptomized most often by poor financial performance. Pain tends to be the major catalyst for seeking help; it is a prime source of motivation. (Of course, there is always the danger that as soon as a minimal amount of progress is made and less "pain" is experienced, the client will "take a flight into health." The client may claim that everything is well just to avoid the pain that might accompany further changes.)

We can make a few broad distinctions among the different forms of therapy. One major difference is between *insight-oriented* and *supportive* intervention. In insight-oriented therapy and consulting, the emphasis is on helping to foster new perceptions, to disentangle the covert forces at hand, to clarify the roots of one's feelings and behavior toward other people and situations. The goal is to achieve what is often called the "aha" experience. The intervention aims to achieve a recognition of improperly assessed or neglected behavioral phenomena. It leads to insights of a cognitive and emotional nature. Insight-oriented therapy or consultancy should reveal resistances and transferential patterns by using the processes of confrontation/clarification, interpretation, and working through, discussed in Chapter Seven. The aim is to resolve conflicts, relieve symptoms, and improve adaptive functioning.

. In contrast to insight-oriented therapy or consulting, supportive psychotherapy reinforces the patient's defenses and helps the patient to suppress and control disturbing thoughts and feelings. It uses techniques of reassurance, suggestion, inspiration, persuasion, and manipulation. Unlike psychoanalytic psychotherapy, supportive therapy focuses mainly on present difficulties and avoids probing into the past or the unconscious. It is limited in its therapeutic objectives rather than in duration.[2]

One type of short-term supportive psychotherapy may be particularly interesting to organizational consultants. It is often called "paradoxical intervention" or "strategic psychotherapy."[3] In this form of treatment the reframing and redefining of the problem stands central. An attempt is made to rid interpersonal relationships of vicious circles. Examples of these brief interventions are the instruction to fail in the most feared manner possible for diagnostic purposes, the request to give up a certain behavior pattern by explicitly instructing the client to perform another mutually exclusive behavior, and the exaggeration of feared scenarios. The therapist may discuss the disadvantages of improvement, thereby highlighting the underlying unconscious elements of the problem. The therapist may even express pessimism about the chances for improvement, inducing rebellion and thus constructive change by the client.

In general, in supportive therapy or consultancy, the aim is to recover a beneficent homeostatic state—that is, to restore and stabilize the individual's defensive structure, to minimize regression, and to reduce anxiety and the fear of new situations. The emphasis is on bringing the person back to her more acceptable level of functioning. To further this end, the consultant is supportive, offering friendly leadership and thereby gratifying some of the dependency needs of the client. The ultimate objectives, however, are to help the client to develop a greater sense of independence, to make her feel more secure, more accepted, and less anxious, and to help her to abandon disruptive behavior patterns. These effects will render her less vulnerable to threats.

Despite the distinctions between insight-oriented and supportive intervention, each contains elements of the other. We might consider these therapies to be end points on a continuum, appropriate for very high or very low tolerance for frustration, respectively, on the part of the client. Depending on the consultant's tolerance assessment, different "doses" and combinations of therapies will have to be given. One might start with a supportive orientation, shifting to insight when the client has strengthened to the point of being able to tolerate more taxing interventions. At other times the client might be too vulnerable to insights that might shatter his fragile estimation of himself.

We can also differentiate between consulting done on a *one-to-one* basis and in a *group* setting. One-to-one consultancy involves in.eraction between only the consultant and one client. In a group setting, one or more consultants deal with a number of executives simultaneously. Again, this is not an either/or proposition. In a typical consulting situation, we often combine both types of intervention, depending on the objectives at hand. Group therapy will illuminate the nature of the interaction between individuals; it may thus foster an understanding of key dysfunctions. During concurrent individual therapy the emerging concerns from the group sessions could be further explored and worked through interpersonally.

The group orientation can take many forms, depending on the number of participants and the role of the consultant or therapist, which can range from very *active* to very *passive*. An active leader may lessen the anxiety of the group by taking it upon himself to solve problems and delineate solutions. But he may thereby (as we saw in Chapters Two and Three) engender excessive expectations in the group members. He might also cause transferential problems if he takes on the role of a parental figure; clients may become too dependent on him, curtailing their own initiatives. A so-called passive leader, in contrast, does not instruct, but puts the onus of interaction in the hands of the group members. He focuses more on making interpretations than suggestions. This format may cause excessive anxiety, provoking the members to rebel against a leader who has frustrated their dependency needs.

Another distinction among therapies is based on the dimension of *depth*. It concerns how "deep" the consultant should go in interpreting the intrapsychic, interpersonal, and group material that emerges. For example, should the consultant point out resistances as they manifest themselves in the organizational group, exposing personality patterns and dormant conflicts? In determining the appropriate depth of a therapeutic intervention, it is again necessary to assess the group members' tolerance for pain. This will determine how much material the consultant should reveal. Some issues will be better handled on a one-to-one basis, particularly where they might induce shame and guilt reactions were the revelations to be made in a group setting or where they might reveal vulnerability in inappropriate surroundings.

Usually the organizational clinician (or the consultant with clinical expertise) will follow this scenario:

1. The clinician conducts interviews individually with all the parties to try to obtain a more precise notion of the nature and source of the dysfunction.

2. He must make some assessment of the severity of the case and the possibilities of using economical short-term therapies, paradoxical interventions, group therapies, or personnel transfers.

3. Having developed a diagnosis and prognosis, the consultant must try to sell his prescription to those in charge. This will be a time for tact and flexibility, especially where top-level managers are involved. It will often become necessary to trade off treatment efficacy for political acceptability. Selling the project must be considered an essential part of any intervention.

4. Only now can the intervention really begin. The most important consideration is to tailor the intervention to the indi-

vidual or group at hand, subject to the parameters of the problem. Depending on time, resources, and personalities, a choice has to be made between supportive (including paradoxical) and insight-oriented therapy. As indicated, one can view the first form of therapy as an initial step leading to the others. Another question is whether individual therapy should be combined with some form of group therapy. In most instances it is best to have both forms of therapy concurrently. For dysfunctional group fantasies or transferential problems, work in groups may suffice. For problems related to career life cycle, individual therapy is the treatment of choice. Of course, where the firm faces an emergency, "first aid" objective approaches must take precedence over psychological ones. Where the problem revolves around a busy executive of much power and talent, it is impractical to have him or her undergo a very lengthy or time-consuming form of psychotherapy.

Preventive Maintenance

The most important recommendation, we have saved for last. The tremendous difficulties of trying to cope with serious maladaptations in organizations make it clear that the best possible way to deal with them is to try to avoid them. There are several ways of doing so.

Psychological Screening in Recruitment, Promotion, and Transfer. Competence, political clout, tact, and kinship have all motivated the recruitment or promotion of key managers. Too often, however, we slight personality and character. It is not that these variables are entirely ignored. Certainly a person's image, the impression he leaves, is often a critical factor in placement decisions. But rarely is personality studied in a systematic and clinical manner. Increasingly, there are better and better interviewing techniques that clinical psychologists, psychiatrists, and psychoanalysts can use to uncover neurotic tendencies and dysfunctional defenses that in an organizational context lead to interpersonal and other problems. Many organizations of mental health professionals are available to do this kind of work. Certainly the mental health of key personnel is something that can vitally influence an entire organization, and so it simply cannot be left to chance. A manager's *professional* competence can best be assessed by other managers in the field. But mental health, a requirement for all stressful positions, can be properly assessed only by professionals using specialized interviewing procedures. Many executives would do well to remember this fact when making their crucial placement decisions.

We must stress that in-depth assessments of mental health should be used only for making the most important placement decisions. In addition, confidentiality of information must be a prime consideration (hence the added desirability, in many cases, of hiring outside consultants). It may also be useful to procure a second opinion if there is any doubt about the assessment.

Employee transfers and promotions, even at lower levels of the organization, can often benefit from the input of career counselors or organizational psychologists. A primary aim is to ensure that grave personality mismatches do not occur between superiors and subordinates. Think, for example, of what would become of a dependent employee assigned to an "expelling" superior. There must be some attempt to match the needs and strengths of the subordinate with those of the superior. In smaller organizations this may not pose a great problem, since the personalities of most key managers are likely to be quite familiar to many of the top executives. In large organizations, however, it may be useful to make sure that this kind of information is systematically taken into consideration by those making key placement decisions. Obviously great care must be taken to guard against a "Big Brother" personnel department—a central agency having intimate information that can make or break a career. Again, it seems that occasional use can be made of external consultants, who may be able to depoliticize placement decisions as much as possible.

Departmental and Organizational Audits. We have shown in Chapter Two how group fantasies can give rise to unrealistic departmental and organizational orientations. Such fantasies are best recognized before they have had a chance to rigidify and influence strategy. The only way to do this effectively is to have someone from outside the department or the organization appraise the departmental myths, culture, and beliefs. Many questions can be asked. Do department members seem to exhibit overwhelming conformity in their views of the environment, mission, problems, and strategies? Is there an obsession with enemies inside or outside the firm? Does *all* initiative lie with the leader or the leader's codified policies? Do utopian wishes supplant practical programs? Someone from outside the group should be asking these sorts of questions every year or two to ensure that the collective sense of reality is not being eroded. Such audits can be done of departments, divisions, or even the dominant coalition of the organization. They can investigate the emergence of both group fantasies and neurotic organizational syndromes. Vigilance against neurotic configurations such as those of Chapter One can help to neutralize them before they do much damage.

Organizational Ombudsmen. A powerful figure in the organization may victimize a number of his subordinates, often without knowing it. This situation poses a touchy dilemma for the subordinate, who may be too afraid to complain directly to the boss or to those still further up the hierarchy. Thus, problems of transference or superior binding behavior can endure and worsen. For prevention it might be useful to have an organizational ombudsman who will hear complaints from subordinates. That way anonymity can be preserved. The ombudsman, preferably someone who has clinical experience, could try to straighten things out with the boss or subordinate before they get out of hand. He or she will also be in a position to become aware of many complaints about the same superior and so be able to help in placement decisions. One natural area from which to select this ombudsman is the personnel department. If so, a serious rethinking of the role of the traditional personnel function may be indicated. If ombudsmen are to be effective, they must have political clout (usually absent in the traditional personnel department). It may therefore become necessary to give a more strategic role to their function. Great care must be taken, of course, to ensure that the ombudsmen are not political opportunists.

Consultants with Tenure. Organizational dysfunctions that

have psychodynamic roots cause peculiar problems for management consultants, no matter how skilled. First, the problems
take a long time to discover, particularly their critical nuances.
Second, they represent areas of emotional sensitivity and defensiveness on the part of very powerful executives. Consultants
who are hired to do a quick assignment are unlikely to have
enough time to be able to discern the source of the difficulties.
Even if they do, they may be thrown out of the organization if
they get too close to the truth in the presence of neurotic senior
executives. One way of avoiding these problems is through
longer-term consulting contracts. The consultant can agree to
spend so many hours per year at the firm, and a contract can be
signed for two or three years. That way, the consultant has a
chance to become much more familiar with the organization
and its key personnel. He may even help to perform the ombudsman role. Contract security may be an impetus to greater
frankness in a consultant's dealings with top managers. Obviously, the organization should have already experienced a favorable relationship with a reputable consultant before embarking
on such a venture. Otherwise the firm could find itself wasting a
great deal of money.

The suggestions we have made in this chapter are quite
tentative and general. Firms will have to adapt them to their
own situations. In fact, the theme of the book stresses that
there are rarely any easy answers when addressing complex organizational problems of the type we have been dealing with.
Each requires individual study and tailor-made solutions. Our
plea is that our suggestions be used to establish a focus for attention and that they not be interpreted as dogma.

9

Organizational Therapy
in Action:
A Case Study

Illness is the doctor to whom we pay most heed: to kind-
ness, to knowledge we make promises only; pain we obey.
—Marcel Proust, *Cities of the Plain*

The previous chapters have dealt with "neurotic" organizations, organizational cultures, transferential processes, dysfunctional interaction patterns, the career life cycle, obstacles
to organizational change, and the process of changing. It will be
appropriate now to give an integrative case example of how
knowledge of these covert organizational forces can be used in
organizational intervention.

A Company in Transition

To illustrate organizational intervention, we have chosen
a family firm in which the psychodynamic forces were very intense. Our contact with the firm was initiated by a call made by
the president of a marketing consulting firm, asking one of the
authors whether he would be willing to attend a meeting between the consultant and one of his clients. This consultant, it
seems, was unable to understand what his client really wanted.

185

He mentioned to us that the company's president had asked him to help develop a marketing and strategic plan. After a few meetings with the executive group, however, the marketing consultant wondered whether a plan was what was really needed. He doubted that he could develop an adequate marketing plan, given that the firm's managers were so secretive and so reluctant to give out any financial information. It was as if they completely distrusted him. If they really wanted help, why was it always so difficult to get the whole executive group together? And when a meeting was finally arranged, it inevitably degenerated into disorderly squabbling as the executives present blamed one another for real or imagined mistakes. In fact, the marketing consultant had begun to wonder about the covert motivations of the senior executive group, since these managers seemed to have such a destructive effect on one another.

The Diana Company was a manufacturer of high-quality lingerie. It was vertically integrated, with its own knitting, fabric development, dyeing, cutting, sewing, and finishing departments. Outside contractors were used for some of the production processes. In addition to buying yarns for knitting, Diana purchased raw fabrics to be further processed. The company's executives were proud of their high-quality product and claimed their distinctive competence to be their innovativeness in fabric development. They were not nearly as good at product styling. Their overall track record as reflected by growth in sales was only mediocre.

The Diana Company was owned and operated by the Adams family. The firm dated back to the late 1920s, when William Adams, previously a foreman in a textile company in Edinburgh, had immigrated from Scotland and started a small manufacturing concern. After many years of hardship and near-bankruptcy, the company finally started to do well.

Although William Adams had died ten years before, he was still vividly remembered by many of the senior employees at Diana. They nostalgically recalled "the old tyrant" and pointed to his stone bust, which still guarded the entry hall of the rather shabby-looking building that housed the administrative offices and the main plant.

William Adams knew everyone on a first-name basis. Company legend had it that he was able to go into the factory, spot the only poorly fabricated piece of lingerie on the entire floor, and know immediately who was responsible. One employee recalled how he had been fired three times by "the old man" during his tenure at the company. He told of how once, in trying to open the door to his own office, he had found that the lock had been changed. He had not even been told he had been dismissed. Many of the employees were rather guarded in their comments about conditions at the company during William's reign. However, there was a general consensus that, in spite of his toughness, if one stood up to William and lived up to his demanding standards, one could expect a certain amount of respect and loyalty in return. But many failed that very demanding test. If one was looking to be complimented for work well done or for a warm, supportive environment, the Diana Company was the wrong place to be.

The company had a history of extremely erratic profits and sales. Many reasons were given for this checkered record. One major contributing factor was that labor/management relationships had never been very good, so that strikes were frequent. These disruptions caused delivery problems, which, given the seasonality of the product line, resulted in lost sales. Another major weakness was the company's inability to take advantage of fashion trends. Its misreading of consumer tastes caused sales to remain fairly stagnant and, indeed, to decline in real terms. Now Diana's yearly sales were on the order of $25 million, but profits had fallen dramatically during the two years immediately preceding our entry into the firm.

When William Adams died, he was succeeded by his son Paul. Since the founder had never explicitly put forward a clear succession plan, his death was followed by a bitter power struggle between Paul and his brother-in-law. A legal technicality discovered by Paul's son Michael eventually made it possible for Paul to remove his brother-in-law from active participation in the company.

At the time Paul took control, the key executive group consisted of himself, his eldest son, David, who was vice-president of sales and marketing, and the controller, John Stoddard. These three men had formed a close coalition to expel Paul's brother-in-law. A number of years later, Paul's two other sons joined the company; the middle son, Michael, eventually became vice-president of manufacturing, and the youngest son, Robert, became director of export operations. After Paul's ascendancy seven years earlier, the company had been quite profitable, one of the main reasons being the attractive product line. The edge Diana had developed over the competition could be attributed largely to Paul's considerable fabric-development talents.

The Objective Problems

The marketing consultant had found many things wrong with the marketing and sales organization. Marketing research was nonexistent and there was very little competitive analysis. Advertising was limited to cooperative arrangements with some of the large chain stores, the main media being newspapers and billboards. Given the emphasis on the identity of the retailing chain in the ads, the consultant seriously questioned the usefulness of these advertising arrangements in creating brand awareness. The senior executives had only a vague notion of the characteristics of the consumers who bought their products. In addition, the sales organization was far from satisfactory. The company employed sales agents who did not have an exclusivity clause and were therefore free to sell the lines of other manufacturers as well. In order to motivate these agents, enticements were required and expensive deals had to be made.

From an "objective" point of view, the causes of these difficulties seemed rather straightforward. First, the organizational structure was very vaguely defined. Lines of authority and responsibility overlapped, so that Paul's sons and the controller were continually skirmishing over their roles and prerogatives. These conflicts also permeated some areas of middle management, especially in the marketing and manufacturing departments. For example, hiring and firing of plant personnel were the prerogatives of the controller rather than the head of manu-

facturing. A second problem was the lack of performance re-
views and control systems, which allowed many inefficiencies
to creep into operations without anyone becoming aware of
them. Diana's plants had become among the least efficient and
productive in the industry. Two major contributing factors
were the dismal labor relations situation and the inappropriate
work-flow organization in the plants. A third problem was that
power for decision making was too tightly centralized in Paul's
hands. He really tried to run the whole show and was kept very
busy doing so, particularly given his need to make bold and
dramatic decisions. As a result, he had too little time left for
formulating long-range strategies, for paying attention to broad
problems of marketing strategy, and for developing or recruiting
managerial talent to take some of the load off his shoulders.
Paul was too preoccupied with putting out fires to pay attention to these matters. Perhaps the most serious result was the
erratic nature and shortsightedness of the marketing strategy.
There was too little marketing research, too many products
were impulsively introduced at too great expense, advertising
was neglected, and the sales force was badly structured. All
these flaws made Diana more vulnerable to increasing competitive threats while straining the firm's resources. By the third
year after Paul's elevation to the presidency, sales were falling
in real terms and profits had declined considerably. What is
more, sales and earnings fluctuations had become more pronounced, owing to the more dramatic changes in consumer
tastes. Diana's problems are summarized in Figure 2.

    All these problems were serious, and they were not par-
ticularly difficult to discover; any competent management consultant could have done so. But it soon became clear to us that
there were many hidden, covert forces at work that had to be
made manifest and resolved before the surface problems could
be addressed. One had first to deal with the prevailing irrationality within the firm. It was necessary to understand why the
president, Paul, behaved as he did—why he hoarded power and
meddled in all levels of operation, why he resisted taking anyone's advice.

    Paul was a handsome man in his late fifties who was capa-

Figure 2. Summary of Concrete Problems at Diana.

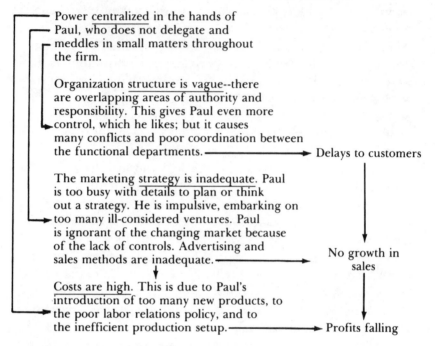

Arrows represent hypothesized causal relations
between problems and symptoms.

ble of considerable charm. His management style was dominated by a strong histrionic component that contributed to
highly dramatic and impulsive decision making. Paul liked to
show off and often would describe in great detail how he had
managed to outwit a competitor. His behavior had a restless
quality in which action often served as a substitute for planning.
Little time was devoted to reflection. Quick alterations in his
mood inhibited effective decision making. Paul seemed unable
to distinguish between important and trivial decisions: The two
received equal amounts of his time.

Paul's distrustful nature created a rather paranoid atmosphere within the company. He believed that there were "many
dangers out there." And, naturally, there were always *real*
threats to feed on, given the competitive nature of the industry. Paul especially feared espionage by competitors as well as

trade union hostility. Information about the company's operations was thus closely guarded. The paranoid firm of Chapter
One is recalled.

An example of Paul's cautious, suspicious nature was his
extremely aggressive approach to labor relations. He had recently bought an overseas plant for the express purpose of using it
as leverage against the union. This seemed rather a draconian
measure at a time when the market for Diana's product was
shrinking. Sometimes it appeared to Paul as if he were living
under a state of siege, surrounded by enemies such as the
unions, the few remaining stockholders, family members, customers, and even the "useless, expensive" consultants. These
thoughts contributed to his irrational decisions, such as his refusal to sell goods in process to a noncompeting business at a
time when machines were idle and employees had been laid off.
Ten years earlier Paul had been burnt by a competitor who had
used his fabrics to manufacture a similar line of products—an
incident his own father had not let him forget. He was not going
to let it happen again. Another indication of trouble was that
the company had worked itself through many consultants. All
were quickly discarded as soon as they expressed some unfavorable view of a previous strategy, made an unpopular recommendation, or began to ask for "secret" information.

We could have developed a strategic action plan and made
recommendations on the basis of the "objective" problems. It
was likely, however, that the president would ignore these recommendations, just like those of three previous consultants.
Much more than a simple report delineating solutions was
needed to produce effective change and to steer the company in
a more successful direction. First, it was necessary to get a better understanding of the more covert forces operating in the
organization—forces which had given rise to the problems to
begin with and which were still likely to impede their resolution.

Family Dynamics

The catalyst for the president's request for a marketing
plan had been David Adams' (the oldest son's) threat to quit.
Bringing in a consultant was the president's way of expressing

his concern over the matter, showing his son that he cared. David's main gripe, we discovered, was the aggravation caused him by his younger brother, Michael, who had recently joined the firm on a full-time basis. David told us that there had been an unwritten agreement in the family that the middle son would enter one of the professions and would never become involved in the family business. David was supposed to be the chosen one, the next in line for the presidency. But now Michael had entered the company through the back door. He had begun by helping part-time and then had started working full-time. David's discontent was dramatically demonstrated by the overt rivalry and envy between himself and the more innovative Michael. Given the interdependency of their functions as heads of marketing and manufacturing, respectively, this conflict had serious organizational repercussions. It resulted in a lack of cooperation that caused late product deliveries, product line stagnation, pricing inequities, and poor customer relations.

The difference in appearance and behavior between the two older brothers during meetings was striking. While David would come in dressed in a dark, conservative business suit, Michael would appear in a worn outfit, usually consisting of an old pair of slacks and an open shirt. The hostility between the two brothers was quite noticeable during these meetings. Each of them would try to show the other in a bad light. A remarkable interplay would occur. Michael engaged in rather childish behavior, playing with paper clips, empty bottles, or whatever was available—to the increasing irritation of David, who would eventually blow up and tell Michael to stop fooling around and deal with the business at hand. In such instances the youngest brother, Robert, if present, would usually intervene to calm things down.

It was also apparent that the two older brothers withheld information from each other, thereby causing costly errors and misunderstandings. Moreover, this behavior had harmful repercussions in their respective departments. Their subordinates would imitate the behavior of the brothers. They too became quite secretive and were unwilling to share information. Severe problems of coordination resulted, causing late deliveries, poor product development, and excessive returns of merchandise by customers.

Besides complaining about stress symptoms that had begun with Michael's entry, David expressed his fear that a coalition might develop between Michael and Robert, the youngest brother. Although David felt that his relationship with Robert was quite good, he could not help remembering what had happened to his uncle, who was ousted from the firm by a similar coalition. He felt that since he was only in his late thirties, there was still time to start something else. He talked nostalgically about the good old days when grandfather William was still in charge and things were really going well. David felt that he had always been the favorite grandson. Although his grandfather might have been tough on others, David remembered him only as a kind, considerate man who always had time for him.

It was interesting to note that David now occupied his late grandfather's office. Pictures of him posing with his grandfather were all over the wall, while photographs of his father, Paul, were conspicuously absent. It also struck us, from looking at the pictures, how much David resembled his grandfather, even in dress and comportment.

Our interviews with Paul revealed that he was quite bitter about his relationship with his late father, William, the "tyrant." Paul felt that his father had never really acknowledged or appreciated his contributions to the company, that he had never given him credit for his considerable talents in fabric development and product design. Instead, William ignored his son's suggestions or perhaps eventually adopted them without giving him credit. During William's presidency, Paul had considered quitting many times. However, every time he threatened to go, William, by subtly evoking feelings of guilt, had coerced him to come back. We can still hear the anger in Paul's voice as he recalled how little time his father had spent with him—even Paul's eldest son, David, was given more. Paul had worked extremely hard all those years. Almost all his time was spent in the plants at the expense of his family life. After coming home he would usually be too tired to pay much attention to the children. Paul was particularly hurt by William's final affront: His father had not even bothered to make provisions in his will that Paul would be his successor.

Through Paul, William's ghost continued to haunt the company. Probably because of his relationship with his father (we knew very little about the mother), Paul had become quite distrustful of others. We have indicated how this distrust was manifested in his relationships with unions, consultants, and customers. It also caused him to centralize power and to "bind" his sons, just as he had been bound by his father. Perhaps as a result of his submissive relationship with his father, Paul found it hard to vent his hostility outwardly. Although he would explode occasionally, he preferred to use more indirect channels. Initially, in our encounters with Paul, we wondered how a man who made such a "charming," often flamboyant impression could condone the violent personnel practices so prevalent in the company. Firing would take place on the spur of the moment, with little consideration for the welfare of the employees. In studying the situation more closely, we realized that the controller, John Stoddard, acted somehow as the "split off," projected, "bad" part of the president. He did all Paul's dirty work. As Paul's proxy, he relished the role of "hatchet man," firing and demoting people, cutting salaries, and obsessively controlling minor expenses. He was the one ostensibly responsible for the dismal labor relations.

Michael's behavior could be seen in a similar "proxy" vein. Michael seemed to play the part of the "rebel," the role Paul might really have liked to act out toward his own father but had never dared to. Now, however, Paul permitted Michael to act irresponsibly toward his oldest son, David, and toward other executives in the company. (Time for a speculation: As we said before, when we entered Diana, the most immediate problem was David's desire to leave. We conjectured that in a symbolic sense Paul saw the oldest son as the "bad" grandfather whom David idolized and resembled both in appearance and in behavior. It seemed that Paul, through his proxy, Michael, was belatedly getting even with his father, using David as a substitute.)

Michael, like his father, used hyperactivity as a way of coping with stress. He was also prone to sudden mood swings.

At times, he could be as impulsive and enthusiastic as his father, a state that could suddenly give way to depression. In the latter mood, Michael felt that all his efforts were hopeless—that it would be better for everybody if he just quit. In our conversations with Michael, we were also struck by his need to get even, to get back at his older brother, David, for certain misdeeds of childhood. Michael once mentioned to us that he had built his "bunker" and from there would like to "shoot at all of them." And Michael was not alone in his "bunker." He shared it with a much older man, Larry Henderson, who, as his assistant, was constantly with him, making suggestions about every aspect of his job. Michael lavishly praised Henderson's abilities, an assessment we did not share. Perhaps, because of the absence of his real father, who had spent all his time in the plants, Michael was using the older man as a substitute. He needed someone to idealize—but this time on *his* terms.

The youngest son, Robert, was very soft-spoken, quite in contrast to Michael. He was the "Hamlet" of the organization, never able to decide which side to take when fights occurred among family members. This was a pattern he seemed to have established in early childhood. His indecisiveness permeated all his activities.

When Paul was asked what he would like to see happening to the company in the future, he spoke of his desire to have "a happy football team" around him, made up of all his sons. He envisioned a state of harmony in which everybody would be equal. We felt that Paul's statement had aspects of a reparative fantasy. He seemed to want to make up for all the wrongs he had inflicted. At the same time, his desire might also have been engendered by his wish to have been treated in a more gentle, understanding manner by his own father. All these relationships and their possible significance are summarized in Table 9.

Planning the Intervention

With our knowledge of these covert organizational processes, the questions become: What steps should be taken to restore health to the organization? What would be the best way to deal with individual and organizational resistances? How could

Table 9. Summary of the Key Interpersonal Relationships at Diana.

Parties	Relationship	Possible Causes	Possible Consequences
William and Paul (father/son)	William ruthlessly dominated and "bound" Paul, never giving him credit		Paul's distrust of unions, consultants, "spies," and so on; his refusal to delegate authority; preference for vague structure, since he has control; preoccupation with minor problems of the firm; dramatic style in which he tries to impress others (read: father)
William and David (grandfather/ grandson)	David was William's favorite grandson; David still idolizes his grandfather	William older and more mellow, wanted a closer relationship that he never had with his own son, Paul	Paul became jealous of David; David has high expectations because he is the "chosen one"; conflict with Michael
Paul and David (father/son)	Paul ignores David	David is like William	David gets frustrated, feels deserted, is envious of Michael; therefore, collaboration among the brothers is poor
	Paul distrusts David and "binds" him	Paul and David's relationship to William	Paul tries to make all decisions himself— does not delegate to sons
	David wants to impress Paul because he loves him	Paul is the busy, absent father whose attention must be fought for	David becomes very frustrated at Paul's neglect and apparent distrust; he becomes jealous of Mi-

Table 9. Summary of the Key Interpersonal Relationships at Diana,
Cont'd.

Parties	Relationship	Possible Causes	Possible Consequences
			chael, suspicious of Michael's and Robert's joining forces
David and Michael (brothers)	Rivals; envious of each other	Childhood battles never resolved; busy parents whose love the brothers had to compete for	Impossible to collaborate with each other—no coordination between marketing and production
Paul and Michael (father/son)	Paul uses Michael as his proxy	Unconsciously, Paul wishes Michael to enact his rebelliousness toward his late father	Friction between Michael and David and between Michael and controller; makes collaboration impossible
	Michael wants more attention from Paul	Paul is the busy, absent father whose attention must be fought for	Michael is looking for older men to assist him; excessive reliance and overvaluation of the capabilities of his assistant; imitation of Paul's management style
Paul and controller (boss and proxy)	Paul uses Stoddard as proxy	Paul needs outlet to channel his hostility indirectly	Stoddard creates havoc with his callousness, destructive labor relations, firings, and meddling with Michael's plants and workers
Robert and brothers	Gets along well with both, but forced to take sides	David and Michael's rivalry	Robert is confused and indecisive

the main actors be helped to develop deeper insights into the sources of their problems? How much interpretation and insight could the key players tolerate? How might they be helped to work through their resistances and arrive at new ways of running the company? Was there a sufficient amount of "pain" to induce them to "live with" the consultant and to form an enduring working alliance? What kind of transference reactions would they have to the consultants?

From the preceding account of the company's situation, we can infer a number of things about its problems. First, it seems that the Diana Company resembles the *dramatic* firm of Chapter One. Firms of this type pursue inconsistent strategies that carry a very high element of risk and cause resources to be squandered. Paul centralized power and impulsively introduced too many new product lines. Dramatic firms also have difficulty controlling operations because of their risky and dangerous expansion policies. There is no competent second tier of management. Paul's unjustified fears and suspicions, however, also gave Diana some of the attributes of the *paranoid* firm.

It also seemed that the prevailing organizational culture of the company was of the *fight/flight* variety (Chapter Two), making for factionalism, stereotyping, suspicion, infighting, and a search for enemies. We can, however, also recognize elements of the *dependency* culture. Many of the executives desired to be "nourished" and protected by the president from the turmoil around them.

Because Diana was a family firm, the destructive two-person interaction patterns described in Chapters Three and Four became very prominent. As is evident, binding and proxy behavior was most common. In addition, all three transference patterns were present, either as directed toward the consultants or among the key executives in the company. We could hypothesize that Paul's desire for admiration from us, shown by his boasting of his successes, was based on the need for "mirroring." Michael's behavior toward his assistant contained all the elements of the idealizing transference, a reaction pattern that would shift to a persecutory one vis-à-vis the controller.

The position of each of the key actors in the career *life*

cycle plays a role in his susceptibility to change. We have seen in Chapter Five how each stage in the life cycle has its special concerns. Paul, being close to the end of his career, when generativity and life review become important issues, would look on events in the company quite differently than his sons. Because the sons were all in their thirties, other needs more in line with the socialization and growth phase and the midlife crisis prevailed.

In the light of all these forces, we might ask whether the president could ever really have a "happy football team," given the existing players and their differences. Would Paul be able to work through his disappointments, or would he resort to "pathological mourning"? Indeed, given his family history and his behavior in the company, how much interpretation and insight could Paul tolerate?

Our Program for Diana

Some of the interventions discussed in Chapter Eight were employed in our work with Diana. We felt that Michael's provocative behavior contributed to the turbulence in the firm. It therefore seemed advisable, as a first step, to create a "holding environment" for him, to prevent further aggressive behavior on his part toward David and Stoddard, the controller. This would defuse the hostile atmosphere within the company. One of the consultants began to see Michael weekly, mixing insight-oriented and supportive intervention. Through the processes of confrontation, clarification, and interpretation, Michael was made more aware of the dysfunctional processes at work in the company. His relationships with his father, his two brothers, and his assistant were also explored. In addition, partly as a way of alleviating the anxiety that accompanied the various interpretations, Michael was given pragmatic business advice. For example, a plan for setting up career paths for key factory personnel was developed. Ways were explored to minimize the friction with the controller and with David.

It was also necessary for us to establish at least a minimal working alliance with the president, Paul. We needed to minimize persecutory transference reactions and build on his ability to "idealize" what we as consultants could do for him. If this could not be accomplished because of Paul's (or, for that matter, our) attitudes or personalities, the consulting effort would soon be aborted. We were quickly able to determine that Paul had a very limited tolerance for frustration. Too much exposure to disruptive family and organizational dynamics might arrest the change process by causing Paul to engage in flight behavior. A more pragmatic approach was used. We set up a number of problem-solving sessions during which Paul was asked to articulate a realistic plan for the future of the company. We made a number of "paradoxical interventions" (Chapter Eight) in which worst-case scenarios were explored. For example, we exaggerated what could happen to family relationships and the company if certain remedial measures were not taken. At other times, we would confess to a sense of pessimism. We told Paul that we might fail like all the other consultants before us—that the situation might just be too tough. We were implicitly inviting him to prove us wrong. These actions made Paul gradually more aware of the problems of his firm. But his reactions had to be monitored carefully to avoid overloading him with negative information about himself, the family, and the company. We had to introduce small, incremental doses of insight so Paul would not marshal his considerable arsenal of resistances.

These sessions eventually made Paul realize that he could not have his happy football team. Too much had happened in the past to make that possible. The few occasions when his wife was present (at the explicit request of the consultant) were particularly enlightening for him. She confirmed many of the consultant's interpretations, putting another source of pressure on Paul. It made him see how much the family situation had deteriorated, how much conflict really existed among his sons, and what his responsibility had been in this matter. His wife told him how difficult it had been to keep up appearances of harmony at family gatherings.

Paul also became more aware of how all this friction had affected the operations of his company. His advanced stage in the career life cycle (he had just become a grandfather) had made him more reflective, especially about the long-term health of the firm, which would be his principal legacy to his family. A certain susceptibility to change seemed to result. It was as if Paul were now trying to repair the wrongs of the past. Even if it might be too late for some of his children, at least he could create a better environment for his grandchildren. After a "push" by the consultants, he expressed his willingness to relinquish some of his control over the company. Paul finally approved a gradual transfer of 75 percent of his shares to his sons. This happened two years after our initial involvement with Diana.

A number of structural changes were made to limit the repercussions of Paul's dysfunctional management style and to reduce conflicts among the brothers. To create more independence for Michael and Robert, two separate divisions were set up. Each was made an independent profit center. Although Paul would be nominally in charge of both divisions, the bulk of his attention would be devoted to the fabric development and production division, clearly his area of expertise. The middle son, Michael, would be in charge of the other division; he would run the lingerie manufacturing operation. A clear organizational structure was set up and new information systems were introduced. The objectives and strategy for each division were clarified.

The youngest son, Robert, joined his father in the fabric development and production division. This gave Paul the opportunity to train Robert in his strongest area of expertise, grooming him as a successor in this division and giving himself a sense of generativity.

The oldest son, David, was encouraged to start an unrelated real estate venture. This would reduce the conflict among the various departments. David had revealed to us in a number of interviews that he had never really been attracted to his father's business. His true interests were in investment banking and venture-capital management. It was only because he wanted to be closer to his grandfather that he had stayed in the business. For reasons of psychological and financial equity, we encouraged Paul to limit his contribution to the new venture to an initial infusion of capital. We felt that a certain amount of distance should be maintained between father and sons, creating the climate for future harmony. It was necessary that the sons be allowed greater freedom—that their bonds to Paul be loosened.

The hostility between the two oldest brothers was unlikely ever to be resolved by any consulting effort. Our analysis of the depth of their feelings indicated that much more work would be needed. Only intensive insight-oriented psychotherapy might show promise of alleviating their strong feelings of envy, spite, and anger. This was beyond the capacity of the consultants, given their mandate to revive the firm in the quickest way possible.

We tried to modify the fight/flight culture prevailing in the company. An early retirement was arranged for the controller, John Stoddard, who was close to the normal retirement age. There were a number of reasons for this recommendation. First, Stoddard's knowledge of information systems and electronic data processing was very limited. Such knowledge was essential, given the size of the company and the cyclical and competitive nature of the industry. Second, Stoddard, not entirely through any fault of his own, had antagonized too many executives with his rather crude power games. His exit would give Michael a freer hand and remove overlap between Stoddard and the director of plants. Third, he had resisted developing a tier of middle managers, as was obvious from the dearth of talent in his department. Here he was playing on the president's fears of managerial espionage. Finally, having him around might tempt Paul to fall back into his old behavior pattern of using him as a proxy.

The youngest son, Robert, was encouraged to join a modified Balint group for executives.[1] He began to meet regularly with executives from other firms to discuss, in a neutral setting, interpersonal problems of management under the guidance of a group specialist. Our subsequent interviews with Robert disclosed that these meetings had helped him to recognize his dysfunctional ways of dealing with others. What he had learned during the sessions had been particularly useful in improving his relationships with his father and brothers. Robert also began to realize how his indecisiveness impaired his functioning and had organizational repercussions. He was now struggling to change it. He became more assertive at meetings and was particularly useful in keeping his father on the topic.

We also helped Diana to recruit a number of capable middle managers who could serve as the managerial foundation of the company in the future. Finally, the union problem was solved through arbitration. With the controller (who had been the main negotiator) out of the way, we hoped that future labor conflicts would be minimized.

For the sake of continuity, even after all these changes were made, the key executives met first on a weekly and later on a monthly basis with the consultants. These meetings were formalized through our membership on a planning and operations committee whose main objectives were to implement the new organization structure, to review policy, to plan strategy, and to review performance.

Table 10 summarizes the various interventions taken.

Table 10. Summary of Interventions Implemented.

Party Treated	Intervention	Rationale
Organization as a whole	Establish profit centers and clearer definition of responsibility and authority; more delegation	Create more independence for Michael and Robert; allow them to develop, freeing Paul to do what he is excellent at and loves to do most—develop new fabrics
	Move David out of Diana	Reduce conflict between manufacturing, sales, and marketing; improve delivery and product line introduction, customer relations, and pricing; permit constructive meetings
	Retire controller	Clear the air for better labor relations, since he was the villain; give Michael a

(continued on next page)

Table 10. Summary of Interventions Implemented, Cont'd.

Party Treated	Intervention	Rationale
		freer hand; remove overlap between responsibilities of controller and director of plants
	Improve advertising and sales strategy and consolidate product line	Boost sales; reduce costs
	Establish more sophisticated financial controls and procedures for scanning the market	Identify areas of promise and inefficiency; keep product lines current
	Do more strategic planning —committee formed to do this	Reduce impulsive strategic decisions, with more points of view brought to bear; prevent Paul from ignoring unpleasant information about Diana
Paul	Supportive psychotherapy and counseling (occasional paradoxical interventions) —give insights slowly and gradually; get Paul to work more closely with Michael and Robert, to increase sense of generativity	Paul has low tolerance for frustration—must be handled gently or whole project might have to be aborted
David	Set him up in his own separate business; provide common-sense advice, mixed with minimal doses of insight-oriented psychotherapy, to help him understand his destructive relationship with Paul and Michael	His departure would make him happier and allow for more harmony in the firm; David is not interested in Diana or industry—was there to fulfill Paul and William's expectations; could never really resolve long-standing conflict with Michael
Michael	Let him run his own independent profit center; insight-oriented psychotherapy mixed with pragmatic business advice	Make him feel more secure about himself, less reliant on assistants or father; stabilize his management style to reduce extreme behavior; reduce his level of aggression

Table 10. Summary of Interventions Implemented, Cont'd.

Party Treated	Intervention	Rationale
Robert	Have him join the fabric division; Balint group to help him explore his management style	Make him more decisive; Robert can fulfill the role of "sounding board" for father; will keep Paul on track, since Robert is the least "bound" of the brothers

We were not entirely pleased with the eventual outcome of our consulting effort. Although the oldest son, David, started his own venture, he never completely severed his ties with the company. He continued to be somewhat involved in sales, mainly in the role of a contact person for a few large accounts. We felt that it would have reduced chances of conflict had David gone his own way entirely. In addition, our membership on the planning and operations committee did not last as long as we would have liked. When Paul saw the improvements in the company's operations, he felt that everything was under control and that he could do without us. Through our contact with the youngest son, we have learned about Paul's occasional "regressive" behavior. Apparently, he sometimes still engages in impulsive exploits, antagonizing the unions and meddling with David's venture. At the time of this writing, however, these actions do not seem sufficiently disruptive to seriously impede the organization's recovery. Sales are now growing at 10 percent real, and the firm is once again solidly in the black.

It might be objected that the Diana case involves a family firm and therefore provides an unreliable vehicle for showing the psychodynamic roots of organizational dysfunction. This is certainly an extreme case. That is the source of its pedagogical utility. We wish, however, to emphasize that many organizations that we have dealt with also exhibit psychological dynamics that account in large part for their strategic and structural problems.

Conclusion

Working for Change— Cautions and Recommendations

The rider must ride the horse,
not be run away with.
          —Donald Winnicott, *Playing and Reality*

This book has done more to pose tough questions than to provide easy answers. It represents still another challenge to the belief that management is a rational task performed by rational people according to sensible organizational objectives. We have tried to show how extrarational, intrapsychic forces can strongly influence organizational strategy, structure, decision making, leadership, and group functioning. These forces are not particularly easy to identify or to diagnose and are harder still to combat. But they are prevalent. They also constitute hazardous and persistent causes of dysfunction within all types of organizations.

Neurotic styles, groups sharing basic assumptions, transference patterns, resistances, superior/subordinate entanglements, and position in the career life cycle can all have a dramatic impact on organizational performance. We have shown how these forces can lead to impulsive decision making, severe morale problems, inadequate leadership, and untenable strategies and structures. Organizational consultants simply cannot afford to ignore these factors as contributors to the problems that they so often find themselves struggling with. We have seen how specific problems in firms often stem directly from the long-standing intrapsychic problems of their managers. For example, dramatic executives overextend their firm's resources and fail to make proper use of managerial information. Utopian organizational cultures might be in pursuit of unrealistic and expensive objectives. Persecutory transferences contribute to interpersonal hostility and a lack of cooperation, while "binding" superiors can cause underdeveloped and conforming subordinates. We have argued that, too often, management consultants see only the surface manifestations of these problems and try to address them directly. They might, for example, introduce capital budgeting and information systems in firms run by dramatic personalities, advocate management by objectives for utopian groups, and suggest the establishment of committees in firms where persecutory transferences lead to uncooperativeness.

It is our opinion that these measures only address symptoms without getting at their root causes. They are therefore unlikely to be of much use. Sometimes the only way to change the organization's behavior is to change the behavior of its principal actors. And the only way to do that is to convince them *that* they are wrong, to show them *why* they are wrong, and to give them at least some insight into the genesis of their dysfunctional attitudes, beliefs, and actions.

This can be done only by gaining insight, not only into organizational problems, but into the people who run the organizations. But that is not easy to accomplish. A good deal of time must be spent talking with executives and with their associates. Attitudes must be observed as well as behaviors. Intrapsychic themes must be studied. Managerial fantasies become as important as objective realities in revealing the genesis of problems. Much time and effort are required to make these discoveries, and the process of diagnosis can be disquieting for both the executives and the consultant. Sensitive issues are raised. Uncomfortable questions are asked. But these travails are necessary to discover the reasons for the organization's problems. Without a sound knowledge of these reasons, no thorough solution will emerge. Only the symptoms will be addressed. The underlying problems will remain, giving rise in the future to similar symptoms. At the same time it is also essential for the consultant to provide a supportive atmosphere for the clients, to help them to cope with and assimilate the new insights and to prevent their progress from becoming arrested at any of the stages of the working-through process.

Although this form of diagnosis and therapy is indispensable to the resolution of many organizational problems, it has a number of limitations. First, it is often unpleasant, time-consuming, and expensive. It is also risky for consultants, who might alienate themselves from top managers through their probing and thus may find themselves without a client. We have seen how difficult it can be to generate insight and how painful the working-through process can be. These are no small disincentives. Second, the form of intervention that we advocate can be carried out only by those who have acquired some understanding of psychodynamics. However, our method is very likely to do more harm than good in the hands of a well-meaning tyro with only a few psychology courses under his belt. As yet, very few management consultants have the training to carry out our suggestions. Third, it is by no means certain that all dysfunctional psychodynamic adjustment patterns can be successfully combated. Our case studies point mostly to our successes, but we have had our share of failures as well. Some intrapsychic problems are so deep-seated or severe that they would not even be amenable to change in any psychiatric or long-term psychoanalytic setting, let alone in the context of an organizational consulting project. At other times, executives are simply not undergoing enough pain (from poor organizational performance or threats to their jobs or well-being) to want to explore sensitive topics or to give up cherished habits or beliefs—and they usually have the power to thwart any meaningful organizational intervention.

Our approach to organizational intervention is not without a certain degree of pessimism. We have stated over and over that intrapsychic forces in organizations may be very resistant to change. They represent long-standing, deeply ingrained ways of perceiving, interpreting, and behaving on the part of coalitions of very powerful members of the organization. These patterns are very hard to alter, even when their dysfunctional consequences are obvious to the consultants. Psychiatric and psychoanalytic research has shown that many of our most problematic behaviors, attitudes, and modes of perception have their roots in early childhood experiences. They often are reinforced throughout adult life and become extremely stable and self-perpetuating. Sometimes, therefore, consultants cannot change an organization by addressing these patterns directly. The problem is that sick firms run by neurotic managers are often the hardest to change. This is not to say that they *cannot* be changed; but change will require a long and arduous intervention process. It is not simply a matter of pointing out dysfunctional behavior and prescribing a more appropriate substitute. Instead, much effort must be devoted to providing managers with insight into their dysfunctional behavior and its genesis and to helping them improve by giving them the necessary incentives and support.

In many cases, the problems faced by organizations are not as deep-seated as the ones at Diana. It may just be a question of replacing a "neurotic" executive or disbanding a destructive interpersonal relationship. These simple measures have done wonders to clear the way toward resolving more concrete structural organizational problems. Just as it is hazardous to be too shallow in diagnosing and treating organizational problems—looking at surface phenomena and ignoring the underlying psychodynamic influences—it is also unwise to go to the other extreme. Not all organizational problems have their roots in widespread or complex psychopathology. So it is best to diagnose with as few preconceptions as possible, always looking for the critical leverage points that will break the problem. In the final analysis, we have to keep in mind that it is the ability to find simplicity within complexity that characterizes effective intervention.

Notes

Introduction

1. See, for example, Fritz J. Roethlisberger and William J. Dickson, *Management and the Worker* (Cambridge, Mass.: Harvard University Press, 1939); Elton Mayo, *Human Problems of an Industrial Civilization* (Cambridge, Mass.: Harvard University Press, 1945); Douglas McGregor, *The Human Side of Enterprise* (New York: McGraw-Hill, 1960); Louis E. Davis and Albert B. Cherns (Eds.), *The Quality of Working Life*, 2 vols. (New York: Free Press, 1975).

2. See David C. McClelland, *Power: The Inner Experience* (New York: Irvington, 1975); David C. McClelland, *The Achieving Society* (New York: Irvington, 1961).

3. See Danny Miller, Manfred F. R. Kets de Vries, and Jean-Marie Toulouse, "Top Executive Locus of Control and Its Relationship to Strategy Making, Structure, and Environment," *Academy of Management Journal*, 1982, *25*, 237–253.

4. See Harold M. Schroder, Michael Driver, and Siegfried

211

Streufert, *Human Information Processing* (New York: Holt, Rinehart and Winston, 1967).

5. Herbert A. Simon, *Administrative Behavior* (New York: Macmillan, 1947).

6. James G. March and Herbert A. Simon, *Organizations* (New York: Wiley, 1958).

7. Richard M. Cyert and James G. March, *A Behavioral Theory of the Firm* (Englewood Cliffs, N.J.: Prentice-Hall, 1963).

8. Wilfred R. Bion, *Experiences in Groups* (London: Tavistock, 1959).

Chapter One

1. For example, the organismic analogy in organizational theory has been exceedingly popular and even of considerable value, but it has resulted in obscuring key differences between organisms and organizations. See, for example, M. Keeley, "Organizational Analogy: A Comparison of Organismic and Social Contract Models," *Administrative Science Quarterly*, 1980, *25*, 337-362.

2. See Danny Miller and Peter Friesen, *Organizations: A Quantum View* (Englewood Cliffs, N.J.: Prentice-Hall, 1984).

3. Among the researchers who have looked at this interface are Elliott Jaques, *The Changing Culture of a Factory* (London: Tavistock, 1951) and *Work, Creativity, and Social Justice* (New York: International Universities Press, 1970); Abraham Zaleznik and Manfred F. R. Kets de Vries, *Power and the Corporate Mind* (Boston: Houghton Mifflin, 1975); Michael Maccoby, *The Gamesman* (New York: Simon & Schuster, 1976); Roy Payne and Derek S. Pugh, "Organization Structure and Climate," in M. D. Dunnette (Ed.), *Handbook of Industrial and Organizational Psychology* (Chicago: Rand McNally, 1976); Otto Kernberg, "Regression in Organizational Leadership," *Psychiatry*, 1979, *42*, 29-39; Manfred F. R. Kets de Vries, *Organizational Paradoxes: Clinical Approaches to Management* (London: Tavistock, 1980); Manfred F. R. Kets de Vries (Ed.),

The Irrational Executive: Psychoanalytic Explorations in Management (New York: International Universities Press, 1984).

4. See Jerry E. Phares, *Locus of Control in Personality* (Morristown, N.J.: General Learning Press, 1976); Herbert M. Lefcourt, *Locus of Control* (New York: Wiley, 1976).

5. See David C. McClelland, *The Achieving Society* (New York: Irvington, 1961).

6. See David C. McClelland, *Power: The Inner Experience* (New York: Irvington, 1975).

7. See Victor H. Vroom, *Some Personality Determinants of the Effects of Participation* (Englewood Cliffs, N.J.: Prentice-Hall, 1960); Henry Tosi, "A Re-examination of Personality as a Determinant of the Effects of Participation," *Personnel Psychology,* 1970, *23,* 91–99.

8. See Robert K. Merton, "Bureaucratic Structure and Personality," in Robert K. Merton, *Social Theory and Social Structure* (New York: Free Press, 1968).

9. We are especially indebted to the work of Otto Fenichel, *The Psychoanalytic Theory of Neurosis* (New York: Norton, 1945); David Shapiro, *Neurotic Styles* (New York: Basic Books, 1965); J. Laplanche and J. B. Pontalis, *The Language of Psychoanalysis* (London: Hogarth Press, 1973); Alfred M. Freedman, Harold I. Kaplan, and Benjamin J. Sadock (Eds.), *Comprehensive Textbook of Psychiatry,* 2 vols. (Baltimore: Williams & Wilkins, 1975); Armand M. Nicholi (Ed.), *The Harvard Guide to Modern Psychiatry* (Cambridge, Mass.: Belknap Press, 1978).

10. *Object* is used in the special sense of the person toward whom instinctual needs are directed.

11. Important researchers in the field are such clinicians as Melanie Klein, *Contributions to Psychoanalysis: 1921-45* (London: Hogarth Press, 1948); W. Ronald D. Fairbairn, *An Object-Relations Theory of Personality* (New York: Basic Books, 1952); Michael Balint, *Primary Love and Psychoanalytic Technique* (London: Liveright, 1965); Harry Guntrip, *Schizoid Phenomena, Object Relations, and the Self* (New York: International Universities Press, 1969); Edith Jacobson, *The Self*

and the Object World (New York: International Universities Press, 1964); Joseph Sandler and Bernard Rosenblatt, "The Concept of the Representational World," *Psychoanalytic Study of the Child*, 1962, *17*, 128–145; Margaret S. Mahler, Fred Pine, and Anni Bergman, *The Psychological Birth of the Human Infant* (New York: Basic Books, 1975); Otto Kernberg, *Object Relations Theory and Clinical Psychoanalysis* (New York: Jason Aronson, 1976).

12. Laplanche and Pontalis, *Language of Psychoanalysis*, p. 318.

13. Josef Breuer and Sigmund Freud, "Studies on Hysteria," in James Strachey (Ed.), *The Standard Edition of the Complete Psychological Works of Sigmund Freud*, Vol. 2 (London: Hogarth Press/Institute of Psychoanalysis, 1893–1895), p. 22. All future references to Freud's works will be designated *Standard Edition*.

14. Ian I. Mitroff and Ralph H. Kilmann, "Organization Stories: An Approach to the Design and Analysis of Organizations Through Myths and Stories," in R. H. Kilmann, L. R. Pondy, and D. P. Slevin (Eds.), *The Management of Organization Design Strategies and Implementation* (New York: Elsevier/North Holland, 1976), p. 190.

15. Jean-Paul Larçon and Roland Reitter, *Structures de pouvoir et identité de l'enterprise* (Paris: Nathan, 1979).

16. These are discussed in the American Psychiatric Association's *Diagnostic and Statistical Manual of Mental Disorders*, 3rd ed. (Washington, D.C.: American Psychiatric Association, 1980). In our framework the "dramatic" style is a mixture of the histrionic and narcissistic styles. In an organizational context we found it difficult to separate elements of the two styles. Actually, in the literature a distinction is often made between two types of histrionics, one genital ("the good hysteric") and one oral ("the so-called good hysteric"). See J. Marmor, "Orality in the Hysterical Personality," *Journal of the American Psychoanalytic Association*, 1953, *1*, 656–667; Elisabeth R. Zetzel, "The So-Called Good Hysteric," *International Journal of Psychoanalysis*, 1968, *49*, 256.

17. We are referring to the types S_3, S_2, F_1, F_2, and F_3 in an empirical taxonomy of organizations by Danny Miller and

Peter Friesen, "Strategy Making in Context: Ten Empirical Archetypes," *Journal of Management Studies,* 1977, *14,* 258-280; Danny Miller and Peter Friesen, "Archetypes of Strategy Formulation," *Management Science,* 1978, *24,* 921-933. The paranoid firms seem also to correspond to some of the "analyzers" as described by Raymond Miles and Charles Snow, *Strategy, Structure, and Process* (New York: McGraw-Hill, 1978). The compulsive firm resembles the "machine bureaucracies" as described by Henry Mintzberg, *The Structuring of Organizations* (Englewood Cliffs, N.J.: Prentice-Hall, 1979). We can find similarities between the dramatic firms and the entrepreneurial types portrayed by Orvis Collins and David Moore, *The Organization Makers* (New York: Appleton-Century-Crofts, 1970). The depressive firms resemble the bureaucracies described by both Victor Thompson, *Modern Organizations* (New York: Knopf, 1961), and William H. Starbuck, A. Greve, and B. Hedberg, "Responding to Crises," *Journal of Business Administration,* 1978, *9,* 111-137. We can also compare the schizoid firms to the political arenas listed by Henry Mintzberg, *Power in and Around Organizations* (Englewood Cliffs, N.J.: Prentice-Hall, 1983).

18. All names and situations in case illustrations have been disguised, the exceptions being references to well-known public figures.

19. See Danny Miller, "Strategy Making in Context: Ten Empirical Archetypes," unpublished doctoral dissertation, McGill University, 1976, and Danny Miller and Peter Friesen, *Organizations: A Quantum View* (Englewood Cliffs, N.J.: Prentice-Hall, 1984).

20. For a description of the "gamesman" see Maccoby, *The Gamesman.* Actually, the "gamesman" seems very similar to what is often described in psychiatric and psychoanalytic literature as the narcissistic personality. Excellent descriptions of this type of personality, each author taking a different perspective, are given by Heinz Kohut, *The Analysis of the Self* (New York: International Universities Press, 1971), and Otto Kernberg, *Borderline Conditions and Pathological Narcissism* (New York: Jason Aronson, 1975). For a description of the narcissistic personality in an organizational context see Manfred F. R.

Kets de Vries and Danny Miller, "Narcissism and Leadership: An Object Relations Perspective," Harvard University Graduate School of Business Administration, 1984.

21. For a study that highlights the process of executive complementarity using a hospital site, see Richard C. Hodgson, Daniel J. Levinson, and Abraham Zaleznik, *The Executive Role Constellation: An Analysis of Personality and Role Relations in Management* (Boston: Division of Research, Graduate School of Business Administration, Harvard University, 1965).

22. A good description of the hermeneutic point of view—in which deciphering the structures of signification stands central—can be found in Robert Palmer, *Hermeneutics* (Evanston, Ill.: Northwestern University Press, 1969), and Paul Ricoeur, *The Conflict of Interpretations: Essays in Hermeneutics,* D. Inde (Ed.), (Evanston, Ill.: Northwestern University Press, 1974). See also Abraham Zaleznik and Manfred F. R. Kets de Vries, "Leadership as a Text: An Essay on Interpretation," Harvard University Graduate School of Business Administration, 1984.

Chapter Two

1. Using the terminology of psychoanalytic theory, fantasies can be defined as basic mental scenarios that evolve in complexity as the individual matures. Desires based on instinctual needs become connected with mental representations of self and others and are expressed through fantasies, which can be considered the building blocks for action. For a review of the meaning and significance of fantasy, see, for example, Melanie Klein, *Contributions to Psychoanalysis 1921-45* (London: Hogarth Press, 1948); Susan Isaacs, "The Nature and Function of Fantasy," *International Journal of Psychoanalysis,* 1948, *29,* 73-97; David Beres, "The Unconscious Fantasy," *Psychoanalytic Quarterly,* 1962, *31,* 309-328; Jean Laplanche and J. B. Pontalis, "Fantasy and the Origins of Sexuality," *International Journal of Psychoanalysis,* 1968, *49,* 1-18.

2. Wilfred R. Bion, *Experiences in Groups* (London: Tavistock, 1959), p. 42.

3. Bion, *Experiences in Groups,* p. 42.

4. Robert Freed Bales, *Personality and Interpersonal Behavior* (New York: Holt, Rinehart and Winston, 1970), p. 138.

5. Bales, *Personality and Interpersonal Behavior,* p. 150.

6. Bion, *Experiences in Groups.*

7. For example, applications of Bion's concepts about groups to organizations can be found in Robert DeBoard, *The Psychoanalysis of Organizations* (London: Tavistock, 1978), and Otto Kernberg, "Leadership and Organizational Functioning: Organizational Regression," *International Journal of Group Psychotherapy,* 1978, *28,* 3-25.

8. What we can observe is that a "schizoid split" is maintained. What is "good" becomes introjected—taken in by the individual—and what is "bad" is projected onto outsiders. According to Laplanche and Pontalis, in "Fantasy and the Origins of Sexuality," such projection is a primitive defense mechanism "whereby qualities, feelings, wishes, or even objects which the subject refuses to recognize or rejects in himself, are expelled from the self and located in another person or thing" (p. 349).

9. See Sigmund Freud, "Group Psychology and the Analysis of the Ego," *Standard Edition,* Vol. 18, 1921; Philip E. Slater, *Microcosm* (New York: Wiley, 1966).

10. Tom Burns and G. M. Stalker, *The Management of Innovation* (London: Tavistock, 1961).

11. For a description of this approach to group work, see Michael Balint, *The Doctor, His Patient, and the Illness* (New York: International Universities Press, 1957).

Chapter Three

1. Josef Breuer and Sigmund Freud, "Studies on Hysteria," *Standard Edition,* Vol. 2, 1893-1895.

2. Sigmund Freud, "Fragment of an Analysis of a Case of Hysteria," *Standard Edition,* Vol. 7, 1905. See also Sigmund Freud, "The Dynamics of Transference," *Standard Edition,* Vol. 12, 1912.

3. James Strachey, "The Nature of the Therapeutic Action of Psychoanalysis," *International Journal of Psychoanalysis,* 1934, *15,* 127-159.

4. See Anthony Storr, *The Art of Psychotherapy* (New York: Methuen, 1979).

5. See, for example, the surveys of Douglas W. Orr, "Transference and Countertransference: A Historical Survey," *Journal of the American Psychoanalytic Association*, 1954, *11*, 621-670; Ralph R. Greenson, *The Technique and Practice of Psychoanalysis*, Vol. 1 (New York: International Universities Press, 1967); Robert Langs, *The Therapeutic Interaction*, 2 vols. (New York: Jason Aronson, 1976).

6. Otto Fenichel, *The Psychoanalytic Theory of Neurosis* (New York: Norton, 1945), p. 30.

7. Storr, *Art of Psychotherapy*, p. 69.

8. Joseph Sandler, Alex Holder, Marie Kawenoka, Hanna Engl Kennedy, and Lily Neurath, "Notes on Some Theoretical and Clinical Aspects of Transference," *International Journal of Psychoanalysis*, 1969, *50*, p. 639.

9. Greenson, *Technique and Practice of Psychoanalysis*, pp. 151-152.

10. See Otto Fenichel, *Problems of Psychoanalytic Technique* (Albany, N.Y.: Psychoanalytic Quarterly, 1941).

11. Greenson, *Technique and Practice of Psychoanalysis*.

12. For a discussion of the etiology of various forms of transference, see Heinz Kohut and Ernest S. Wolf, "The Disorders of the Self and Their Treatment: An Outline," *International Journal of Psychoanalysis*, 1978, *59*, 413-425.

13. To mention only a few, the literature distinguishes between neurotic and nonneurotic transference, the latter being transference manifestations of a severe psychotic or borderline nature. Heinz Kohut's interest in narcissistic personality disorders led him to recognize two types of transference manifestations, which he termed *mirror* and *idealizing* types (*The Analysis of the Self* [New York: International Universities Press, 1971]). According to his observations, in the mirror transference, the *self* takes on a grandiose, exhibitionistic image, while in the complementary idealizing transference, the *other* is seen in the image of the idealized parent. Both transference patterns can be viewed as attempts to restore a previously existing state of perfection, a period in time when one felt properly responded to, before serious unempathic reactions by the parent occurred.

Many therapists have pointed out the instinctualized nature of transference, referring to interaction patterns of an eroticized and aggressive nature. Leo Stone, in *The Psychoanalytic Situation* (New York: International Universities Press, 1961) and in "The Psychoanalytic Situation and Transference: Postscript to an Earlier Communication," *Journal of the American Psychoanalytic Association,* 1967, *15,* 3–58, distinguishes primordial from mature transference, both of which are responses to the early separation/individuation process of the child but date back to different phases of the human life cycle. See also Margaret S. Mahler, Fred Pine, and Anni Bergman, *The Psychological Birth of the Human Infant* (New York: Basic Books, 1975). The work of the Kleinians—see, for example, Melanie Klein, "The Origins of Transference," *International Journal of Psychoanalysis,* 1952, *33,* 433–438; Hanna Segal, *Introduction to the Work of Melanie Klein* (New York: Basic Books, 1964); Heinrich Racker, *Transference and Countertransference* (New York: International Universities Press, 1968)—has led to a distinction between transferences based on projective and introjective mechanisms, both of which are distortive processes. In projective mechanisms the individual attributes to other people his own emotions and perceptions. In introjective mechanisms he assimilates and internalizes personality qualities of another person.

Joseph Sandler and his associates (see Joseph Sandler, Christopher Dare, and Alex Holder, *The Patient and the Analyst: The Basis of the Psychoanalytic Process* [New York: International Universities Press, 1970], and Sandler and others, "Notes on Some Theoretical and Clinical Aspects of Transference") introduced three general types of transferences, which have different origins in time. The first are genetic transferences —unconscious perceptual distortions derived from early disruptive childhood relationships, from experiences with parental and other significant figures. The second type of transference is based on the externalization of stable inner psychological states (see Sigmund Freud, "The Ego and the Id," *Standard Edition,* Vol. 19, 1923), such as instinctual wishes, guilt, conscience, and self-representations. The final type of transference derives from the most current relationships. Robert Langs, in his monumental work *The Therapeutic Interaction,* distinguishes between matrix and reactive transferences, viewed as extremes on a continuum, whereby the former are based on the earliest experiences of the individual while the latter are reactions of a more contemporary origin.

Another distinction found in the literature is that between transference patterns characterized by attempts to harm others —see, for example, Harold F. Searles, *Collected Papers on Schizophrenia and Related Subjects* (New York: International Universities Press, 1965); Brian Bird, "Notes on Transference: Universal Phenomenon and the Hardest Part of Analysis," *Journal of the American Psychoanalytic Association,* 1972, *20,* 267–301; Langs, *The Therapeutic Interaction*—or to help them—see Margaret Little, "Countertransference and the Patient's Response to It," *International Journal of Psychoanalysis,* 1951, *33,* 32-40; Searles, *Collected Papers*; Langs, *The Therapeutic Interaction.* A number of writers have emphasized the interpersonal dependency relationship implied in the transference process; see, for example, D. W. Winnicott, *Through Pediatrics to Psychoanalysis* (New York: Basic Books, 1975); Michael Balint, *The Basic Fault: Therapeutic Aspects of Regression* (London: Tavistock, 1968).

14. See Kohut, *Analysis of the Self.*

15. See Kohut, *Analysis of the Self.*

16. For a discussion of the narcissistic executive see Manfred F. R. Kets de Vries, "Leiderschap in een narcistisch tijdperk," *Management Totaal,* 1981, *5,* 20-25, based on the working paper "Leadership in a Narcissistic Age," Faculty of Management, McGill University, 1980.

17. See Michael Maccoby, *The Gamesman* (New York: Simon & Schuster, 1976).

18. For an elaborate description of this process, see Otto Kernberg, *Borderline Conditions and Pathological Narcissism* (New York: Jason Aronson, 1975).

19. See Fenichel, *Psychoanalytic Theory of Neurosis.*

20. For a discussion of the psychological dimensions of power, see Abraham Zaleznik and Manfred F. R. Kets de Vries, *Power and the Corporate Mind* (Boston: Houghton Mifflin,

1975); Manfred F. R. Kets de Vries, *Organizational Paradoxes: Clinical Approaches to Management* (London: Tavistock, 1980).

Chapter Four

1. Gregory Bateson, Don D. Jackson, Jay Haley, and John H. Weakland, "Toward a Theory of Schizophrenia," *Behavioral Science,* 1956, *1,* 251-264.

2. Lyman C. Wynne, Irving M. Ryckoff, Juliana Day, and Stanley I. Hirsch, "Pseudo-Mutuality in the Family Relations of Schizophrenics," *Psychiatry,* 1958, *21,* 205-220.

3. An extensive literature exists about these dysfunctional family relationships. See, for example, the work of Don D. Jackson: "The Question of Family Homeostasis," *Psychiatric Quarterly Supplement,* 1957, *3,* 79-90, pt. 1; "Interactional Psychotherapy," in Morris I. Stein (Ed.), *Contemporary Psychotherapies* (New York: Free Press, 1962); "The Study of the Family," *Family Process,* 1965, *4,* 1-20; *The Mirages of Marriage* (New York: Norton, 1968). See also the research of Theodore Lidz and associates: Theodore Lidz, "The Influence of Family Studies on the Treatment of Schizophrenia," *Psychiatry,* 1969, *32,* 237-251; Theodore Lidz, Alice Cornelison, Stephen Fleck, and Dorothy Terry, "The Intrafamilial Environment of Schizophrenic Patients: II. Marital Schism and Marital Skew," *American Journal of Psychiatry,* 1957, *114,* 241-248; Theodore Lidz, Alice Cornelison, Dorothy Terry, and Stephen Fleck, "Intrafamilial Environment of Schizophrenic Patients: VI. The Transmission of Irrationality," *A.M.A. Archives of Neurology and Psychiatry,* 1958, *79,* 305-316. See also the work of Jay Haley: "The Family of the Schizophrenic: A Model System," *Journal of Nervous and Mental Disease,* 1959, *129,* 357-374; *Strategies of Psychotherapy* (New York: Grune & Stratton, 1963); "Research on Family Patterns: An Instrument Measurement," *Family Process,* 1964, *3,* 41-65; *Problem-Solving Therapy: New Strategies for Effective Family Therapy* (San Francisco: Jossey-Bass, 1976). Other important researchers in this field are Albert E. Scheffen, "Regressive One-to-One Relationships," *Psychiatric Quarterly,* 1960, *23,* 692-709; M. Acker-

man, *Treating the Troubled Family* (New York: Basic Books, 1966); Paul Watzlawick, Janet Helmick Beavin, and Don D. Jackson, *Pragmatics of Human Communication* (New York: Norton, 1967); Salvatore Minuchin, *Families and Family Therapy* (Cambridge, Mass.: Harvard University Press, 1974); Mara Selvini Palazzoli, Gianfranco Cecchin, Giuliana Prata, and Luigi Boscolo, *Paradox and Counterparadox* (New York: Jason Aronson, 1978); Lynn Hoffman, *Foundations of Family Therapy* (New York: Basic Books, 1981); J. Boszormenyi-Nagy and G. Spark, *Invisible Loyalties: Reciprocity in Inter-Generational Family Therapy* (New York: Harper & Row, 1973); Gerald R. Weeks and Lucciano L'Abate, *Paradoxical Psychotherapy: Theory and Practice with Individuals, Couples, and Families* (New York: Brunner/Mazel, 1982).

4. See, for example, Carlos E. Sluzki, Janet Beavin, Alejandro Tarnopolsky, and Eliseo Veron, "Transactional Disqualification: Research on the Double Bind," in P. Watzlawick and J. Weakland (Eds.), *The Interactional View* (New York: Norton, 1977).

5. See Lidz and others, "The Transmission of Irrationality"; see also Ronald D. Laing, "Mystification, Confession, and Conflict," in J. Boszormenyi-Nagy and J. L. Franco (Eds.), *Intensive Family Therapy: Theoretical and Practical Aspects* (New York: Harper & Row, 1965).

6. See Harold F. Searles, "The Effort to Drive the Other Person Crazy—An Element in the Aetiology and Psychotherapy of Schizophrenia," *British Journal of Medical Psychology,* 1959, *32,* 1-18, pt. 1. See also Margaret Mahler, Fred Pine, and Anni Bergman, *The Psychological Birth of the Human Infant* (New York: Basic Books, 1975).

7. See Minuchin, *Families and Family Therapy*; Helm Stierlin, *Separating Parents and Adolescents* (New York: Quadrangle/New York Times Book Co., 1974).

8. See Searles, "The Effort to Drive the Other Person Crazy."

9. See Antonio J. Ferreira, "Family Myth and Homeostasis," *Archives of General Psychiatry,* 1963, *9,* 457-463; Helm Stierlin, "Group Fantasies and Family Myths—Some The-

oretical and Practical Aspects," *Family Process*, 1973, *12*, 111–125.

10. See Lidz and others, "The Transmission of Irrationality."

11. See Wynne and others, "Pseudo-Mutuality in the Family Relations of Schizophrenics."

12. See Murray Bowen, "The Use of Family Theory in Clinical Practice," *Comprehensive Psychiatry*, 1966, 7, 345–374; Bowen, *Family Therapy in Clinical Practice* (New York: Jason Aronson, 1978).

13. See Minuchin, *Families and Family Therapy*.

14. See Stierlin, *Separating Parents and Adolescents*.

15. See Stierlin, *Separating Parents and Adolescents*.

16. Stierlin, *Separating Parents and Adolescents*, p. xii.

17. Stierlin, *Separating Parents and Adolescents*, p. xiii.

18. Stierlin, *Separating Parents and Adolescents*, pp. xii–xiii.

19. Stierlin, *Separating Parents and Adolescents*, p. 52.

20. For an elaboration of this process, see Ezra F. Vogel and Norman W. Bell, "The Emotionally Disturbed Child as the Family Scapegoat," in Norman W. Bell and Ezra F. Vogel, *A Modern Introduction to the Family* (New York: Free Press, 1968); John Zinner and Roger Shapiro, "Projective Identification as a Mode of Perception and Behavior in Families of Adolescents," *International Journal of Psychoanalysis*, 1972, *53*, 523–530; John Zinner and Roger Shapiro, "The Family Group as a Single Psychic Entity: Implications for Acting Out in Adolescence," *International Review of Psychoanalysis*, 1974, *1*, 169–186; Stierlin, *Separating Parents and Adolescents*; Hoffman, *Foundations of Family Therapy*.

21. For a description of the double-bind phenomenon, see Bateson and others, "Toward a Theory of Schizophrenia"; Milton M. Berger (Ed.), *Beyond the Double Bind* (New York: Brunner/Mazel, 1978).

22. Joseph Heller, *Catch-22* (New York: Dell, 1974).

23. Heller, *Catch-22*, p. 23.

24. For a description of folie à deux see Manfred F. R. Kets de Vries, "Managers Can Drive Their Subordinates Mad,"

Harvard Business Review, 1979 (July-August), 125-135. See also Manfred F. R. Kets de Vries, *Organizational Paradoxes: Clinical Approaches to Management* (London: Tavistock, 1980).

25. Izabel E. P. Menzies, in her study of the nursing service of a general hospital ("A Case Study in the Functioning of Social Systems as a Defense Against Anxiety," *Human Relations,* 1960, *13*, 95-121), points out how "purposeful obscurity in the formal distribution of responsibility" can be used to cope with emerging anxiety.

26. See Stierlin, *Separating Parents and Adolescents.*

Chapter Five

1. See Manfred F. R. Kets de Vries, Danny Miller, Jean-Marie Toulouse, Peter Friesen, Maurice Boivert, and R. Theriault, "Using the Life Cycle to Anticipate Satisfaction at Work," *Journal of Forecasting,* Fall 1984 (in press).

2. Edwin A. Locke, "The Nature and Causes of Job Satisfaction," in Marvin D. Dunnette (Ed.), *Handbook of Industrial and Organizational Psychology* (Chicago: Rand McNally, 1976), p. 129.

3. Debates about linearity and curvilinearity abound as findings conflict. See, for example, S. D. Saleh and J. L. Otis, "Age and Level of Job Satisfaction," *Personnel Psychology,* 1964, *17*, 425-430; C. L. Hulin and P. C. Smith, "A Linear Model of Job Satisfaction," *Journal of Applied Psychology,* 1965, *49*, 209-216; G. P. Fournet, M. K. DiStefano, and M. W. Pryer, "Job Satisfaction: Issues and Problems," *Personnel Psychology,* 1966, *19*, 165-184; L. H. Lofquist and R. V. Dawis, *Adjustment to Work* (New York: Appleton-Century-Crofts, 1969); J. L. Gibson and S. M. Klein, "Employee Attitudes as a Function of Age and Length of Service: A Reconceptualization," *Academy of Management Journal,* 1970, *13*, 411-425; J. W. Hunt and P. N. Saul, "The Relationship of Age, Tenure, and Job Satisfaction in Males and Females," *Academy of Management Journal,* 1975, *18*, 690-702.

4. See the research of J. A. Weitz, "A Neglected Concept in the Study of Job Satisfaction," *Personnel Psychology,* 1952,

5, 201-205; Patricia C. Smith, "The Prediction of Individual Differences in Susceptibility to Industrial Monotony," *Journal of Applied Psychology,* 1955, *39,* 322-329; A. W. Kornhauser, *Mental Health and the Industrial Worker: A Detroit Study* (New York: Wiley, 1965); B. Iris and G. V. Barrett, "Some Relations Between Job and Life Satisfaction and Job Importance," *Journal of Applied Psychology,* 1972, *56,* 301-304; C. Bühler, "General Structures of Human Life Cycle," in C. Bühler and F. Mesarick, *The Course of Life* (New York: Springer, 1968).

5. See, for example, Sigmund Freud, "Three Essays on the Theory of Sexuality," *Standard Edition,* Vol. 7, 1905; Margaret S. Mahler, Fred Pine, and Anni Bergman, *The Psychological Birth of the Human Infant* (New York: Basic Books, 1975).

6. Erik H. Erikson, *Identity and the Life Cycle: Selected Papers* (New York: International Universities Press, 1959); Erik H. Erikson, *Childhood and Society,* 2nd ed. (New York: Norton, 1963).

7. Robert W. White, *Lives in Progress* (New York: Holt, Rinehart and Winston, 1966).

8. Else Frenkel-Brunswik, "Adjustments and Reorientation in the Course of the Life Span," in B. Neugarten (Ed.), *Middle Age and Aging* (Chicago: University of Chicago Press, 1968).

9. Daniel J. Levinson, Charlotte M. Darrow, Edward B. Klein, Maria H. Levinson, and Braxton McKee, "The Psychosocial Development of Men in Early Adulthood and the Mid-Life Transition," in *Life History Research in Psychopathology,* Vol. 3 (Minneapolis: University of Minnesota Press, 1974), pp. 343-357; Daniel J. Levinson, *The Seasons of a Man's Life* (New York: Knopf, 1978).

10. Roger L. Gould, "The Phases of Adult Life: A Study in Developmental Psychology," *American Journal of Psychiatry,* 1972, *129,* 33-43; Roger L. Gould, *Transformation: Growth and Change in Adult Life* (New York: Simon & Schuster, 1978).

11. George E. Vaillant, *Adaptation to Life* (Boston: Little, Brown, 1977).

12. See Lewis B. Ward and Anthony G. Athos, *Student*

Expectations of Corporate Life: Implications for Management Recruiting (Boston: Division of Research, Graduate School of Business Administration, Harvard University, 1972); Daniel C. Feldman, "A Practical Program for Employee Socialization," *Organizational Dynamics,* 1976 (Autumn), 64–80; John P. Wanous, "Organizational Entry: From Naive Expectations to Realistic Beliefs," *Journal of Applied Psychology,* 1976, *61,* 22–29; Ross A. Webber, "Career Problems of Young Managers," *California Management Review,* 1976, *19,* 19–33; Meryl Reis Louis, "Surprise and Sense Making: What Newcomers Experience in Entering Unfamiliar Organizational Settings," *Administrative Science Quarterly,* 1980, *25,* 226–249.

13. See, for example, Ian C. Ross and Alvin Zander, "Need Satisfaction and Employee Turnover," *Personnel Psychology,* 1957, *10,* 327–338; Marvin D. Dunnette, Richard D. Arvey, and Paul A. Banas, "Why Do They Leave," *Personnel,* 1973, *50,* 25–39.

14. Edgar H. Schein, "The Individual, the Organization, and the Career: A Conceptual Scheme," *Journal of Applied Behavioral Science,* 1971, *7,* 401–427.

15. Schein, "The Individual, the Organization, and the Career."

16. J. Rosenbaum, "Tournament Mobility: Career Patterns in a Corporation," *Administrative Science Quarterly,* 1979, *24,* 220–241.

17. See Kets de Vries and others, "Using the Life Cycle to Anticipate Satisfaction at Work."

18. See Orville G. Brim, Jr., "Socialization Through the Life Cycle," in Orville G. Brim, Jr., and Stanton Wheeler (Eds.), *Socialization After Childhood: Two Essays* (New York: Wiley, 1966); John Van Maanen, "Experiencing Organization: Notes on the Meaning of Careers and Socialization," in John Van Maanen (Ed.), *Organizational Careers: Some New Perspectives* (New York: Wiley, 1977); Feldman, "A Practical Program for Employee Socialization"; Edgar H. Schein, *Career Dynamics: Matching Individual and Organizational Needs* (Reading, Mass.: Addison-Wesley, 1980).

19. See Samuel A. Culbert and John J. McDonough, *The*

Invisible War: Pursuing Self-Interest at Work (New York: Wiley, 1980).

20. See Chris Argyris, *Integrating Individual and Organization* (New York: Wiley, 1964); E. Lawler, *Motivation in Work Organizations* (Monterey, Calif.: Brooks/Cole, 1973).

21. Levinson and others, "The Psychosocial Development of Men in Early Adulthood and the Mid-Life Transition"; Levinson, *The Seasons of a Man's Life.*

22. Elliott Jaques, "Death and the Mid-Life Crisis," *International Journal of Psychoanalysis*, 1965, *46*, 502–514.

23. Bernice L. Neugarten, "The Awareness of Middle Age," in B. L. Neurgarten (Ed.), *Middle Age and Aging* (Chicago: University of Chicago Press, 1968), p. 97.

24. Erikson, *Childhood and Society.*

25. Cyril Sofer, *Men in Mid-Career* (Cambridge: Cambridge University Press, 1970).

26. B. Lawrence, "The Work of the Mid-Life Crisis," *Sloan Management Review*, 1980, *29*, 35–49.

27. Gould, *Transformation.*

28. See Manfred F. R. Kets de Vries, "The Mid-Career Conundrum," *Organizational Dynamics*, 1978 (Autumn), 45–62.

29. Levinson and others, "The Psychosocial Development of Men in Early Adulthood and the Mid-Life Transition"; Levinson, *The Seasons of a Man's Life.*

30. See D. D. Miller and William H. Form, *Industrial Sociology* (New York: Harper & Row, 1951).

31. See Manfred F. R. Kets de Vries, *Organizational Paradoxes: Clinical Approaches to Management* (London: Tavistock, 1980), chap. 10.

32. See Peter C. Pineo, "Disenchantment in the Later Years of Marriage," in Neugarten (Ed.), *Middle Age and Aging*; Gould, *Transformation.*

33. See Carl G. Jung, "The Stages of Life," in J. Campbell (Ed.), *The Portable Jung* (New York: Viking Press, 1971).

34. Erikson, *Identity and the Life Cycle*; Erikson, *Childhood and Society.*

35. See, for example, the study by Jean-Marie Toulouse,

Les reussites quebécoises: Défi des hommes d'affaires (Montreal: Agence d'Arc, 1980).

Chapter Six

1. For a psychoanalytic discussion of resistances, see Anna Freud, *The Ego and the Mechanisms of Defense,* rev. ed. (New York: International Universities Press, 1966); Otto Fenichel, *The Psychoanalytic Theory of Neurosis* (New York: International Universities Press, 1945); Charles Brenner, *An Elementary Textbook of Psychoanalysis* (New York: International Universities Press, 1955); Charles Brenner, *Psychoanalytic Technique and Psychic Conflict* (New York: Norton, 1976); Karl Menninger, *Theory of Psychoanalytic Technique* (New York: Basic Books, 1958); Ralph R. Greenson, *The Technique and Practice of Psychoanalysis* (New York: International Universities Press, 1967).

2. In a general sense we can distinguish among "ego," "superego," and "id" resistances. The ego resistances are so called because they are originated by the ego, a metapsychological construct representing the executive agency of the mind. The ego tries to mediate between a person's internal and external worlds in an effort to maintain a stable, homeostatic state (see Sigmund Freud, "Inhibitions, Symptoms, and Anxiety," *Standard Edition,* Vol. 20, 1926).

According to Sigmund Freud ("The Ego and the Id," *Standard Edition,* Vol. 19, 1923), the superego, in a metapsychological sense, represents society within the psyche and gives rise to conscience, morality, and ideals. It internalizes the demands of socializing forces, thereby fulfilling a self-observation function. The superego also affirms and disapproves of one's actions and executes demands for the reparation of wrongdoing, occasionally inflicting self-punishment in the process.

"Id" resistances remain after "ego" and "superego" resistances have been dismantled. They give rise to a compulsion to repeat earlier experiences and situations, whatever the costs, and to the tendency of the organism toward a state of entropy (see Sigmund Freud, "Beyond the Pleasure Principle," *Standard*

Edition, Vol. 18, 1920)—necessitating the strenuous effort of further "working through" (see Sigmund Freud, "Remembering, Repeating, and Working Through," *Standard Edition,* Vol. 12, 1914; Greenson, *Technique and Practice of Psychoanalysis.* Our discussion of resistances will concentrate on the first two forms, since id resistances are very poorly understood.

Psychoanalysts also discuss transference resistances. As we have seen in our discussion of transference, in such instances experiences are *relived* rather than simply *remembered.* The person seems to be stuck in his ways, unwilling to recognize the reasons for a particular way of behaving. Instead, "acting out" replaces insight; it blocks change and leads to repetitive growth-inhibiting behavior. Menninger calls this form of resistance "frustration" or "revenge" resistance, since hostility is often expressed toward disappointing and frustrating key persons. These usually stand for the parental figures of childhood. Since we have already dealt with transference and its vicissitudes, we shall focus on the other resistances.

3. See Freud, *The Ego and the Mechanisms of Defense;* Brenner, *Elementary Textbook of Psychoanalysis.*

4. See Freud, *The Ego and the Mechanisms of Defense;* Fenichel, *Psychoanalytic Theory of Neurosis.*

5. See Brenner, *Elementary Textbook of Psychoanalysis;* John C. Nemiah, "The Dynamic Bases of Psychopathology," in Armand M. Nicholi (Ed.), *The Harvard Guide to Modern Psychiatry* (Cambridge, Mass.: Belknap Press, 1978).

6. See Freud, *The Ego and the Mechanisms of Defense;* Brenner, *Elementary Textbook of Psychoanalysis.*

7. See Brenner, *Elementary Textbook of Psychoanalysis;* Nemiah, "Dynamic Bases of Psychopathology."

8. Freud, *The Ego and the Mechanisms of Defense,* p. 113.

9. See Brenner, *Elementary Textbook of Psychoanalysis.*

10. For a psychohistorical study of the life of Frederick Taylor, see Sudhir Kakar, *Frederick Taylor: A Study in Personality and Innovation* (Cambridge, Mass.: M.I.T. Press, 1970).

11. Kakar, *Frederick Taylor,* p. 20.

12. See Freud, *The Ego and the Mechanisms of Defense.*

13. See Fenichel, *Psychoanalytic Theory of Neurosis.*

Chapter Seven

1. For an excellent clinical approach to organizational diagnosis, see Harry Levinson, *Organizational Diagnosis* (Cambridge, Mass.: Harvard University Press, 1972).

2. For a discussion of these processes, see Ralph R. Greenson, *The Technique and Practice of Psychoanalysis* (New York: International Universities Press, 1967); Charles Brenner, *Psychoanalytic Technique and Psychic Conflict* (New York: International Universities Press, 1976); William M. Meissner and Armand M. Nicholi, "The Psychotherapies: Individual, Family, and Groups," in Armand M. Nicholi (Ed.), *The Harvard Guide to Modern Psychiatry* (Cambridge, Mass.: Belknap Press, 1978).

3. See Otto Fenichel, *Problems of Psychoanalytic Technique* (New York: Psychoanalytic Quarterly, 1941); Edward Glover, *The Technique of Psychoanalysis* (New York: International Universities Press, 1955); Karl Menninger, *Theory of Psychoanalytic Technique* (New York: Basic Books, 1958).

4. Sigmund Freud, "Remembering, Repeating, and Working Through," *Standard Edition,* Vol. 20, 1914; Freud, "Constructions in Analysis," *Standard Edition,* Vol. 23, 1937.

5. John Bowlby, *Attachment and Loss*: Vol. 1, *Attachment* (New York: Basic Books, 1969); Vol. 2, *Separation* (New York: Basic Books, 1973); Vol. 3, *Loss* (New York: Basic Books, 1980).

6. Bowlby, *Loss*, p. 18.

7. Bowlby, *Loss*, p. 85.

8. Bowlby, *Loss*.

9. We were particularly influenced by the research done by Bowlby, *Loss,* but also by that of George H. Pollock, "Mourning and Adaptation," *International Journal of Psychoanalysis,* 1961, *42,* 341–361; G. Gorer, *Death, Grief, and Mourning in Contemporary Britain* (London: Tavistock, 1965); G. Gorer, "Death, Grief, and Mourning in Britain," in E. J. Anthony and C. Koupernik (Eds.), *The Child in His Family: The Impact of Disease and Death* (New York: Wiley, 1973); C. M. Parkes, " 'Seeking' and 'Finding' a Lost Object: Evidence from Recent Studies of the Reaction of Bereavement," *Social Sci-*

ence and Medicine, 1970, *4*, 187-201; C. M. Parkes, *Bereavement: Studies of Grief in Adult Life* (New York: International Universities Press, 1972); C. M. Parkes, "Unexpected and Untimely Bereavement: A Statistical Study of Young Boston Widows," in B. Schoenberg and others (Eds.), *Bereavement: Its Psychosocial Aspects* (New York: Columbia University Press, 1972); Peter Marris, *Widows and Their Families* (London: Routledge & Kegan Paul, 1958); Peter Marris, *Loss and Change* (London: Routledge & Kegan Paul, 1974); Erich Lindemann, *Beyond Grief: Studies in Crisis Intervention* (New York: Jason Aronson, 1979).

   10. See John Bowlby, "Processes of Mourning," *International Journal of Psychoanalysis*, 1961, *42*, 317-340; Parkes, *Bereavement*.

   11. See Marris, *Widows and Their Families*; John Bowlby, "Grief and Mourning in Infancy and Early Adulthood," *Psychoanalytic Study of the Child*, 1960, *15*, 9-52; Bowlby, "Processes of Mourning"; John Bowlby, "Pathological Mourning and Childhood Mourning," *Journal of the American Psychoanalytic Association*, 1961, *11*, 500-541; Parkes, *Bereavement*; Parkes, "Unexpected and Untimely Bereavement."

   12. See I. O. Glick, R. S. Weiss, and C. M. Parkes, *The First Year of Bereavement* (New York: Wiley, 1974); Gorer, *Death, Grief, and Mourning in Contemporary Britain*; Parkes, *Bereavement*.

   13. See Glick, Weiss, and Parkes, *The First Year of Bereavement*; Gorer, *Death, Grief, and Mourning in Contemporary Britain*; Parkes, *Bereavement*; Marris, *Widows and Their Families*.

   14. See Bowlby, "Pathological Mourning and Childhood Mourning"; Lindemann, *Beyond Grief*.

Chapter Eight

   1. For a description of the working alliance or therapeutic alliance, see Elisabeth R. Zetzel, "Current Concepts of Transference," *International Journal of Psychoanalysis*, 1956, *37*, 369-378; Elisabeth R. Zetzel, "The Analytic Situation," in

R. E. Litman (Ed.), *Psychoanalysis in the Americas* (New York: International Universities Press, 1966); Homer C. Curtis, "The Concept of Therapeutic Alliance: Implications for the 'Widening Scope,'" *Journal of the American Psychoanalytic Association,* 1979, *27,* 159-192, supplement.

    2. See William M. Meissner and Armand M. Nicholi, "The Psychotherapies: Individual, Family, and Group," in Armand M. Nicholi (Ed.), *The Harvard Guide to Modern Psychiatry* (Cambridge, Mass.: Belknap Press, 1978).

    3. For a description of paradoxical intervention techniques, particularly in family therapy, see Paul Watzlawick, Janet Helmick Beavin, and Don D. Jackson, *Pragmatics of Human Communication* (New York: Norton, 1967); Paul Watzlawick, John H. Weakland, and Richard Fisch, *Change: Principles of Problem Formation and Problem Resolution* (New York: Norton, 1974); Mara Selvini Palazzoli, Gianfranco Cecchin, Giuliana Prata, and Luigi Boscolo, *Paradox and Counterparadox* (New York: Jason Aronson, 1978); Gerald R. Weeks and Luciano L'Abate, *Paradoxical Psychotherapy: Theory and Practice with Individuals, Couples, and Families* (New York: Brunner/Mazel, 1982); Richard Fisch, John H. Weakland, and Lynn Segal, *The Tactics of Change: Doing Therapy Briefly* (San Francisco: Jossey-Bass, 1982).

Chapter Nine

    1. A description of this technique can be found in Michael Balint, *The Doctor, His Patient, and the Illness* (New York: International Universities Press, 1957).

Index